LAST OF THE MAYA

LAST OF THE MAYA

★

**HERBERT
RITTLINGER**

TAPLINGER PUBLISHING COMPANY
NEW YORK

First American Edition published
by Taplinger Publishing Co., Inc., 1962

© F. A. Brockhaus, Wiesbaden, 1959

Originally published in Germany
by F. A. Brockhaus under the title *Ins Land der Lacandonen*

First published in Great Britain, 1961

English translation © Odhams Press Limited, 1961
under the title *Jungle Quest*

Library of Congress Catalog Card Number: 62–21628

Printed in the U.S.A.

CONTENTS

ILLUSTRATIONS

ILLUSTRATIONS

The Blond God of the Lacandones

AT half past nine on a grey morning we saw the blond god of the Lacandones. He had a mighty beard and flowing, golden hair. Although he wore blue jeans and an ordinary bush shirt we noticed at once that he was holy. He was running across the courtyard of the Dolphin Hotel in the direction of the lavatories. We were speechless.

I do not know if you know what a Mexican hotel and its lavatories are like. Delightful. Of course, Kliesing and I would have been speechless if *any* gringo should have crossed our path in this godforsaken hole. For days we had been the only gringos in Comitán, and objects of great curiosity. Actually, we were not gringos at all. In contrast to most other Latin Americans the Mexicans call only North Americans gringos. When they called *us* gringos, Kliesing said: we're no gringos, we're Alemanes. But when they did not know that we were Alemanes they called us gringos because that was easier for them. I did not mind, because I like things to be easy. But Kliesing and Paulchen (Paulchen was not there at the moment), who had been living in Mexico for fifteen and thirty years respectively, set great store on being Alemanes and not gringos. Old German Alemanes. We would have been very happy to meet a gringo here, but we were not quite prepared to meet a holy gringo, or whatever he was.

We were lying on rickety wicker chairs with our feet up on the patio railing, and as the juke-box paused we heard the gringo singing in the lavatory.

9

"Now he's singing," Kliesing said. "You wait. He's the blond god of the Lacandones."

It was a terrible exaggeration. Kliesing had just made it up. We were sitting in Comitán because we wanted to go to the country of the Lacandones. These Lacandones are pure Maya Indians who live, remote from all contact with the other Mexican Indians, in the jungles between Guatemala and Chiapas. Chiapas is the most southerly and the most interesting Mexican state. It lies on the same latitude as the southern Sahara, Central India and Siam, and is as big as Austria.

But back to the Lacandones. Once a strong and warlike people, today they number only a hundred and sixty-seven souls, belonging to three clans. Dispersed as families and even individuals they lead a hidden, semi-nomadic life on the rivers of the great forests. The most significant and surprising fact about them is that they have never been christianized to this day.

The first time I came on this rarity was in a book by Traven. Then came Healey's discovery.

Giles Healey, an American journalist whose expedition had been financed by the United Fruit Company, had only intended to write a report about the *chicle* collectors. (*Chicle* is a special kind of gum used in the manufacture of chewing gum.) Another American, Charles Frey, who lived in Chiapas and was married to an Indian, had drawn his attention to the ruins of a Maya city on the river Lacanja which had hitherto remained unexplored. The small group of northern Lacandones who lived there called the city Bonampak, which means "city of the painted walls".

This was in 1946.

It was another two years before a well-equipped American expedition reached Bonampak from the other side, from the lowlands. It led to the discovery of the greatest murals of ancient America.

Thanks to this discovery, and to the presence of the small group of Lacandones who lived near Bonampak, this strange forest-people was wrested from ethnological oblivion. Such is the remoteness of the great cordillera and jungle country to the south of the isthmus of Tehuantepec.

We were very happy that a country like this still existed and I saw at once that nothing had changed since Traven's days. But we did not want to go to Bonampak. Bonampak can be reached with comparative ease by taking the railway to Tenosique and crossing the river Usumacinta. I thought: there will be the usual landing-strip for single-engined aircraft and helicopters, and with plenty of money and a little time everybody can fly to this Maya city, take some photographs, and fly away again. (I thought wrong, by the way: the nearest landing-strip is two days' strenuous ride from Bonampak. A little while before, two Americans had been waiting there for the next aircraft for thirty days.) However that may be, beyond these few points the country is as inaccessible as before. Most of it is still unexplored.

Friend Kliesing found out that there was a big lake somewhere in the area of the river Jataté, one of the sources of the Usumacinta. This lake, the Miramar lagoon, with its rock islands and forgotten pyramids and temples, was said to have been the centre of the old empire of the Lacandones, but for more than two hundred years a terrible curse had lain on the lake. The decline of the Lacandones began there. Ever since then its shores had remained uninhabited, its mirror-like surface unbroken by boat or canoe.

That was where we wanted to go.

But first we wanted to pay the Lacandones a visit. We hoped they enjoyed visits. It was far from certain. Then we wanted to cross the accursed lake with its mysterious islands —a more certain and less difficult project.

We hoped very much that we would find the Lacandones. Somewhere on the Jataté there was said to be a group: a pretty mythical group. Neither in Mexico City nor anywhere else had we been able to get information about them. In Mexico City a lot of people had a lot of information on all kinds of subjects. For instance, they knew for a fact that one was killed on sight and chopped up with razor-sharp machetes if one pitched camp anywhere in the Mexican provinces and particularly in Chiapas. But about the Lacandones nobody knew anything, not even government departments.

So we had tried to get used to the idea of travelling to the country of the Lacandones without ever meeting a single one of its inhabitants. Even Kliesing with his sunny optimism had tried to get used to the idea. Now we were sitting a thousand miles out of Mexico City by the Pan American Highway, in Comitán on the border of Guatemala, strenuously wondering on which rivers and where in the vast forest we were likely to meet Lacandones; and in Comitán we had found out even less than in Mexico City. We were entirely in the dark. That was why we were speechless when we saw the gringo with the long hair. It was obvious that he came from the bush and that he was our man, despite his appearance. That was why we leapt at the wildest deductions—without ever guessing that they would be surpassed by reality. That was why we had to get hold of him—without knowing whether he would welcome our advances or spit at us. For you never know how holy men from the bush will react. They are quite capable of spitting at you. But even if he were to have spat at us it would have been something—though admittedly not very much.

*　　　*　　　*

"We heard you sing," Kliesing said, in Spanish.

"Yes," the holy man said in American, "this is a strange country with strange privies or none at all." His eyes were blue and clear, like rainwater in spring. He was a handsome man, no more than forty. With his clear blue eyes he looked at us curiously:

"The gentlemen are tourists?"

"*No somos turistas*," Kliesing said in Spanish, by mistake. He spoke Spanish better than American. "We want to go to the Jataté."

"Really?" said the man with the blond hair and the yellow topee, genuinely surprised.

"Yes," I said, "we could even be important tourists."

"You know the bush? If you want to go to the Jataté you'll have something in front of you. I once went with a young American from the Upper Jataté across the Paso Soledad and the Sierra Colmena to the Rio Euseba. I only went along because he wouldn't listen and insisted on doing it, and because I didn't want the boy to die. That's where we got lost. Fortunately he had enough *tortillas* for a week in his rucksack. But after four days in the rain the tortillas were sodden and mouldy and no longer eatable. We were sick and had to throw them away. I knew of a waterfall which I could reorientate myself by, and the sixth day we found this waterfall. That was our salvation. On the ninth day we got to the village of Porvenir, hungry and in rags and exhausted. The boy looked like this——"

He pulled in his cheeks, making terrible hollows. His long beard trembled. We watched the performance cynically. Kind as the holy man was, we looked at him cynically.

"But it's not just because of this that I think people have no idea of the size and proportions of the forest. For this or that reason you go into the bush and think you can smile at all the good advice. But then the bush hits out at you. It hits at you hard and without mercy. It hits at you with swamp, torrential rain, rivers, mountains, thickets, lakes, vultures and thunder. It's a snake with six hundred thousand coils. This is the most virgin country of the earth. That's why I ask you if you know the bush."

"This señor knows the bush all over Mexico. And I know the bush from the Cape to Cooch Behar."

"Yes," Kliesing said. "We know the bush pretty well."

"Are you a missionary?" I asked.

"No," he said. "I just live in the forest."

"On a *finca* (a farm)?"

"No. Just on my own."

"On your own?"

"That's what I mean."

"*Where* in the forest?"

"Pretty far down. On a little river near the Savannah of San Quintin."

"Well," Kliesing said. "A hermit!"

"If you like," said the hermit. "But you—are you on your own?"

"No. There are five of us. My friend Kliesing, and then my wife, and Timber and Paulchen. Paulchen is a chef. Timber is a young German who became a Canadian lumberjack, but a little while ago he decided that Canada was too cold for him. So he tramped down to Mexico and Kliesing picked him up. He's a valuable addition to our expedition. We've sent the three of them with our kit in Don Herlindo's pick-up to San José del Arco to hire horses, mules, *arrieros* and guides. Because we want to take the Santo Domingo Trail down to the Jataté.'

"That's a difficult trail," the hermit said matter-of-factly. "It runs past a nine-hundred-foot waterfall. I doubt that you'll find highland people to go down there with you. It's a difficult trail."

"We only want to go down to a point where we can put our boats into the Santo Domingo river. We've got folding canoes—a kind of collapsible *cayugi*."

"God be with you, gentlemen!"

"That's why we want to have a look at the trail and the river from the air first. That's why we're sitting here and waiting for the aircraft. We've found somebody with an aircraft who'll fly us there."

"Castellanos?"

"Castellanos. Don Gustavo."

"Good old Spanish family. Been here since the days of the conquistadores. One of the three or four good old Spanish families in Comitán."

"Yes. Don Gustavo came specially over in his Cessna from his finca near Ocosingo. But we can't start because of the weather over the forest. Although here it's only the mornings that are grey and the afternoons are marvellous, we can't fly down to the forest. That's why we're sitting where we are."

"Furthermore, I don't think your wife and your two friends will find enough horses and mules in San José. It's just the time of the maize harvest."

"Do *you* know where we could get animals?"

"Let me think. Go to Las Margaritas, fifteen miles from here. There look for Don Emilio and mention my name. Don Emilio will help you."

"What is your name?"

"Enrique Pequeño."

"You're not a Mexican——"

"No, of course not. I'm a gringo. It's only a translation. A translation of Harry. But everybody here knows me as Don Enrique."

We introduced ourselves. We were suspicious, although it became more and more interesting. We were full of childish suspicion, only because this Enrique looked like a strange apostle. We left the patio of the Dolphin Hotel and walked out into the *zócalo* (market square) of Comitán. But the Indios in the zócalo did not seem to find it strange that on this grey morning an apostle walked among them. Rather it was Kliesing and myself at whom they stared, although we looked perfectly normal and ordinary. We *were* perfectly normal and ordinary; that is to say, Kliesing was perhaps not quite as ordinary as myself. Kliesing was a great vegetarian and astrologer. An even greater vegetarian and astrologer was Paulchen, the oldest of us, who had gone with my wife and Timber to act as an interpreter, because he had been in the country for thirty years. Paulchen was a chef from Vienna who had changed over to vegetarian diets. He had been a dietary chef in a sanatorium on the Semmering, and he was a firm vegetarian and believed in cosmic vibrations. Apart from that he was a nice man. I only wondered how our two vegetarian friends—who had been joined by Timber— would fare in the jungle when they ran out of provisions. It may sound strange, but in the jungle one cannot live off the fruits of the forest. I will be more explicit later on. Anyway, I declared categorically that I would take a gun.

Kliesing, with his experience of the bush, had immediately agreed. Kliesing had said from the very beginning that in the bush it was a matter of life and death. We would have to be prepared for extraordinary situations, and when it was a matter of life and death he would eat meat. He was quite sure it would not do him any harm to eat meat if it was a matter of life and death, and also that in these circumstances it would agree with him.

But Paulchen had merely asked: "Why don't we simply buy tortillas?"

"Tortillas? Where, Paulchen?"

"Well, from the Indios."

"But if there are no Indios."

"Indios? There'll always be Indios."

That is how Paulchen was, the dear chap. We looked at him thoughtfully and for a long time. Then we decided to mess separately.

Paulchen was a first-class chef and made marvellous waffles. He took a Swedish waffle-iron with him into the bush. Even so, we decided to mess separately, my wife and

I, because it was already difficult enough to go into the bush with vegetarians and people who are affected by vibrations without adding further complications. I only mention this because it added a touch of the fantastic to our comedy. Luckily neither Kliesing nor Paulchen were fanatics, and on the trip each in his own way turned out to be very practical men. All the same, Kliesing (and some time later Paulchen) was much less favourably disposed towards our saint from the woods than we others. True, in the beginning I was not sure of him myself. It would not have been a good idea to tell everybody that we wanted to go not just to the Jataté, but to the Lacandones as well. That is why I did not mention it to Don Enrique, but I was glad we had met him. During our short conversation he had given us a lot of useful information which showed that he really knew the country. (He did not have much time because he wanted to catch the bus to Las Casas.) All the same we always got off the topic—instead of asking him about the Lacandones—and during one of these digressions he told us he was a naturalist.

"What's that? Is it something like a naturist?"

"I don't know what a naturist is," he replied. "I've got an 'al' in between. I simply do some gardening, planting and harvesting. I don't keep domestic animals. I don't like domestic animals because they make a mess everywhere, but round my hut you find all the animals of the forest; they're my friends. When the day comes to an end, at dusk, it's the time for jaguars——"

"Have you a gun?"

"I never kill."

"How do you get along with the people?"

"Fine. The nearest natives live a few miles from my hut. They helped me to build the hut. They're my special friends. It's because of them that I live there."

"Tolojabales?"

"No," said Harry. "Not Tolojabales. Lacandones."

That was Harry, the hermit from the forest. Not only was he the first person in Mexico who did not raise his arms and declare that we were mad, that we would meet a violent end (if we did not die naturally from typhus, dysentery and fever) and who gave us good and useful information—but he was also a person, and the only one, who lived as a kind of Robinson Crusoe in the forest of the Lacandones!

He had built his hut near the river where the *casique* "Bor" and his clan lived. For five years Harry had lived near the Bor clan—for reasons which we did not understand right away. To these Indians of the forest, who were called *caribes* (savages) by the highland Indians, he must have appeared as a being from another, incomprehensible world.

"It was all I could do to prevent them from regarding me as a kind of white god and prostrating themselves before me. They began to offer the maize sacrifice, not only to the moon, the fire and the river god, but to me as well!"

"The blond god of the Lacandones!"

"Something like that. A white god who gives away machetes, shirt material and rubber balls. But they soon found me out—in spite of machetes, shirt material and rubber balls. If you stay any length of time with these children of the forest they soon see through the white man's equivocal position."

"Nowhere in the world are the natives what they used to be," I said. "Did they become dangerous?"

"Not they. Their adoration, if one might call it that, soon changed to light-hearted profanity."

"We must come to pay them a visit."

"O.K.," said Harry, "when shall I have the honour?"

"We want to go to the Jataté," Kliesing said.

"When you're at the mouth of the Rio Santo Domingo," Harry said, "you're four days' travel upstream from the Savannah of San Quintin. My hut is five miles to the east from there. If you go on travelling upstream you'll soon meet Lacandones. Only you may not see them if they don't like you. If they don't like you, there's nothing you can do. The best thing is to give up your idea of the Santo Domingo Trail and go to Las Margaritas. Wait for me there. I'm only going to Las Casas to buy machetes, shirt material and rubber balls, and a few provisions for myself. In a fortnight I'll be back in Las Margaritas. Then we'll ride the Euseba Trail together, down to my hut and on to the Lacandones . . ."

Kliesing stepped on my foot. He did not like the proposition. I did not like the idea of giving up our beautiful Santo Domingo plan, either. For one thing, our advance guard was already in San José with all our luggage. They had probably hired a lot of animals and arrieros so that we could start at once. We were very anxious to start at once. Harry was a great and surprising find for us, but we could not quite make him out. I thought he was sympathetic—but perhaps he was not our man.

We accompanied him to the bus and said that all the same we would like to try the Santo Domingo. We were very grateful to him—good-bye, Harry! Perhaps—no, *certainly*— we would meet again down in the forest, ha-ha, ho-ho, in the forest of the Lacandones.

And Harry got into the bus.

*   *   *

Thoughtfully we returned to the Dolphin Hotel.

There we were awaited by one of Castellanos' peons, a gentle Indian—gentle and inscrutable like almost all Indians there. He said we were to come to Castellanos' house right away. Don Gustavo would also arrive right away.

The fog which had hung over Comitán and probably over the whole of this part of the *tierra fria*, the Mexican highland, was about to clear. During the short walk to Castellanos' house the sun broke through.

Castellanos was burning to fly with us over the (according to Harry) earth's most virgin jungle, the jungle on whose edges he was living and which was remoter to him than the Club Social in Mexico City or the daily price of coffee on the New York stock exchange. He had a rancho in the *tierra templada* on the slopes of the highland at Ocosingo, and he owned his Cessna as we own a car. With a car he wouldn't have reached his rancho from Comitán at all, and from Las Casas he would only have got half-way. But during the rainy period when the landing-strips turned into swamps there was still no other way than to go on horseback.

Now, at the beginning of February, the dry period was well advanced. The bad weather could only have been the effect of a "low" over the Gulf. So we had thought. But we had thought wrong, Castellanos explained. The farther south you go, the more the weather over the tropical forests was an individual weather, independent of the general weather situation. That was why he was anxious to start that morning and forget about lunch. Castellanos was a reserve officer of the Mexican Air Force and likely to be an excellent bush pilot. He was very keen on this reconnaissance flight over the tropical jungle, for which we were to pay eight hundred pesos (but that was not why he was keen). For a flight of four hours on high-octane petrol which had to be imported from the United States, eight hundred pesos (twenty-two pounds) was a very modest price. He was looking forward to it because he had never flown over this area and wanted to see it, and because we were important *expedicionistas*. We had studied the aerial maps very carefully and shown him all the places where we wanted to go and which we wanted to see from above if the fuel lasted, and off we went.

The airstrip of Comitán was a stretch of smooth steppe with fuel drums and a decrepit repair shed. In the shed stood a two-engined aircraft, quietly rusting away. This, too, belonged to Castellanos. He was going to have it put right and use it for air-charter business with rich American tourists. In view of the special low fee he was charging us we said we would give him publicity among any rich Americans we came across, but we did not meet any, or not the right ones.

The Cessna was gleaming in the sun. It was brand-new, a proper gem of a plane, the four-seater cabin in cream and pink, something between a beauty parlour and a luxury perambulator. Two peons loosened the ropes—the aircraft had been moored to the ground because of the wind. Kliesing sat in front next to Castellanos, and I went to the back because there was more room for taking photographs. In the cockpit, up on the left, was a picture of the Mother of God; by its side a picture of a patron saint of aeronautics, but I forget which saint it was. Then Castellanos started the engine. We rolled on to the runway, the plane left the ground smoothly and elegantly, and rose into the vast, airy, sun-flooded sky.

The country stretched out like an enormous platform, yellow and dry, with toy mountains round the edges, dropping off into dark horizons. In the east, the straight ribbon of the *Panamericana*—the short stretch from Comitán to the border asphalted—disappeared. The yellow steppe was flecked here and there with herds of cattle which collected round waterholes and salt-licks and lined all over with Indian and mule tracks, and small, torn, half-dry river beds. Over the dark horizons for which we were heading, in the east, lay motionless white cloud masses.

Then came pine trees, ninety to a hundred and fifty feet high. We were approaching the lake district of Montebello and the settlements of Santa Helena and San José del Arco. We had hoped to catch sight of our vanguard's tents, and Don Gustavo was to roar across the tents while our friends and my wife waved to us. That was how we had imagined it, but we had hardly reached the edge of the mountains and started over the pine forest when somebody seemed to have punctured a steam boiler. From every valley and gorge torrents of clouds gushed up.

It all happened so quickly. We plummeted crazily and the trees raced towards us. The aircraft was forced down to thirty feet above the treetops. At first we thought Castellanos was having fun. Then we saw Castellanos was *not* having fun and we had some uncomfortable minutes. When he had worked out the thermostatic difference we managed to break away; we flew up and down over the lakes of Montebello and between small ranchos and small, flat houses white among the pines, and Mexicans with large sombreros waving to us.

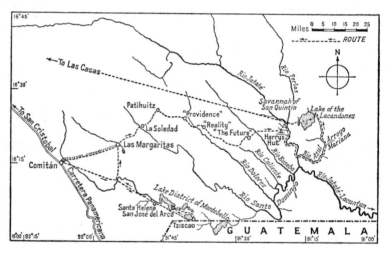

Of our vanguard and tents not a trace.

The vapours which rose from the valleys and gorges and the hot tropical lowlands closed in more and more. Although Castellanos now had the aircraft well under control we told him to forget the damned tents altogether and get out of this wash-house. I was furious with our vanguard and my wife because we had not seen their tents and because they had failed to put out any signs.

Castellanos flew on through thin, drifting mists close to a mountainside, not more than thirty or forty feet over the trees, but this time intentionally, and we all watched the treetops with great care. Then the treetops, and the mountain ridge which formed the frontier with Guatemala, grew distant, and we plunged into a dense fog. Next we were out of the fog and suddenly surrounded by light and blue sky again, the dazzling cloudbanks below us, close enough to walk on. Then we flew straight into the brilliant sun.

It was a magnificent cloudbank, an arctic landscape of overpowering beauty. It lay across the whole of the Santo Domingo area, and over the Jataté area, and over the jungles farther south. But over Guatemala it was cut off as if with a knife, and you could look down on Guatemala. We flew fifty or sixty miles into Guatemala—they are not very particular about such things. Mexico and Guatemala are not quite in step politically, but all the same they are not very particular. They are not yet advanced enough to quarrel over air-space. Anyway, we only tried to fly round these clouds and find a gap to get through to the Santo Domingo.

We could not find a gap. We circled round and round, and then we began to run low on petrol. A final attempt to fly below the cloudbank ended in a dangerous loss of height. We quickly climbed back into the blue-golden sun and went home.

Normally, a Cessna like ours can stay in the air for four hours. Castellanos had taken on the maximum of fuel, but we could not risk staying up for more than half an hour beyond normal. It was not really permitted to go above the clouds, Castellanos explained, and up to those heights. That was what it said in the handbook. Castellanos let go of the elevator control, leaned back, and searched through his side-pockets for the handbook so that we could read it. We were flying about three hundred feet above the clouds, at twelve thousand six hundred feet. The aircraft was humming along

23

beautifully without any rolling and we could have played a comfortable game of chess.

Then we were over the mountain ranges again, and the clouds which were hiding the land of the Lacandones came as abruptly to an end as they had over Guatemala. The highland steppe lay full in the sunshine, and once again we saw herds of cattle at the water-holes, the criss-cross lines of paths, and Indians and Mexicans in their sombreros. Castellanos said we were to pay only five hundred pesos because we had not seen anything, and we said: *muchas gracias, Señor.* Perhaps we would try again another day, we said, if he felt like it, but actually we were already prepared to forgo a second reconnaissance flight. For had not we had ideal weather and still not seen anything of the land of the Lacandones? It all depended on chance. We were burning to get on and get some ground under our feet, or rather under the feet of the horses which we believed were waiting for us with steaming nostrils in the village of San José in the valley of the thundering hooves.

For fun Castellanos flew a few rounds over Comitán. The Indians stopped in the streets and waved. Then he flew very low over his house so that they would start warming up his lunch. Finally he came down on the bumpy steppe more lightly and gently than any Stratocruiser ever manages it on the concrete runway of Idlewild. Boy, can flying be wonderful! Particularly when it serves no purpose.

*   *   *

Towards evening Don Herlindo came back with his pickup. He came to the Dolphin Hotel and asked us if we wanted to start next morning, and we said we certainly did. We asked him how our vanguard was faring and whether they had horses and mules. He said they were very well, and they would soon have animals. He looked like Sancho Panza. He was a six-foot tall Sancho Panza, with a monster of a sombrero on his head. He brought a letter from my wife, written on pieces of scrap paper:

Montebello, Monday afternoon

My dear—thick fog, rather lonely and shivering. There's nothing much to tell about the road here, we just hope that you won't be as cold as we were. Our caballero has just made me a present of an orchid. He has a rancho here in a colonia *which is called Santa Helena, and there he breeds orchids among the bananas.*

Now he's putting on snow chains! Because of the mud! To take us to the lakes of Montebello. Madre de Dios, we're looking forward to our tents and sleeping bags. Don't forget the rum. Try and come soon. It's not all that wonderful here at present, but mañana it will be better, they say.

Now we're in the mud.

Now we've gone on another 200 yards.

The lakes are deep down in wooded valleys, with hardly any banks, very steep. How we're going to get the animals isn't certain. You know, I don't think Paulchen has quite realized that we need animals. Although he's been in the country for thirty years and speaks fluent Spanish he hasn't yet taken a single step in the matter. He doesn't speak a word with Don Herlindo, although he is such a splendid caballero. He leaves everything to me with my five words of Spanish, and to Timber without any word at all. He tells us to take it easy. But apart from that he's a dear. All the same, come soon. But bear in mind that we may have to come back with all the stuff!

Now we're going back to Santa Helena. (It's five p.m.)

Six p.m. We're still in the mud. It's raining. The snow chains have broken.

Santa Helena, Tuesday

We sleep in a hut, that is to say, we have slept. We arrived in Santa Helena in the dark. Don Herlindo was furious. But he had a room cleared for us and somehow feels responsible for us. We assume that we're on his rancho.

The road practically stops at the first lake. After that you sink into mud. We walked another couple of miles to an abandoned rancho. We didn't see any other ranchos. But we met Indians who told us there were plenty of horses and mules. Will explore on foot.

The lakes look romantic. You can see one going into the next. As far as we could make out the valleys, they stretch for miles. Also they lie deep and the shores are precipitous, but one can get down to them; we've tried it. The water is crystal-clear. We must try to get animals which can take our stuff far enough for us to start living in tents; and we must be certain we can get other animals and drivers to take us to the river.

If this letter gets to you before your flight: have a look at the Rio Euseba, in case the road there is better, even if it's longer. Today you probably won't get your reconnaissance flight either—it's still raining here. Last night, in the yard of the rancho, the Indians were sitting with their wives and babies round the fire. What a sight. Darkness all round. Try to pin down Don Herlindo, he's promised to get animals. We're not going to pay the remaining money. We leave that to you. So that he brings you here.

Your Vanguard.

PS. The Indians are sitting round the fire again. They're roasting tortillas. But it looks less romantic than at night.

PS. (2) It's cold!!!!!

PS. (3) Santa Helena, Wednesday.

No aircraft! What's happened to you heroes?

*　　　*　　　*

We started in the morning and drove with Don Herlindo to Montebello. We drove through the same country with its criss-cross tracks and river beds which we had seen from the air. Only now we very rarely saw any track but our own. Later we no longer drove on a track, but straight across the steppe. We made very good progress across the short grass of the steppe, up and down, up and down, accompanied by Don Herlindo's jokes. Don Herlindo was a great joker, particularly when we met colourful troupes of women, balancing large baskets of orchids on their heads—and

26

pumpkins and fettered chickens and, once, a baby. When the pines started there was a recognizable road again. It was still dry, but so much ploughed up that we had to drive at walking pace. Then the pines grew thicker and we came into the region of mist and rain of which my wife had written and which we had seen from the air. From far down, from the steaming jungles of the Lacandones, rose the white clouds as they had done on the previous day. They rose like an immense curtain which only stopped at the blue sky of the highlands. Down on the ground, in front of this curtain, we started slithering every ten yards or so because of the muddy road. Sometimes Kliesing and I jumped out to push, but in spite of it all we reached Don Herlindo's rancho by noon, which meant that we had taken only six hours for thirty miles.

Don Herlindo's rancho was the centre of a small *colonia* of a few Indian and mestizo huts scattered in the pine forest. A colonia is not an old-established village, but a new settlement —generally a settlement of colonists in virgin country. The rancho consisted of a mud house with a wooden veranda, a tiled roof, a kitchen-house on the right and a *tienda* on the left—a den-like shop for the needs of the Indians, kept by Don Herlindo's señora. To the back was the garden with the orchids between the bananas, and an open pigsty. The pigs looked after the sanitation in the simplest possible manner. For, as Harry had already remarked, this was a country without privies.

The rancho was surrounded by a stockade. Everything smelled of galloping horses, looked like sudden attack and wild shooting. On and around the little wooden veranda our kit was stacked up. To Kliesing and myself, who had not seen it for some days, it appeared completely mad to have dragged all that luggage along: four folding canoes, four tents, sleeping-bags, air-mattresses, guns and ammunition, cameras, numbered boxes with gifts for the Lacandones (in case we tracked them down) and lots of numbered boxes with our provisions for two months in the wilderness. All these things had been selected as rationally as possible. It was splendid equipment. Only it wasn't quite clear how we would transport it in the jungle, once we were on our own. We looked at it with amusement.

Of our vanguard nobody was to be seen.

Don Herlindo's señora said my wife and the two caballeros had started early in the morning for San José del Arco to look for animals. We were happy they had shown some action.

Kliesing and I decided during lunch that we would go for a walk. We would walk down the road where the snow chains had torn. Gaily we went on our way. Soon we came to the first lakes.

I must say something about these lakes of Montebello, mainly because I am fascinated by any kind of water-formation on the earth's surface. There are thirty-five medium-sized and small lakes, almost every one having a different colour. In all probability they are so-called secondary lakes, that is to say, lakes in the creation of which several phenomena, such as volcanic explosions or tectonic upheavals, have been concerned at the same time. They have never been properly surveyed. It is also interesting that those on the Mexican side have no connection with the upper courses of the Rio Santo Domingo, while some of those on the Guatemalan side have an outlet to the Santo Domingo. The lakes on the Mexican side can have only subterranean outlets.

After two hours' strenuous marching on a well-defined forest path we had put the upper lake-region behind us and came to San José. This is a village, not a colonia, because there has always been a settlement here. With its Indian gardens, huts and stockades, it lies on a hill above a little wooded valley, where a small river—not connected with the lakes—rushes down towards the Rio Santo Domingo.

Shortly below the village the river breaks through a rock barrier which shuts off the valley.

In the village there seemed to be only women and children. The men were all away, or were sleeping in the huts, for it was the time of the siesta and fairly warm. We could not imagine that two days ago it was cold here. Even of the cloud curtain nothing was to be seen any more, because the narrow valley and the narrow mountains shut out the view. We asked some women about our people and the women said yes, the señora and the two gringos were down by the river, over there. . . .

We went down; not even the children followed us; and we gave our usual piercing cries. We took off our shoes and crossed the river by the stones placed there by the Indians and climbed up into the wood on the other side. The wood was no longer a pine wood, I noticed, but a sub-tropical deciduous wood. Then we gave another series of cries, and suddenly we heard an answer from close by. My wife cried out, and Timber cried out, and we cried out they should stop crying out and instead tell us just where they were because we could not see them. They were on the other side down by the river and had been bathing. We had to climb down again and take off our clothes and wade through the river with the water coming up to our chests, holding our clothes over our heads, and my wife said happily: well, there you are. I was pretty furious, because a blind man could have seen that they had not bothered about animals but just gone for a bathe.

My wife said: come on, be happy, you idiot, aren't you glad we're together again? And I said I was glad and we all shook hands. I said to Paulchen: come on, be happy, because I could not think of anything else and because Paulchen was just sitting there, sorting out something, and I said the same thing to Timber, although Timber was not sorting out any-thing and was happy anyway. They did not have any animals, but they had achieved something all the same. They had found the only man in the whole area who was able to find animals and who did not just talk and do nothing like Don Herlindo. His name was Don Rafael; but he was not there at the moment, he was coming home in the evening his señora had said. They had spoken to his señora. That is to say, my wife had spoken with the señora in her hut, and Paulchen should have acted as interpreter.

"But do you think we could get him to utter a word?" my wife said. "He simply sat and said: take it easy. Let's wait for the others, we'll only do the wrong thing."

"You know," my wife went on, "I've a feeling Paulchen doesn't know where we're going."

"What makes you think that?"

"I'm sure he hasn't a clue where we're going."

This disclosure was a little startling, but on the whole it made Paulchen seem even more sympathetic. At least it would discourage future arguments. Paulchen was sitting on a rock, sorting strange leaves from a strange shrub from which he was going to brew tea. Paulchen collected leaves from all kinds of shrubs and trees to make tea. He knew the special characteristics and virtues of each kind of tea. To begin with my wife and I were much amused by Paulchen's strange teas, but after a fortnight we drank them ourselves every evening.

Then Paulchen rolled himself a cigarette. He could not quite do without cigarettes—three or four a day perhaps—and from time to time he even fancied a little drink, although he never drank much. That would have interfered with the vibrations.

"Tell me," I said to Paulchen, "geography isn't one of your strong points, is it?"

"How do you mean?" Paulchen asked. He looked at me over his hawk's nose with his gentle partridge's eyes as if to say that it was impossible to offend him. Probably Kliesing and I had not informed him properly, or we had not noticed that he had never listened properly to our valuable information. After he had made a horoscope for Kliesing and himself —we never heard how it had come out—he simply came along, because he had always come along with Kliesing and because he liked to travel and be useful (except as an interpreter).

"Forget it," I said.

Kliesing told them the results of our fruitless flight. When he had finished I said:

"And then we met a curious saint with hair that reached to his shoulders. The blond god of the Lacandones."

"Come off it," said Timber.

"It's true," I said. "Or it was in the beginning. These days he's simply a hermit with long hair. A hermit in the jungle."

"Yes," Kliesing said, "but he's of no use to us."

"No," I said. "Probably not."

After this chat we walked back to the village and looked for Don Rafael's house. It was a simple hut built over a mud floor and contained a bedstead and some seating accommodation. It was kept scrupulously clean. There were arms and hunting equipment on the walls. As everywhere else, the kitchen was separate, across the yard. There were some nice-looking children about. Don Rafael's wife made us coffee in the usual way, by first roasting the beans and then grinding them in a mortar. As usual, it was excellent. She also produced tortillas and even *frejoles* and *mole*, although we tried to stop her. Frejoles are black or brown beans, and mole is a dark sauce made from finely-ground maize powder and chillies and many more ingredients which are the secret of every Mexican housewife. Mole is generally served with meat dishes, in many parts of Mexico mainly with turkey, and is as hot as hell. When you have burnt your mouth a few times you cannot do without it any more.

Don Rafael's wife said she would inform her husband

when he came back in the evening. We asked her to inform her husband instantly.

She said: *si, Señores, mañana. Mañana* she would tell her husband. *Mañana* she would tell him that we were quick-action gringos.

"*No somos gringos*," Kliesing said. "*Somos——*"

The señora stared at Kliesing uncomprehendingly. She looked very efficient. We had a high opinion of her. But we had not a very high opinion of Mexican promptness. If it was not *mañana*, it was *mañana-mañana*, and if it was not *mañana-mañana*, then it was *mañana²*—*mañana* squared. We were still far too quick-action. We left full of doubts.

We reached Don Herlindo's ranch in the dark. The Indians were crouching round the fire. The moon rose. We installed ourselves and ate our dinner and did some hard thinking. We were very tired.

When we were even more tired we heard the clattering of hooves outside. Three caballeros came riding in, armed to the teeth. They dismounted. The horses put their heads together. Their bodies were steaming in the moonlight and by the flickering fire of the Indians. It was Don Rafael with his son and his brother. The brother's face was marked with a machete cut which ran right across one cheek. The son had a fat cartridge belt and a fat Colt sticking out from one of his pockets.

We introduced ourselves.

Really—to think they had come so promptly! The moon, Don Rafael said. It was light till midnight and favourable. That was why they had come right away.

"Marvellous," my wife said. "Such handsome men."

"Wait a minute," Timber said. "When we take a little trouble . . ."

"Well," my wife said pleasantly, "why don't you take a little trouble?"

Luckily Don Herlindo had a little barrel of *comiteco* in his

At the Rancho Patihuitz, 5,700 ft. above sea-level, the highest stopping place on the journey to the Lacandones.

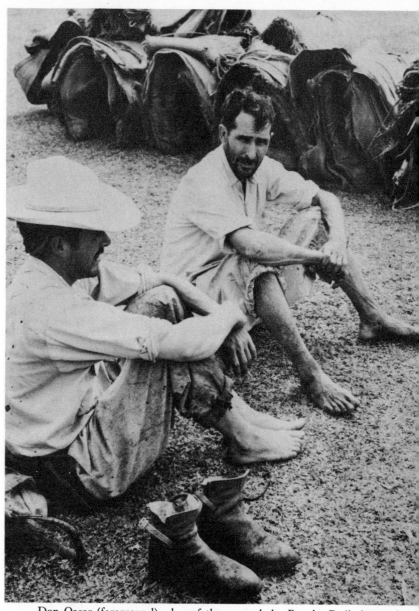

Don Oscar (foreground) whose father owned the Rancho Patihuitz, and Don Emilio, guide, who joined the expedition at Las Margaritas.

tienda. Comiteco is a spirit which is famous in all Chiapas and beyond. Comiteco must not be sold to Indians, and nobody sells it to Indians—not from fear of the legal consequences, but simply because the Indians cannot take any alcohol and get riotously drunk after one or two glasses of good comiteco.

In Chiapas, which is an isolated mountain country, the cheap agave spirit called *pulque* is unobtainable. Pulque is drunk in large quantities all over the rest of Mexico. It has a nasty musty taste, and suddenly you are on the floor and lost to the world. No, in Chiapas there is no need to drink pulque. In these wonderful tropical and sub-tropical highlands you need only scratch every sixth or seventh plant, help the fermentation along a little, or make a still from three clay pots—and you have the most intoxicating drink. If this is too much trouble you go to the nearest market and for a few centavos buy *aquardiente*, firewater. To sell this to the Indians is not prohibited because it contains more water than fire. If it were prohibited the Indians would make much worse stuff themselves.

*　　*　　*

The fire was blazing. The comiteco was warming. The Indians round the fire made jokes about us. We probably gave them ample reason. They never made jokes right away; normally they accepted our presence with great gravity. The Indians are gentlemen and rarely laugh, but when they got to know us a little more intimately they saw the joke.

We explained our plan to Don Rafael. Animals—yes. Of course it would take several days to get them together. They would come with us, all three of them, and a few arrieros as well.

The Santo Domingo trail!

Si.

Down to there, Don Rafael——

We spread out the maps and stood the petrol lamp on top of them. We had a very fine archaeological map, plus an official Mexican map, also two very handsome American maps, surveyed by air with the latest corrections. We had every map of the area that exists. On all maps the Rio Santo Domingo trail was prominently marked like a motor road elsewhere. (Jokers, those cartographers!) Don Rafael took a close look. He could read maps very well, of course; he had spent last year's dry season with a Mexican boundary commission in the jungle. Don Rafael said:

"No, Señores. You can't go there."

"Why not, Don Rafael?"

"Because all the maps are wrong, Señores . . ."

"What—wrong?"

"This trail doesn't exist."

"But it's down here! In black and white. Red and white, even."

"It's a trail from the *chiclero* days. During the last war the chicleros still went down there. But nobody afterwards. The trail doesn't exist any more."

We had already taken possession of this path—"our" path we called it—and after thinking so much about it, it was a shock to have to think of it as non-existent. We had foreseen all kinds of difficulties. With the exception of one: that the trail was not there . . .

There could be no doubting Don Rafael's word. He knew the area better than anybody. He was reliability personified.

"I can take you to the Rio Dolores, Señores, no farther. The Rio Dolores is the end. What comes after is impenetrable wilderness. *Completamente*, Señores. Completely impenetrable."

The Rio Dolores was useless to us if we would get stuck there.

"Pointless," said Paulchen.

"My brother and I once even took a cayugi, a canoe, overland to the Rio Santo Domingo. We were trying to penetrate farther by using the river—*mandarlo al carajo: Permittame*, excuse me, the señora . . ."

"The señora just knows enough Spanish not to understand this."

"I noticed right away that she is a remarkable señora," said Don Rafael.

"Yes, sometimes she is pretty outstanding."

"After five kilometres we were all but drowned," Don Rafael said. "We got to the river bank—but only with the clothes we stood up in. The cayugi and everything went over a cataract. We had to get back via the Rio Dolores. After ten days we came to the village of Chayabe—like this!"

He sucked his cheeks into terrible hollows. Just like Harry when he had told us the story of the American who would not listen to advice. So now we had heard two tales of the jungle which featured not poisonous snakes, ravenous tigers or arrows from an ambush, but fallen-in cheeks, prominent cheek-bones, hunger and exhaustion.

"*Por Dios*," the experienced bushman said, "we were so weak we were dying. I don't want another experience like it as long as I live! That's how weak we were."

"Yes," I said. "That's what it's like when one has lost one's equipment and is stranded in the bush without a gun."

"But you can find tea everywhere," Paulchen said.

Don Rafael looked at Paulchen with amazement. We cut Paulchen's further explanations short. He didn't mind: Paulchen generally started minding only three days after the event, and then for reasons which took us another three days to find out. At the moment we were too busy with the shock we had just had—the shock of learning that our wonderful trail did not exist, even though it was marked on all the maps.

Don Rafael suggested that we should take a trail he had

cut with the boundary commission the previous year. Needless to say, even this would be overgrown and there would be hard work with the machetes, but he knew the area. He would guarantee to take us to the place where the Jataté joins the Lacuntún. Ten or twelve days and we would be there.

"Just wait," I said to Kliesing, "we'll have to go back with all our stuff."

As for Lacandones, he had not met them in the whole area. Nobody had ever met them there, not even the crocodile hunters who went in with their cayugis. We would have liked this new route if we had not intended to do anything but go with our canoes down the Jataté, the Lacuntún and the Usumacinta. These were the only waterways along which the country was considered more or less explored, although, except on the Usumacinta, nobody lived there. Although there were no settlements till one came down to the Usumacinta—an ideal area for the unsociable Lacandones—it struck me as unlikely that we would meet Lacandones there. And then we had this mad idea to penetrate to the Lagoon of the Lacandones—this mysterious lake hidden in the jungle. Don Rafael knew about the lake, too, but he had never been there. From the point where Don Rafael wanted to take us we should have been obliged, according to the maps (I'll return to our maps and their draughtsmen, those gifted humorists, several times during this narrative), to penetrate at least eighty miles upstream over unknown, but doubtless considerable, obstacles. Kliesing was all for it, but I managed to convince him by quoting a few facts.

We had to take a simpler route, even if the approach march took longer. The most logical and simple route was the one which Harry the hermit had pointed out to us in Comitán. We had to go back.

We were sorry. Don Rafael and his brother were splendid, tough, capable men for any enterprise, but we could not accept their services because the other route was far too long for animals from this area, and their hire would have been far too expensive for us. Don Rafael and his brother realized this, too. Like all real Mexicans, like all *hombres de razón*, they were not anxious to make money out of us or even to cheat us. Of course, they would not have minded earning a little money on this tour if it had worked out like that. We must have seemed pretty mad to them. All the same, I had the impression that they would have liked to come along, just for the fun of it.

The Indians were still lying round the fire. They stayed there throughout the whole cool highland night. We accompanied our friends to the wooden gate and said good-bye. They mounted and galloped away and disappeared in the bright moonlight between the pine trees, and for a while the earth still rang with the sound of their horses' hooves.

*   *   *

We asked Don Herlindo when he could take us all back with his pick-up, and what he would charge for the return journey. Paulchen said we should be careful, and Paulchen was right, but unfortunately we were completely in the hands of Don Herlindo, and Don Herlindo was a businessman without machete scars. But even he did not abuse his transport monopoly. He quoted us a decent price and said whenever we wanted.

We wanted the day after tomorrow. *Mañana* we wanted to go bathing. We happened to be in an exceptionally charming neighbourhood, on the edge of the high plateau where there are many delightful lakes. The weather was at its best. We were simply optimistic enough to want nothing more than to go bathing. Even before we had achieved anything we wanted to waste a day and "relax".

In the main we achieved our object. The fact that afterwards we stumbled behind Timber's torch through the forest in the moonlight, lost our way, and arrived at the rancho at midnight, parched with thirst and dead-beat after a day's march of twenty-two miles—all that was not due to intentional wanderlust.

We had not planned for *that* much wanderlust.

I do not know how it happened. Perhaps it was the country, after all. Perhaps it was just the beautiful day.

I do not want to dwell too long on this beautiful day. Nothing happens on beautiful days. We had started early, with some snacks packed for lunch, and light hearts. We had discovered a new, beautiful lake, with lovely shores. There we had bathed for a long time and enjoyed the sun. Then we had wandered on and found another lake, and then another one, and finally the biggest of them all which was called *Tziscao* which means magpie-muck. That had been in the afternoon when it was already high time to turn back, but just when we meant to leave we heard strange music from across the lake.

It was celestial music which rang like a gentle magic over the forests and hills and the glittering water. We listened to these marvellously gentle sounds of mysterious instruments, which in a strange, quick rhythm repeated a tune of few bars. It was a marimba coming from an unseen village. We took the path round the lake, up and down and up again, always following the marvellous sounds. Thus we stumbled into the southernmost Mexican village, the Colonia Tziscao.

The settlement, with its mud-and-slat huts crowned by thick grass roofs, lay hard on the frontier of Guatemala. The frontier was marked by a stone. On one side of it was written in weather-washed letters MEXICO, on the other GUATEMALA. Apart from that there were none of the things which otherwise endear frontiers to us: no customs, no silly searchings of luggage, no police, no barriers, no passport and visa difficulties. It was one of the most casual and charming frontiers I have ever seen. Yet Mexicans and Guatemalans do not even like each other. I do not know why. (We couldn't tell the difference between them.) I suppose they dislike each other because patriots of all nations dislike other patriots.

Patriots of the world, unite!

We photographed the frontier stone between Guatemala and Mexico from the front, the back and the side.

Our invasion of the southernmost Mexican village was received with friendliness tempered by incredulity. "*Ah, arquelogicos,*" a few educated citizens cried out, explaining us. "*Gringos arquelogicos.*"

"*No somos gringos,*" Kliesing corrected them. "*Somos Alemanes.*"

"*Si,*" one of the educated citizens replied. "*'eil 'itler :*" (One and a half decades after the event!)

"*Gringos de ciencia!*" others insisted. Scientific gringos.

We smiled, flattered. We told Timber not to laugh, because Timber had a way of laughing which, although it was kind laughter, burst out like steam from inside him and could not be stopped. We were always afraid that people who did not know him might take offence.

Timber tried to remain solemn.

We were served coffee and lemonade. We had a shameless thirst.

The marvellous sounds had been silenced.

Mexico is a democracy, and in Tziscao they had just elected the casique, the mayor. Hence the fiesta with the green, white and red Mexican tricolour on the flagstaff and the marimba band. It was a clean village and the people were overwhelmingly kind. We apologized for our intrusion and begged them to go on with their fiesta.

They said we had not intruded, but they did not go on.

They had danced in a large hut to the sounds of the marimba. We had not intruded on the marimba players either, although they had stopped playing. They stood immovable in the doorway of the hut, wearing blue bush shirts and the inevitable sombreros, and holding the marimba-sticks in their hands. They were three friendly but serious men. A further hundred friendly but serious men stood around us and watched us quench our shameless thirst. The women stayed modestly in the background. No, we had not intruded. We were the great surprise, the highlight of their fiesta.

We asked the educated citizens—the teacher, the dignified mayor, the Nazi and some of the younger men—whether one could not carry the marimba into the open and photograph it. One could. The marimba was carried into the open.

The marimba is a xylophone which consists of a row of wooden slats of different lengths. To increase resonance a number of bodies, such as gourds, are suspended from the slats. In this case they were constructions made of thin red sheets of wood, looking rather like crystalline wooden bells hung upside down. The largest was about four and a half feet long with a two-foot cross-section at the bottom; the twenty-third and smallest was a pocket edition. I hope you can visualize it.

The marimba sounded gently across hills, woods and lake again. The three musicians played solemnly and beautifully without once striking a wrong note. In any European café they would have been a sensation.

The marimba bands one occasionally hears at home are sentimentalized and spoilt. You need the hard-beaten earth of the village square and the sky and the great spaces of the highlands, or the paled huts on a lowland lagoon, or any old tienda full of smoke and pulque and vomit in any old village in the provinces sufficiently far from Mexico City. Of course, it would be difficult for our solemn friends to fill an evening's programme with their stereotyped tunes and the crazy tempo of seven or fifteen beats (seven-eight or fifteen-sixteen time). We had better leave them where they are. There they fill much more than a single evening. A Mexican fiesta of less than three days is not a fiesta.

We photographed the marimba band from every angle. Kliesing, the optimist, asked the musicians for a genuine camera smile. The musicians looked at Kliesing solemnly but unresponsively. That was when Timber could no longer restrain himself. He laughed his kind and solvent laughter so that the village square echoed with it. There was a certain amount of general mirth, but not much. The highland Indians are a very solemn race, as I have mentioned before. Marimba players are even more solemn. Their play went on with undisturbed, superb precision. They did not bat an eyelid. They looked at Timber solemnly but unresponsively.

My wife showed the marimba players how to smile at a camera. The marimba players looked attentively at my wife. Then their honest Indian faces broke into a broad grin for about five seconds.

During those five seconds Kliesing filmed like mad, and I too took some pictures. It was a good thing that Kliesing was an optimist and that we had my wife with us. Women are always useful for photography.

Then we photographed the Mexican flag and everybody was delighted.

After half an hour we had to leave. We paid the three marimba players, who were still playing, thus probably ruining their integrity. The others were allowed to look through my precious Zeiss-Ikon cameras by way of reward. The children got empty film boxes, and my wife distributed sweets. Only the women got nothing. But then the women, at least the young and pretty ones, had had eyes only for Timber. With a cordial handshake—every inhabitant crowded around us (I would never have believed that shaking hands was an Indian custom)—we departed from the hospitable village. Some pleasant young men accompanied us to a path round the lake which was said to be much shorter than the one we had taken.

True, it was shorter, but I had been against taking it all the same, because night would soon fall and then it would probably become surprisingly long, whereas our old path would be shorter, for the simple reason that we knew it. Kliesing, the great optimist, was all for taking the "short" one and I allowed myself to be persuaded by Kliesing, more or less for the last time on this trip. With this I do not want to say that I was always right and Kliesing wrong—quite the contrary. It was only that slowly I was reaching an age when you prefer doing things your own way. On my expeditions I had always done things my own way and now I had grown rigid and insisted, without exactly saying so, on my enormous experience, not only in the Mexican bush (where I had never been before) but in any bush or non-bush anywhere. I realized that this enormous so-called experience could be cancelled out by the most absurd chance, but the Mexican bush, I thought, would not be different from any other bush, although in the end we nearly died. All I am trying to say is that Kliesing's optimism sometimes irritated, and that my suggestions were not always clever either. In contrast to me, who from pig-headedness preferred to do things my own way, Kliesing, who was the same age, always gave in immediately. That explains why we never quarrelled seriously. This alone does not explain, of course, why Kliesing was such a good travelling companion—the best, apart from my wife, that one could imagine. A little frivolous with his dangerous optimism, but reliable—and on the whole even more amiable than Timber. Not that I am saying anything against Timber! One simply had to love Timber, whereas among the rest of us men there could not be any question of love: at the most, a kind of grumpy benevolence.

Well, in the darkness we lost our way, got off our path and on to another one which we did not recognize. We spent some unpleasant hours groping through the darkness, reconciled ourselves to a night in the woods, till finally, towards midnight, we got home to Don Herlindo's rancho.

The next morning, somewhat sleepily, we drove to Las Margaritas.

*   *   *

Geographically I must have muddled the reader hopelessly by now. It would probably be best if we start again at the beginning and state that we started from Comitán at the frontier of Guatemala. From Comitán we had driven thirty miles south-east to the lake district of Montebello where we had got stuck. It now turned out that there was another place at the edge of the wilderness, a proper "town", from which it would be easier to get on. This town was in the opposite direction from Comitán, about seventeen miles north-east.

We did not have to go back to Comitán, and for some childish reason this filled us with satisfaction. I say for some reason, because Kliesing and I were not quite sure. Perhaps we did not want to admit a defeat and provoke the people of Comitán to demonstrations of sympathy. Or perhaps somehow we did not want to associate ourselves with the saint from the bush, but preferred to remain independent and free of the usual "old-timber" tutelage.

We climbed aboard Sancho Panza's pick-up again, overloaded with our boats, tents, numbered cases and odds and ends, and set off through the region of the pine wood. Two were sitting in front with him; three were trying not to fall off the back.

The pine wood was thinning, the recognizable road petered out. About half-way to Comitán Don Herlindo turned right at a place which was not marked at all, and he did it so unexpectedly that the three of us at the back were hurled first against the roof and then against each other. This happened fairly regularly, for Don Herlindo was an impetuous driver who spared neither his vehicle nor ourselves.

We were now in the *meseta alta*. The open, undulating country was broken here and there by low mud or stone walls, by ranchos and groups of trees under which cattle were grazing. Occasionally there were hills with Indian villages, their huts lying low, flat and brown as if dried out by the wind and the sun. Then there was nothing—nothing except the blue distance with white clouds at the edge of the mountain ranges.

We rose and fell in the undulating country like a lone diesel schooner on a yellow-green sea with soft, soundless breakers on the horizon.

Towards noon we climbed through erosion gorges across a small, bare mountain range which had suddenly appeared. In the hot gorges it was jump down and push till the sweat poured off us—up-down, up-down, because stones were in the way; then we were up again, with the upland wind blowing through our sticky shirts. On the other side of the mountain range the country became green and violet with sugar cane, and after that yellow with the harvested maize fields. The small mud walls appeared again, a proper road with holes and stones. Finally dusty trees; huts; a vast plaza of uneven earth with two horsemen galloping across it, and trees round the plaza and rows of houses. We had reached Las Margaritas. At two o'clock on a Friday afternoon we reached Las Margaritas which was just then taking its siesta. Not that anything happens there at any time; but at this hour even the vultures were sleeping.

We woke up an Indian who was asleep in the porch of the church and asked him for Don Emilio's house. There, unfortunately, we had to wake up the whole family. We knocked at the yard gate and the señora was the first to come shuffling out. Doña Elvira, brown with black plaits, the wife of the man we were looking for. We were in luck, Don Emilio was at home: a wiry, upright Mexican.

He looked us over suspiciously.

We decided at once to use "Don Enrique", Harry, as a reference.

Don Emilio's features lit up.

We unloaded everything and dragged it into the portico of Don Emilio's house. Opposite was the realm of Doña Elvira—a single-story kitchen-hut. We paid Don Herlindo, and Don Herlindo prayed for a great number of blessings on ourselves and our enterprise. Since nobody in the Mexican provinces would dream of expecting payment for time and trouble, but only for tangible goods and materials, Don Herlindo had the feeling of having made a lot of money out of us. He rattled away without disturbing Las Margaritas in its sweet slumber. We are happy to recommend him.

In the garden behind Don Emilio's house we set up our tents under beautiful citrus trees. The fruit was large and ripe like oranges, but yellow like lemons, and the flesh was light in colour like that of lemons or grapefruit. The flavour, however, was sweet and insipid, and we did not much like it. Then after three days we liked it more and more. The garden bordered on a small bamboo thicket and a little river, which supplied Las Margaritas with drinking, cooking and washing water, and which (as we learnt later) served also as the village sewer. We had our paradise garden to ourselves. We washed and bathed happily in the river. From the high trees of the other bank forty-three large vultures, zopilotes, as they are called, followed our activities with interest. These zopilotes sit in a row and wait till a dog starves, a mule dies, a horse is given the *coup de grâce*. Then they come fluttering down. They are mainly interested in the intestines.

It was a pretty spot to bathe and pitch one's tent—an oasis of a place. I would never have thought that camping in Las Margaritas could be so pleasant, for over Las Margaritas fly hawks and flocks of screaming birds: black vultures and red kites and silver herons. It is a town with a pestilential stench and no drainage; no sockets for electricity and television, no sockets for anything—only a post office, which is kept by a mustachioed señora and her daughter, with flowers in the patio and a tienda next door—and a police station, of course with policemen who regard foreigners with amused benevolence. In Mexico a foreigner can go where he wants, even to hell, without once having to report his arrival or departure. Las Margaritas—a town with the stench of excrement, a waste of bumpy earth, stamped firm every day by a thousand Indian feet, a town with unpaved alleys and a white baroque church, built of mud, tall and ornate under the blinding light of the sun. The last town at the edge of the wilderness.

Perhaps you will not follow me when I say that with all its screaming birds against the fiery evening sky, its cholera, its pestilence, its swarming life, it was a better place than Mexico City or dull Acapulco or any of the world's great capitals—more beautiful even than the hanging gardens of Semiramis. You think I exaggerate? Perhaps I do. But perhaps I do not.

*　　　*　　　*

The next morning my wife came back from shopping on the zócalo, very excited.

"Just look at *that!*"

I stepped out of the garden and into the street and looked. Like columns of ants they came up into the town from the green valleys below, up through our alley, up to the zócalo. Their heads bent down, the loads held on their backs by a strap across the forehead, brown and sturdy with blue-black hair, the women in colourful skirts, their legs brown and grey like the earth itself, the men with the indispensable razor-sharp machete at their side—that's how they came by in a queer tripping run—tup-tup-tup—tup-tup-tup——

The first bush Indios we had seen.

Small and dark, shy and wild with their yard-long razor-sharp weapons.

You can easily chop off somebody's head with a machete.

From far away they came to the town, which was stranger to them than to any foreigner, to sell a few beans, a bunch of bananas, a sack of charcoal, a captive iguana or some other strange object. Mute and immovable they squatted in the market. The Mexican housewives looked at the displayed goods or picked them up for inspection. If they wanted to buy, they threw a coin on the ground in front of the Indian. If the coin was too small, the Indian said: "No." Except for this "no" the Indian does not speak during the whole transaction, and he never once raises his eyes. Except for "no" he hardly knows a word of Spanish. If the housewife will not pay more, no amount of cajolery will make any difference. There is nothing left for her but to bend down, return the vegetable, or the egg, or the chicken, pick up her coin and leave. Simply to walk away with the goods is a course of action not to be recommended. Without raising his eyes, showing anger or particular hurry, the Indian will gather up his shop and silently follow his customer. Without speaking a single word or once raising his eyes he will squat in front of her house for days and nights till at last her nerves cannot stand the strain any more. There is no bargaining. If the Indian does not sell his stuff, he packs up his vegetables, charcoal or iguanas, and treks the twenty or thirty miles back to his home in the bush.

They were the most uncanny Indians we saw in all Mexico. They were even more uncanny than the Seri whom we—my wife and I by ourselves—later visited on the Tiburón Islands. Until ten years before, those Seri were said to have killed everybody who landed on their islands. But the Seri—the most primitive Indians of both Americas, more primitive than the bush Indians from Chiapas—were gay and carefree in comparison with these creatures of the forest. I do not even know what kind of Indians they were. Possibly they are an isolated tribe of the Tzotzil group.

They were uncanny and harmless. They seemed to have only one desire: to be left in peace.

Their dangerous appearance was due to their long, sharp machetes. For all Indians the machete is their most precious possession. Everybody else who seeks to go into the bush needs it too, of course. The Indians handle it very skilfully, and although they do not use it for picking their teeth, because it is too big, and not for cleaning their fingernails, because they do not clean their fingernails, they use it for nearly everything else: for felling trees, for beating and marking horses, for building huts, for hunting and for self-defence. They file and grind these machetes so lovingly to such a sharp edge, that, as I said, one can chop off a person's head with them. It is a very dangerous weapon. The North American tomahawk is a toy by comparison.

That in spite of this it is very rarely used as a murder weapon speaks for the Indians' peaceful character. But from time to time it happens—after all, murder is statistically established as the second cause of death in Mexico. (The first is malaria.)

Just a year before us a young German painter had come to Las Casas. On the way to a village of the comparatively civilized Huitzteco Indians he met a group of men walking to their fields. They greeted the foreigner politely, as is their custom. For some reason, perhaps because he just happened to be far away in his thoughts, or perhaps because he was embarrassed by his ignorance of the language, instead of replying to the greeting the young artist gave a little laugh, and his laughter was misinterpreted. The men did not like it at all. Perhaps they took it for derision. They walked on, wondering about him.

In the village the painter found only women and children. He looked round for a bit, the women suspiciously watching him. When he started to draw them they ran away, screaming. The women ran to their men in the fields and excitedly told them about the foreigner with the evil eye who was trying to ensnare their souls with his black art.

All this was very unsatisfactory, and the young man at least wanted to make friends with such children as had not run away with their mothers. He gave them sweets and began to play with them. To amuse them and calm their fright he went down on all fours and hopped around, barking like a dog. (All this was put on record afterwards.) Just at that moment the men came back with their women. When they saw the gringo hopping among their children on all fours they were struck with sheer terror, for in the opinion and tradition of the Huitzteco Indians—good Catholics all—a man who hops on the ground on all fours can only be the devil.

They lifted their machetes and struck——

The head clean off the body.

When the authorities found the rest of him it was not far away, but it was far from being in one piece. It was, even in the official consular jargon, a devil of a mess.

*　　　*　　　*

Don Emilio—our man!

He knew the difficult path to the last settlement in the hills, and from there to the hut of Harry the hermit. After that it could not be very far to the Jataté. He promised to take us the last stretch, too.

The animal situation did not look very promising. Even the whole of Las Margaritas was unable to provide the number of mules we needed, and for a very plausible reason: the small amount of barley straw and green oats from the surrounding fields was insufficient, and the maize far too precious, to give to the mules for fodder. Idle animals would have been an expensive hobby, and Indians do not keep mules, nor donkeys, nor horses. Indians walk and carry their loads themselves—up to a hundred and forty pounds on their necks, held by a strap across the forehead. That was the explanation of the stooping posture and tripping run. The bush Indians of Las Margaritas practised it even when they were not carrying anything, or only an empty sack or raffia bag, but we could not hire fifty or sixty Indians as porters as you can still do in some parts of Africa, in the best colonial tradition. Apart from the fact that we would have felt like the lowest of exploiters, the Indians would not have let us hire them. Not because they dislike work—that applies only to the more progressive among them—but simply because they are not as fond of travelling as the Africans are and hate leaving their tribal area. Perhaps they are also more proud. It is the impossibility of finding native porters which makes overland expeditions in tropical America so difficult. Only Mexicans, proper rancheros, keep horses and mules. When Don Emilio, who only owned a grey himself, found that he could not get any animals in the neighbourhood, he declared he would have to ride to La Soledad and Patihuitz —nebulous names to us—to collect animals. It would take two or three days. He demanded an advance.

Paulchen said we ought to be careful.

We gave Don Emilio the advance.

On our first evening in Las Margaritas we stumbled up the dark alley to the zócalo. From tiendas round the huge square fell the peaceful light of oil lamps. We drank comiteco in all the tiendas which were still open, so as not to offend any one proprietor. The tiendas were dens of wood and mud, filled to the ceiling with boxes and sacks, tins and sweets, rope and salt, machetes and tools, candles and soap, Carta Blanca beer and Pepsi-Cola and what have you—most of it not for the needs of the town's population but rather for the Indians of the neighbourhood. For Las Margaritas is an important market, a town that lives by trade and barter with the Indians, who have an insatiable appetite for Pepsi-Cola. That is why there were so many tiendas in Las Margaritas.

The more important ones offered seating accommodation at a table covered with fly-blown oil-cloth. It was all very cosy. Luckily the comiteco glasses were very small and not many of the tiendas stayed open in the evening. The comiteco was extremely good and mild, hardly more than thirty degrees proof, guaranteed pure and therefore acceptable to our vegetarians. Later on we no longer minded about offending other proprietors, but chose our "local"; whose comforting light shone out into the night, waiting for us when all the other tiendas had closed. It was kept by a señora with two daughters (not the post office señora) who watched us being merry and (all three of them) cast fiery glances at Timber.

Saturday night was cinema night.

It was the most remarkable cinema in the world. The film was a Mexican one, featuring elegant men-about-town in the Paris of the 'nineties, with passionate love in marbled halls, evening dress, many Can-Can interludes and all the trimmings, shown in a barn-like building. The audience was composed of mestizos and Indians. None of the uncanny bush Indians were there, only educated townspeople, mainly teddy boys, but also women and girls. The women sat on one side, many of them with babies sucking at their ample breasts. The teddy boys screamed and laughed when the Can-Can girls kicked their legs and showed their black stockings, which they did quite often. It was not that they thought this sexy: they thought it was devastatingly funny.

The original film had been copied on to 16 mm. Because Las Margaritas had no electricity, the cinema people—a melancholy lady and two dim caballeros—were obliged to bring their own generator set which puffed away outside the barn and would never have had the power to pull a 35-mm. film through the projector. All this did nothing to spoil the general enjoyment, and the only sad thing was that the public preferred to give their attention to us instead of the

Parisian masterpiece from Mexico City. I cannot pretend that this attention—flattering in its way—was in the least embarrassing. There being five of us we felt our strength and solidity. We attended the performance for about twenty-five minutes and then left the theatre, mainly because Timber laughed even louder over the Can-Can ladies than the teddy boys, and because we were afraid of lice, and the fleas were already making a welcome change of diet on us.

General regret at our early departure.

"They don't like it!" cried the people of Las Margaritas in disappointment.

My wife was so touched by this that she said we ought to sit down again to show goodwill and lack of haughtiness. My wife likes to be kind to people, and we nearly weakened, but then Timber broke out laughing again, and so resoundingly that the rest of us were infected, too, and had to leave the world's most remarkable cinema in a hurry.

*   *   *

On Monday evening—to our great surprise—who should appear but Don Enrique. Not a fortnight, barely a week, had passed since our meeting in Comitán. His early arrival, a week before the time he had mentioned, seemed somehow suspicious.

Kliesing and I put up all kinds of theories about it. Paulchen said at once that we ought to be on our guard. (Our suspicions were contemptible. I am still ashamed about it.)

"I heard in Comitán that your Santo Domingo trail was a wash-out," cried Harry with outstretched arms. "That's why I did everything to get here as quickly as possible and meet the rest of your party!"

We greeted him with exaggerated heartiness.

My wife and Timber liked him at once. Kliesing and I suddenly thought that the saint was not so extraordinarily saintly any more, but quite a normal person.

"What a handsome man!" my wife exclaimed.

His beard was not as long as it had been. He had had it cut in Las Casas, but only cut short, not cut off completely. His hair still flowed in natural golden waves down to his shoulders.

We invited our friend to dinner outside our tent. My wife and I had a very beautiful, roomy and comfortable Klepper tent with a useful porch which was highly suitable to the occasion. Kliesing had a normal tent with a back entrance. He had had this back entrance made specially in order to ensure a steady current of air and to be able to get away quickly in case he was attacked or in case a snake, jaguar or wild boar came rushing in through the front. Paulchen and Timber did not have such a safety exit. They each had a small U.S. Army tropical tent with a strange, mosquito-proof ventilating device at the back. They could look out through it, but not escape. Therefore, if something rushed in through the front, or if they were attacked, they would be in a comparatively less favourable position than Kliesing and ourselves (whose Klepper tent also boasted a kind of emergency exit).

"I see," said Harry, "that you're excellently equipped! That's the most important thing in the bush. If you're not excellently equipped you won't last a week."

He was pleased that Don Emilio had gone to look for animals. He said we could rely on Don Emilio. We ventured to offer him rice and sardines in tomato sauce. The sardines gave no offence to his vegetarian convictions. Cold-blooded animals. No, it wasn't a dogma. After all, even plants were higher life-forms which we killed to eat. Comiteco? Ugh!

He told us breath-taking tales about his protégés, the Lacandones. He explained to us all the ramifications of the Bor Group. We immediately got it all muddled. We put off taking notes till later; we did not want to interrupt his stories. He intended to bring the three remaining groups of

Lacandones together and settle them in a reservation. The centre of this reservation was to be the Miramar Lagoon—the ancient centre of the country of the Lacandones—that mysterious lake which all Lacandones have been avoiding like the plague for the last two hundred and fifty years and which we meant to reach.

Did he think they would settle there? He said it was a question of subtle psychological preparation and education. He had already approached the government of Chiapas in Tuxtla Guiterrez. The government of Chiapas had listened to his propositions with the greatest benevolence. But you know the Mexicans. They always listen, but they do nothing —not the slightest concern for their ethnologically interesting compatriots! He had now approached UNESCO. That was more promising.

Meanwhile he was doing some journalism to enlighten the world about the fate of the Lacandones. That was why he had hurried back as quickly as possible from Las Casas, to join us because I was a writer. As a writer I, too, could enlighten the world on his idea of a reservation for a dying people.

He told us enthusiastic stories about the Lacandones. Secretly I took it with a large pinch of salt, although he spoke convincingly. I found it hard to imagine the Lacandones as anything but the usual unwashed, slightly rancid-smelling savages, as I had met them on the Amazon, in New Guinea, in the South Seas, in South-East Asia and in the remoter parts of Ethiopia. Sometimes, if they liked you, they were gay and communicative. Cheerful as children. Only they did not have any more children, unfortunately. Inbreeding, brother-sister and father-daughter marriages— amazingly healthy in spite of it. You could not apply our own moral values to them. For instance, in their marital relations they did not take notice of any chance spectators. When they felt like it, they did it amidst joking and laughing, wherever they just happened to be and without letting anything interrupt them . . . We hoped that they would not take any notice of us.

They were very religious. They took their old myths seriously: the moon, the sun, the river; the rain and the maize, the mountains and the caves, the fire and the underworld. Before every meal they sacrificed to the river god. For religious reasons they wore their hair long and flowing down their shoulders.

"Ah," we said. "That's why you wear yours——"

"Yes," said Harry. "For the last five years. Since I've lived with the Lacandones."

Harry came of a wealthy family in Vermont and had once wanted to study literature or something like that, but when his family lost a great part of their money in the crash of 1929, they insisted on his taking a more practical course. He read law, and in the course of this got interested in co-operative societies. The co-operative movement was almost unknown in America at that time, although it was already well developed in Great Britain, Germany and Scandinavia. In the 'thirties, at the time of Roosevelt's New Deal, there was a rising interest in it, so, as a student and with very little money, Harry went to England and studied the co-operatives. On the way over he met his wife, a young teacher, who had been given a grant for post-graduate study. (He did not tell us all this right away, of course; he told it to us later at camp fires and in his hut. I am summing up his story now— in the idyllic garden of Las Margaritas, so to speak—because later I may not find the space for it.)

After a short while it turned out that he was one of five or six students in the whole of the United States who was working on this subject. His institute gave him small bonuses of fifty dollars, sometimes a hundred dollars. Later, after some successful work, a hundred and fifty, once even five hundred. Finally he got a small permanent grant.

"With that I could manage quite well."

He travelled all over Europe with the exception of Italy and Germany, because he liked "neither Mussolini nor Herr Hitler". Shortly before the outbreak of war he returned to the United States. He met Eleanor Roosevelt who was very interested in the co-operative movement and his work on it. At that time Harry gathered round him a number of disciples. Not on account of the co-operatives, but because of his naturalism.

When America entered the war, Harry declared himself and his small community conscientious objectors. As an all-out non-killer of higher forms of life Harry, naturally, had to be an all-out pacifist.

He was told that a collective conscientious objection was not acceptable. It could only be done individually. Well, Harry had replied, then he would dissolve his small community and herewith declare his individual objection.

He went to Sing-Sing for two years.

Not even his friendship with the wife of the President could help him there, for pacifists are notorious for being particularly nasty specimens. That is why in Sing-Sing they were treated in a much tougher fashion than honourable professional criminals. In spite of this Harry only lost a total of six teeth. And these only right at the beginning, in the course of the reception ceremony.

Two years passed. The war came to an end. The interest in the co-operatives and the New Deal came to an end, too. There was no need for it any more in boom times like the Korean War and so on. There came also the McCarthy era, and McCarthy considered all co-operatives as the devil's own creation and Communist-infested. Harry bought a farm in Montana. His wife bore him a son. They lived according to the principles of the simple life as preached by Thoreau. They grew their own vegetables. They also spun and wove their own cloth, but it seems that today you cannot even spin in Montana without being considered a noisome pestilence. Their neighbours began to regard them with mounting suspicion.

"But that wasn't the main reason why we wanted to leave," said Harry. "For our way of living and our way of gardening we simply needed a warmer climate. A tropical or at least sub-tropical climate."

Together with a like-minded friend he bought a South Sea schooner in San Francisco. With a small auxiliary engine and the blessings of all their friends the two of them set sail.

They almost foundered right outside the bay of San Francisco, because Harry's friend had fallen asleep at the helm, and they were drifting towards the rocky coast, and because the auxiliary engine refused to come to life at the decisive moment. But they got clear and managed to set course for the Marquesas Islands and Tahiti.

Sixty days later they suffered the usual shipwreck on a coral reef off Uahuka. The schooner had run aground. The natives brought cushions and bolsters and shored her up.

"Cushions, Harry?"

"Yes," Harry said. "Cushions."

We were surprised. I had never seen anything resembling cushions among the South Sea islanders. Heaven knows what kind of cushion it was. We did not ask Harry, in order not to interrupt him any further, and later we forgot to bring up the question. Anyway, the friendly islanders dragged up a lot of these items, and when the tide rose the schooner got clear of the reef. It was leaking mightily, but it was possible to have it repaired on the Marquesas.

They liked the islanders immensely, but they could not get on with the French officials. The French officials on the Marquesas were not immensely likeable. Officials have a distaste for idealists, because idealists always mean a lot of

work and trouble. That is why officials everywhere have
developed an almost unerring instinct for recognizing and
classifying such people. The officials disliked the two
Americans and cold-shouldered them. Therefore the Marquesas were a wash-out, and the two friends separated.
Harry's friend went to Tonga. There, from Queen Salote
who was not as suspicious as the French officials, he received
an island in exchange for the schooner.

He still lives there, and very happily, too.

Harry had meant to go back to the States via Panama, but
in Panama he left the ship and joined an expedition to
Chiapas. There he heard for the first time of the Lacandones.

The expedition took almost the same route as we were
going to take. For some reason they did not meet with any
Lacandones. Harry found something else: between the two
rivers Euseba and Jataté, on the slope of the Sierra Colmena,
he discovered a forest clearing of breath-taking beauty.
Below the clearing, between orchids and liana-covered trees,
flowed a murmuring river. It came from the darkness of the
forest—colibris, gorgeous butterflies and dragonflies were
dancing about its peaceful mirror—then the mysterious half-
light of the forest closed in again on its calm course. The
strange clearing breathed the peace of the world, the pure
breath of creation, as he had never felt it before . . .

"This is the place!" said Harry.

The others wanted to go on, and Harry, with the picture of
this clearing in the jungle in his heart, travelled home to the
States.

His wife had divorced him.

"A tragedy in itself," he said regretfully, "because on the
whole we understood each other perfectly. But she came
from a wealthy Mid-Western family, and the family had
been against it from the beginning. As long as I had the grant
for my work on the co-operatives everything was more or
less all right. But then they threatened to disinherit her.

You cannot blame decent citizens becoming uneasy at the thought of their daughter being married to a convict in Sing-Sing. After the war, when we wanted to lead our own lives and spin—that was too much. Of course, they thought I was a complete fool. While I was in the South Seas she collapsed under her family's pressure. I was really sorry . . ."

Harry's ideas about women: no more intellectuals! No more white women! At least not for him. That was why he had an Indian girl friend nowadays. No, not one of the Lacandones. An Indian from Guatemala. To educate an unspoilt child of nature! Sometimes she came and cooked *pozole* for him, a kind of porridge made from fermented maize and water, the classical Maya dish. Also tortillas. For the rest of the time she lived with her family in the mountains. He didn't know where she was right now.

Since Harry had returned to his paradise in Chiapas, he spent five months of each year—during the dry period from December to April—as a hermit in the hut he had built with the help of the Lacandones. (The business of his Indian girl friend remained a mystery to us.) During the desolate rainy period, which is particularly horrible in Chiapas, he returned to the United States and managed a friend's farm in Vermont.

"But soon," said Harry, "I'll be able to stay down here the whole year, even during the rainy period."

*   *   *

I return to earth. To the earth of Las Margaritas.

Don Emilio did not come back. In the mornings we bathed in the idyllic river behind the garden. Harry began to upbraid us.

"For heaven's sake," he shouted, "don't bathe!"

"Why ever not?"

"You'll all get cholera. I caught it two years ago! Right in this garden! You should have seen me hanging over the balustrade by the house there—like this!"

He held one hand over his mouth and the other vaguely behind him. He had not known any more what was front and what was behind, he said. Cramps, blue skin: when you lifted it the folds just stood up by themselves . . .

"That was something! My life was hanging by a thread. But for Doña Elvira and some of the neighbouring women . . ."

They dosed him with Indian herbs and *chicalote*, till he was so exhausted that he stopped spitting gall. Chicalote is a Mexican poppy, not the opium poppy, *Papaver somniferum*, but *Argemone mexicana*, from which they manage to extract some kind of opium. Anyway, these Indian and mestizo women got Harry over the crisis with their magic herbs and saved his life.

Yes. And all this from our sweet little river.

"Listen," Harry said. "There are no privies here."

The thought that we would not be able to wash for days, possibly for more than a week, was too painful to contemplate. From then on we washed secretly (and not quite as often and luxuriously) in the cholera river. We had to take cooking and drinking water from it, anyway, like everybody in Las Margaritas. But that was not as bad as bathing, said Harry. For drinking and for making tea one merely had to boil it thoroughly. Down in the forest, he said, everything was quite, quite different. There one could bathe to one's heart's content and drink the water just like that—he made a scooping gesture with his hand.

We boiled the water for our tea very thoroughly.

Then Harry went to bed. He had slung his hammock between two citrus trees.

The rest of us went into the town for a comiteco, and we drank the comiteco in the company of the men of Las Margaritas who were waiting for us in the tienda, and we joked with the señora and her two daughters, and my wife joked with Timber because of the fiery glances the señora and her daughters gave him. Otherwise there was nothing much going on in Las Margaritas at eight-thirty in the evening. We went home in the dark, joking, home to our tents. At home we joked about Harry who lay quietly snoring in his hammock. In his hammock with the mosquito net on top Harry looked like the cocoon of a giant silkworm. Towards morning it became cold in the highlands, and that is why Harry always got up about five and stumped about and disturbed our slumber in our cosy sleeping bags and warm tents, and we did not think kindly of Harry when he stumped about, beating his arms, disturbing us and jokingly announcing: *Emilio no parece!* Emilio won't appear!

Every day, from about three in the afternoon till sunset we expected Don Emilio to appear, but he had not.

He appeared one glorious morning shortly after eight o'clock. Suddenly this morning there was a lot of noise outside the gate. The sound of horses' hooves, neighing, a cloud of dust. Don Emilio had arrived, together with two arrieros, five horses, sixteen pack mules and the son of the animals' owner.

Great joy. The inhabitants of Las Margaritas hurried to the spot. We packed sleeping-bags and tents and all our odds and ends in exaggerated hurry. We were as excited as chickens. At eleven-thirty we were ready to mount. The population applauded us good-naturedly. Even the bush Indians hurrying past seemed suddenly good-natured.

With many speeches, including prominent references to the promiscuity of the female mule, our men set the loaded animals in motion. In a cloud of dust, and cries, and the smell of horses in the hot sun, and laughter, and the curses of the muleteers, we poured out of Las Margaritas.

The expedition was under way.

CHAPTER TWO

Children of the Forest

IN the burning heat we rode across the high plateau of Chiapas.

Slowly order came into the caravan. Each mule sought and demanded his place according to an order of rank which remained mysterious to us. This order was strictly adhered to right to the end. Woe to the mule who left the ranks or even wanted to push ahead! It was put back in his place by the other mules with bites and kicks.

Indians in white trousers and straw hats and machetes met us. They were of a different tribe from our crouching demons of Las Margaritas. They held their hats to their chests and said in Spanish: may you have a good journey!

We came through a village that was called *Gracias a Dios*, Thanks be to God.

After two and a half hours on this our first day we stopped for the night at a hill which was covered with tall pines. In spite of this charming camping spot we protested. Our guides said we must stop for the night because of the water and because the animals still needed some rest.

The animals were unsaddled, the saddles and the baggage piled round the camp, and the tents erected. Camping like this, with horses, always has the same rhythm, which is dictated by the animals. The animals turned us into nomads with an ordered way of life. But for the first day it was a disappointing way of life, however well ordered.

The early camp in the pine wood above a little river had one great advantage. We could bathe. Harry declared bathing to be quite safe, although not nearly as safe as down in the forest, but he himself only took off his sweaty shirt. He did not go into the water with us, not because of cholera but because he felt unwell. He ran a sudden temperature, but he said it was nothing. It always appeared when he came up from the forest and it reappeared when he went down again. It was simply the change of climate and a touch of malaria. Then he showed us a carbuncle on his back, a real prize carbuncle. But Harry said it was not a carbuncle. He said there was a worm inside. He asked us to look closely and see if we could spot the worm. My wife, Timber and I examined it closely. It was a carbuncle the size of two fists together, yellow in the middle, but still quite hard.

"No worm," said Timber.

"There must be a worm," said Harry.

"If there is a worm, then it's simply one of the kind the dentists in the Middle Ages believed in. They thought the pulp of a tooth was a worm which had to be pulled out. What you've got there, my dear Harry, is nothing but a monster boil, a furuncle, an inflammation, a carbuncle——"

Did he not feel it move? Had we not noticed a black spot under the yellow?

Yes, said my wife. She had seen something black, but it was tiny. It was only the speck of dirt which had caused the whole inflammation.

"No, that is the worm," said Harry, but if it was only tiny it was too soon to do anything. He would leave it till he got to his Lacandones. They would burst the thing, and if the worm didn't come out they would smear tobacco juice on it. Then it was sure to come out. With great rings of fat (like the tyre-men of the Michelin advertisements) and a black head and sometimes thicker and longer than a thumb. A fat ringed worm . . .

"Ugh," my wife said. "Some paradise where worms like that creep under one's skin!"

They came, Harry assured us, from a fly, *musca gusanera*, which laid its eggs under one's skin. The worms were called *colmijotes*. Nothing much to worry about, since a little tobacco juice would do the trick.

"Thanks very much," said my wife.

"It's only a bit unpleasant," said Harry, "when you feel them move."

With awe we contemplated Harry's carbuncle which was supposed to house a worm. For some reason we did not quite believe in this worm. We would have forgotten it if Harry had not told us repeatedly during the following days that he could feel the worm moving. Then we forgot the worm entirely, but a few weeks later we were reminded of it, and then we never forgot it again.

*　　　*　　　*

The lazy afternoon at our first camp might have been happy and harmonious. That it was not was due to Paulchen. Paulchen was not only one of the most modest, but also one of the most zealous of men. You could not have wished for a better travelling companion. Paulchen thought of nothing but his duty, i.e. acting as (vegetarian) cook to Kliesing, Timber and himself. I think I have already mentioned that he had once been a first-class professional cook. Several times my wife and I had occasion to regret that we had light-heartedly dispensed with his services. For with his Swedish waffle-iron, maize-meal, water and a little vegetable oil Paulchen made waffles of such crispness, delicacy and even nutritive value, that they were absolutely out of this world. Even Aveckle, my wife, herself a very good cook, learnt a lot from Paulchen. Timber, for his part, enjoyed all the advantages of a two-kitchen expedition, gladly accepting our invitations to have "a second helping". Later he was fed for a time by both parties, and finally only by us.

But—as I was going to say—as soon as we had set foot on

Above: Don Oscar is amused by the antics of the *gringos*: on his plate black beans with chilli and oil. *Below:* Aveckle outside Harry's hut.

Above : Harry leads a flotilla of laughing Lacandones.

Below : The "blond god of the Lacandones" in his hut.

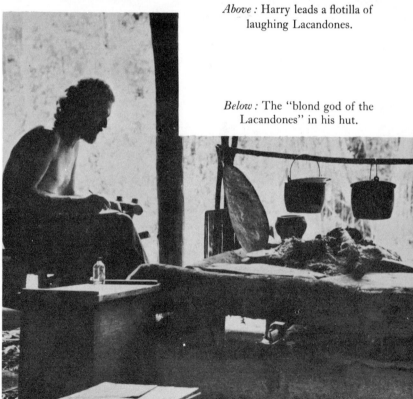

even the most inhospitable shore, Paulchen's first thought was of nothing but his duties as a cook. He built his stove, went looking for the right kind of wood, lit a fire and began to brew one of his weird teas.

He was wonderful at getting a fire going. When it was wet and pouring with rain, in the middle of the jungle, he could make a roaring fire in a matter of minutes. It's an old forest-ranger's trick, which depends on an instinct in finding the "right" kind of wood. For the "right", or seasoned, wood is only wet on the outside, and with a little skill and very little trouble you can cut it up with the machete in the wettest place.

That afternoon, Paul had straightaway remembered his duties, built his stove and lit a fire.

But he had set fire to the pine trees as well.

From the river we saw Paulchen running about excitedly on the hill. Then, in the bright sunshine, we saw thin wisps of smoke, the top edges small, black, and broken. The horses and mules, which were grazing unfettered, galloped wildly away. The dry ground underneath the pines was burning merrily. The fire was darting like lightning in every direction. It was only an inch or so high as yet. We raced after it with sticks and whatever we could lay hands on and tried to put it out. It sprang up in the most unlikely places and we worked like mad. Luckily there was only a very light breeze; but it was enough to drive the fire away from the camp and towards a fence and a field of maize. If the wind had been blowing from a different quarter the expedition would have come to an inglorious end, and our first camp would have been our last. For then we could only have saved the animals and ourselves. We should have lost all the tents, our equipment, boats, saddles and everything else. But we were lucky and worked till the sweat was streaming off us.

We all smelt a bit singed and we laughed. At the end of

two hours we had the fire under control. Only the fence was still burning. We spent a further hour fetching water to put it out. Then we cleaned ourselves in the river and brewed lashings of tea on our Enders petrol stove, about which Paulchen and Kliesing had said some pretty caustic things in the past. We were glad that we had the petrol stove, because we were all parched and thirsty. Later, on many occasions when the business with the "right" firewood did not work, Paul and Kliesing were very glad my wife could make tea on the Enders right away.

In the evening the sky became overcast and we talked with Don Emilio and Don Oscar about the best way to make a fire in a dry forest without setting the forest on fire. Don Oscar was the son of the man who owned the animals. He was a smart young man with a black moustache and carried an alarm horn like those blown by gangers' look-outs at the approach of a train, as well as a fat six-shooter, in his ammunition belt. He was even-tempered—even later, when he did not want to go on—not without wit, and decent. We liked him very much.

Then we were joined by an Indian from the neighbouring village, who listened attentively to our conversation the whole evening, but when he was about to leave he asked for ten pesos (five and sixpence).

"Why, *amigo*?"

"I am the owner of the fence."

We paid for the fence. True, it had been a fairly rough fence, but all the same, we had burned a hundred yards of it. We were glad that fences were cheap in Chiapas. We did not feel like spoiling the market so we gave the man his ten pesos, feeling rather bad about it. The man thanked us politely and left. We felt pretty low.

It began to drizzle, although we were in the highlands and it was the middle of the dry season. We turned in, and in the wet everything smelt even more of charred wood. The

66

arrieros and the two Mexicans lay down somewhere on their horse blankets, and Harry was already in his hammock. He had a temperature, but he said it would be down in two days.

* * *

The next day we left the high plateau of Chiapas and entered the high mountain range which shuts off the Lacandones' country like a wall.

We rode for seven hours, and Harry became very ill. It was hard going, because we had to cross valleys and to negotiate a lot of steep slopes. Harry often had to put his arms round his horse's neck to save himself from falling off. He said he was sorry that he was in such bad shape, and we said we were very sorry for *him*.

We came to a place in a large valley, a place consisting of a few huts and a ruined church which was called La Soledad, "Solitude". From above it looked just like that, but when we came down the coffee had just been harvested, and the valley was filled with a curious sound. As we were riding through small pineapple plantations we noticed that the sound came from the hard leaves of the pineapple plants as the wind blew through them.

On the bridle-path some eight or nine hundred feet higher up on the other side of the valley we got into a bramble thicket with fat, juicy blackberries—such as you find in Europe in the autumn. Six hundred feet higher we emerged into spring. One lone farm was surrounded by flowering almond trees.

Fresh mountain wind. Eagles in the transparent blue. White clouds rising from the invisible sea of the forest.

Later, grey clouds and rain.

Early in the afternoon we reached the Rancho Patihuitz. At five thousand seven hundred feet it was the highest stopping place on our journey to the Lacandones. The rancho was Don Oscar's home, and belonged to his father. It was from here that our animals came.

We lifted Harry from his horse. He was promptly sick. Harry said he was sorry. He lay down at once in one of the huts and we saw nothing of him until the next morning.

Don Oscar's father was a cantankerous old patriarch and inclined to be familiar. We disliked him from the word go. We liked Oscar but not his father. The father seized the opportunity to raise the price of his animals. The animals needed maize, and he wanted a lot more money for maize, but the maize had been included in the price. Don Emilio withdrew discreetly.

Kliesing asked Don Oscar's father whether he had ever been to the capital.

"*Claro*," said Don Oscar's father.

Did he know what a taxi was?

"*Naturalmente*."

Well, then he would know that you did not have to pay for the *gasolina*. That was included in the fare.

Yes, Don Oscar's father said. But maize was the gasolina of the mule: "*La gasolina de la mula es el maíze!*"

He liked this argument so much that he kept repeating the sentence.

"*La gasolina de la mula es el maíz.*"

He kept repeating it even when we bought twenty pesos' worth of extra maize from him just to stop him saying it, because it began to get on our nerves. Although Don Oscar's father was satisfied and triumphant that he had done us so easily he did not stop proclaiming his new-found wisdom as soon as he got hold of one of us. To this day he probably still says, "*La gasolina de la mula es el maíz*", whenever he comes across an expert.

Don Oscar's mama was a tough señora who probably ruled her family and her servants with a pretty heavy hand, but for fifteen pesos she prepared for us—my wife, myself and Timber, who also got a helping—a great meal of beans, two chickens, rice, chilli sauce, of such superb quality that it would not have disgraced the table of the Hotel del Prado in Mexico City. In this strange place, Patihuitz, our tents stood behind the huts of the rancho on a piece of grass land, on a hill between two deep valleys. We might have been able to admire a grand, sub-tropical, mountain landscape if it had not been raining miserably and if it had not been so cold.

*   *   *

On the third day of our trek we did not get into our saddles till ten o'clock.

Harry's temperature had gone. He still felt weak—but his malaria had nearly disappeared, as far as you can ever say that of malaria.

That day we rode for six hours, up and down, across country which became progressively hotter and more tropical.

Steaming valleys.

The mule path became slippery and muddy. At the height of the dry season it was muddy. But it had been well hacked out of the dense forest. We were still travelling on recognized paths which led to the last remote settlements. In Patihuitz we had even been joined by a man with four animals. For a long time we could not make out why he was travelling in these parts and why he joined us. It turned out that he was a salesman who supplied the remoter settlements with elegant consumer goods such as elastic bands, safety-pins, cotton, machetes, chamber-pots, nylon stockings, hairpins, soap, tinned fish, Pepsi-Cola, chewing gum and other useful things in exchange for coffee. He was a gay Mexican who contributed much to the general fun and at the same time gave our caravan a more solid and business-like look.

At four o'clock in the afternoon we set up camp in a village called "Providence". It lay in a lovely valley near the Rio Dolores. Harry was already so much better that, on the following morning, he resumed his old habit of getting up two hours before sunrise, and walking about the camp, disturbing our sleep. In this respect he was utterly insensitive. Paulchen was also inclined to get up before sunrise, and you could hear him busying himself with his stove, quietly breaking wood, lighting the fire, and doing all kinds of things with the utmost quiet, since he was a most considerate man, who did not want to disturb anybody.

And so, that dark morning, we heard Harry stamping about and talking to Paulchen, who was quietly breaking wood, and we wished Harry to the devil, for Harry was raising his voice because Paulchen did not answer him, and because Harry thought Paulchen did not understand his English. But Paulchen did not answer simply because he disliked Harry. We wished Harry even more to the devil.

We also began to suspect that Harry, now that his temperature had gone down, was becoming dictatorial. The evening before he had solemnly declared that he had no wish to be dictatorial. Nothing was farther from his mind! Kliesing and I had declared that nothing was farther from our minds, either. It was pointless being dictatorial.

Excellent, Harry had replied, because after tomorrow everything would be different. We were now coming to the real forest, and things were tough in the real forest, where tough men were sometimes faced with ticklish situations. It was sometimes necessary to make snap decisions. Kliesing and I had said: "Well, when things were tough . . ."

After that we had not known how to go on, but Harry asked us for permission to make certain decisions when things were tough.

I did not mind, and I had asked Kliesing to agree, which he had done at once. I had told Harry that amongst ourselves we were pretty democratic and, what is more, all grown-up. We were therefore likely to act reasonably and logically. Since we were more or less intruders in the realm where he had held sway for five years, and where he knew every path and every twist and turn, nothing would be more logical than to entrust him with the leadership of this part of our expedition. . . .

Harry thanked us profusely for our trust.

It had been a typical piece of expedition-nonsense. The stage had been set for a first-rate comedy. That it did not come to that—at least not as long as Harry was with us—was not just due to the fact that things did not get tough. That came much later. It was due to the fact that Harry, although he had struck a rather theatrical note, was a very capable, sympathetic, decent man. All of us had to admit that very soon. Except Paulchen. Paulchen never admitted it.

Perhaps I am repeating myself: Harry was for us *the* chance to get an immediate contact with the Lacandones— if everything went well. The Lacandones knew that their friend would return during the days of the new moon. They were waiting for the rocket which would announce his arrival. Then the whole tribe would gather at the confluence of the Jataté and the Rio Perlas. Harry said they were sure to come to receive the presents he was bringing.

We were very curious to see whether everything would work out like this and we were very curious to see the Lacandones.

Harry did not normally travel with animals. Usually he walked; carefree, with just rucksack, hammock and machete. Indians brought him supplies down from the highlands— also travelling on foot. The few tracks which lead from the *meseta alta* down to the jungle are made by naked Indian feet. Somewhere in the jungle the tracks get lost, but long before that they have become almost impassable even for mules. It is walking country. Harry liked to start very early in the morning, rest during the hot midday hours, and then walk again till sunset. He tried to sell us the idea, but we could never manage it. Not our fault, though. Harry had not realized that a caravan adopts a very different rhythm.

The reason is obvious. It takes two people at least ten to fifteen minutes to load a mule. Saddling the horses is a little quicker. We had four experts, and at first twenty-one, later nineteen animals. The whole business took at least two hours.

There are many advantages in all this, but at first we had a hellish struggle convincing the experts that it was quite unnecessary to begin the loading with our sleeping-bags and the breakfast things, as some strange tradition apparently required.

Arrieros loading up offer a spectacle which is well worth seeing. It is always the same: the mule is caught, a dirty rag is tied over its eyes to prevent it from kicking and bolting, then it gets a few boots in the belly just to remind it of what will happen if it is stubborn. Then the animal's back is plastered with sheepskins, the driest one at the bottom. The sheepskins are always wet and stinking. On top of this spongy plaster are laid straps of raw-hide with dangling loops. Then two men lift the heavy load, press it against the mule's flanks with their chests till somebody throws the loops across so that they can be tied. I have watched the performance carefully several times, but to this day I do not know exactly how it is done.

The side-loads form a kind of platform, on which the arrieros pile as many packs as they think the animal can carry. All this to the accompaniment of picturesque but invariably obscene language; knowing old mules start groaning and wobbling their knees very early on. When at last a compromise has been struck between the animal's acting ability and the arrieros' opinion, a large number of lassos are wound round load and belly. While this goes on, the men plant one foot firmly against the animal's ribs, while the crafty mule blows itself up like an "escapologist" submitting to chains. The result lasts till the evening—unless the country is too difficult, or the mules intentionally bump against trees or rocks, or roll with the load in the water when crossing a river, or the arrieros have not kicked them often enough in the belly. It sounds a little barbaric. All the same, we had the feeling that the protagonists were evenly matched. More so: the mules had the advantage over the arrieros because they had a greater sense of humour. Each one had a definite character of its own. Much more character than our horses, which did everything they were told.

We thought highly of the mules and tried to make friends with them. We tried, for instance, to ease their lot. But their lot was not really hard enough for our efforts to make any appreciable difference. At the end of their eight-hour-day— but some days it was only six, or even five, because we had to adapt our route to take in the few Indian villages in the vicinity—they were free mules and could go where they fancied.

When, early or late in the afternoon, we set up camp near some remote village, the following pantomime took place: As soon as its load was taken off, each mule took a few slow steps to the side. Then one after another they threw themselves on their backs, legs in the air, and rolled several times from side to side. Sometimes four or five mules rolled at the same time. Then they slowly got up and disappeared. The horses never did this. They simply stood around and watched.

Sometimes we grabbed a mule which we knew had particularly nasty sores on its back. Aveckle, my wife, washed the sores with disinfectant and put on some of the Vaseline which we really meant for ourselves. Or we put iodine on wounds on their feet. Usually the mules patiently endured our efforts, but if these went on too long they grew angry and kicked out. They wanted to join their fellows already enjoying their precious freedom and gorging themselves on tit-bits from bushes, tree and grass, for we were entering a country where the mules could fend for themselves; they could get away from their strict maize diet. Sometimes we saw none of our animals about at all (except, of course, the horses) but they never strayed very far from our camp or the village. The next morning they all were back promptly and never had to be laboriously rounded up.

On the fourth day we started at a quarter past eight—Harry's first success in getting us up good and early.

Rock, mould, clay. Then, more and more frequently, sticky mud. The narrow mud track threaded up the mountain in a series of hairpin bends. Far down below we saw the tail-end of our party: minute riders with only the nodding heads of their horses visible. All this against the backcloth of a vast light-green amphitheatre.

At 2 p.m. we finished up in a village which was called "Reality". We camped in a meadow beside a delightful river and grumbled. We had to halt so early because next day came the most difficult part and there was no settlement thereafter where we could stop. Harry was in a "responsible" mood and told us not to grumble.

Our Mexicans mingled affably with the inhabitants and disappeared into their huts. In almost every settlement Don Oscar had uncles and aunts who had to be visited. This, too, was the place where we saw the traveller in elastic bands and safety-pins for the last time. We, that is to say, my wife and I, asked Don Emilio to get the Indians to sell us a few chickens.

At three o'clock, in spite of the previous sunshine, we were deluged in a tropical rainstorm which covered everything in water and steam for two hours. At the height of the dry season this was a most unnatural phenomenon.

At five o'clock the sun came out again. Some Indian children appeared dragging two buckets, full of chicken meat. We burst into hysterical laughter. We paid the agreed sum to a responsible-looking grown-up girl of twelve, and distributed sweets all round. It was lucky we had Timber.

We could not invite Harry because it was meat and chilli, and not Paulchen's group either, because of their principles. Harry had no victualling problems. He went into this or that hut, and somewhere he always got a handful of beans and tortillas, and perhaps some *piloncillo*, sticks of brown sugar. Sometimes we caught a glimpse of him walking with tortillas in one hand and sugar in the other, occasionally biting into the blackish-brown lump of raw sugar, meditating and enjoying the ascetic meal.

Back to the buckets filled with ten pesos' worth of chicken with all the trappings: frejoles, chilli, mole, and a pile of tortillas on a tin plate covered with a cloth. It did not look appetizing, but it was even better than the chicken prepared by Don Oscar's mother. Sometimes we still dream of it.

*   *   *

The next day we rode strenuously for seven hours through woods, mud and dirt, but it did not get really bad till the day after, when once again we had to cross steaming, muddy valleys and steep mountain ranges with wooded slopes freely exposed to the rainclouds from the lowlands. Sometimes the narrow track revealed the bare rock. On the rock lay a thin layer of earth, but by the side of the path was deep red clay in which horses and mules sank up to their bellies. Sometimes the rock was covered with a grey, greasy clay which caused the animals to slide backwards.

Eight mules stumbled and fell. One mule fell a hundred and twenty feet and somersaulted three times with all its load. We would not have given tuppence for the chance of its being any good after that, but when we had hauled it up and made the load fast again, it just shook its sides and immediately joined its companions in the line.

My wife's horse got so confused that it ran blindly against trees. When she could stand it no longer, she jumped off and immediately sank up to her chest in mud. After that she

75

strangled any further humanitarian impulses and the horse even preferred her to be on its back, because for some time after that it kept clear of trees. The woods up here were not so fresh and overwhelmingly green as they had been two days before.

After five hours of toil we left the wood and crossed a steep slope which seemed to consist of nothing but oozing mud. We literally slid down with our exhausted animals and reached an open plateau. Shortly after one o'clock we reached a village called "The Future".

Our Mexicans unsaddled without even waiting for our superfluous protests. As soon as the loads were off their backs the mules threw themselves on the ground and rolled about.

Porvenir was a village inhabited by Tolojabales Indians. Our men did not like the Tolojabales. The village was the last settlement before the wilderness. It lay, clean and friendly-looking, on an open plateau above the steaming valley of the Rio Euseba. The Rio Euseba is one of the larger rivers which all flow into the great heart-shaped triangle of the Jataté and Lacuntún, which surrounds one of the "dark" spots of the earth.

Hemmed in by its dark mountains, the valley of the Euseba ran south-eastwards, and we saw many other dark mountain ridges running in the same direction. It seemed as if the mighty Euseba valley drew all the other valleys along with it towards the land of the Lacandones, towards the heart of darkness. For the first and perhaps the last time we had a fabulous view over all these sun-flecked mountains, forests and river, and in the uttermost distance at the end of this dark mass floated the delicate table-summit of a high mountain.

Harry said: "That's it. The Monto Blanco, the mountain of the white monkeys. That's where we shall meet the Lacandones."

And suddenly I began to understand Harry as I never had before.

"How far is it to your place, Harry?"

"Two days' journey."

This village of the Tolojabales, linked with the outside world only by the thin thread of the mud track (which became totally impassable during the rain periods), was the nearest "civilized" place to Harry's hut. Everybody knew Don Enrique. It was here that he could always stock up when the need arose.

It was a clean, lively village, which was actually rich and entirely self-sufficient. In this climate there grew more than man or beast could ever eat. The villagers grew excellent coffee. Some of them had mules, and once a year, during the dry season, they transported their coffee to the faraway cities of Las Margaritas or Comitán. The Tolojabales were splendid people, although our Mexicans did not like them very much. The men were friendly. The women and girls dressed gaily like gipsies, only they were plumper and cleaner.

We washed under magnificent cedars—deciduous tropical cedars—in a clear, bubbling mountain stream above the village, and changed our clothes. We had to dry the mud on out khaki bush clothes, later peel and scrape it off and brush it out—washing the clothes would have been hopeless. In the evening young girls with large calabashes and clay jars came to fetch water, their picturesque costume of highly ornate blouses and colourful aprons and their gleaming, blue-black plaits of hair making a charming picture. This was not Aztec Mexico with its ecstasy of blood and sun and ever-present death—this was the gentler world of the Maya: an idyllic, archaic world.

Kliesing and I raced after these enchanting girls to take a few idyllic pictures. This chase of ours greatly amused the Tolojabales. Nobody minded, not even the girls. Kliesing

77

stood with legs astride and constantly changed position to do his filming, and I flung myself down on the ground or climbed on a boulder or squatted on my haunches and took a lot of shots which never yielded a single picture because they all came out blurred. In the dying light I had to give an exposure of a fifth of a second, and my arms were not steady enough after the long ride. Kliesing was better off, because in a picture taken on the run lack of definition and a shaky horizon can be considered as contributing dynamic strength . . .

We stopped taking pictures and trotted after the girls who went back to the village, their calabashes and jars on their heads. The village, on its plateau above the valleys, caught the last evening light. In the middle of it, between the far-flung huts lay our tents and the mounds of saddles and baggage, the grazing animals and the smoke curling up from the camp fires. There was a smell of coffee and of eggs and bacon, and from the black kettle of Paulchen's group the smell of bean soup. All this made a wonderful sight. Everything was wonderful that evening, and we felt on top of the world in this Indian village which seemed to float like an island above the dark seas of the forests. Night came, and the stars, and we all sat outside our tents with the casique and other men of the village.

Don Emilio told the Tolojabales that we had the strange notion of going down to the caribes, and all the Indians laughed like mad. I have already mentioned that they called all "savages" caribes, and to them, naturally, the Lacandones were more savage than most. That is why they laughed like mad when they heard that we wanted to go and visit them.

When they were laughing particularly heartily we saw a green-blue light in the sky suddenly flash across the darkness of the immense forests. It shot across the dark earth in a shallow arc from south-west to north-east. For a moment the reflection lit up the jagged, fang-like edges of mountainous tropical clouds on the horizon. The whole phenomenon lasted no more than a second or two. Then the distant fangs and the fantastic cloud formations sank back into darkness.

Above us the stars.

All five of us had seen the flash. The casique had seen it, Don Emilio had seen it, and another Indian had seen it—the others had not seen it because they had their backs to it, but they had seen its reflection. Harry had not seen it because he had been in one of the huts.

"Sputnik," Don Emilio cried.

In a frenzy of excitement we ran to the hut into which Harry had disappeared; he was sitting among the women. The women were breaking dried tortillas into pieces. Harry was going to take two sacks of them with him. We reported our extraordinary experience.

"That reminds me of our rockets," said Harry. "I hope they didn't get wet. You've got a rifle?"

"Yes. After all——"

"Quite. You need a rifle in the forest. But don't go shooting when you're with the Lacandones."

"No. I only shoot what I need for the pot."

"If the wet rockets won't go off," said Harry, "we'll have to fire a rifle—but the sound of a rifle is swallowed up by the trees, while a rocket explodes above them."

"Couldn't we get there in a day?"

The flying saucer on the dinner table must have inspired in me an idea of crazy speed.

"Well," Harry said, "If we start at six and don't rest during the hottest hours of the day we ought to make it."

"Perhaps we'd better not try," I said.

*   *   *

But we did try. Harry was the driving force. At first it looked as if we should do it without any trouble. We made a quick, easy crossing of the Rio Euseba. The river was very low, and there was no need to unload the animals. Only one mule lost its footing and was in danger of drowning with its load. It was the mule carrying all our cameras and film, and we said good-bye to our dreams. But Emilio and the two arrieros—splendid fellows, by the way—acted like lightning. They got hold of the mule at the very last moment, and we moved on again straight away as if nothing had happened.

We now came to lower-lying forests and into country where hardly anyone travelled and to a track which hardly anyone ever trod. The forest suddenly became dry, the ground hard. No more toiling! No more messing about in the mud! We were in the lee of the Sierra Colmena (or some other unknown sierra). We made excellent time. As they rode along our Mexicans cut great notches in the trees with their machetes in order to recognize the track on the way back.

The first giant tucans.

In a thicket, high up on some mountain, far away from any river, we discovered a cayugi, a large, newly scooped-out canoe. Nobody to be seen. Even Harry was unable to say who the owner might be. It was a mysterious canoe, far from any water, and lying on a mountain like an ark left high and dry after a flood. Later, in a valley, we passed a deserted and overgrown settlement. All the inhabitants had died of yellow fever—all together, like a ship's company. The new, luxuriant growth had produced strange plants: lush fruits and vegetables which had reverted to an earlier type. We plucked ripe, golden oranges that were as large as grapefruit. They were bitter and quite uneatable. Snakes and spiders inhabited the huts. A sinister place.

We rode on through the midday heat, taking no more than two fifteen-minute breaks. It really looked as if we should make it, but we did not.

Harry was riding ahead, storming on as if he had never known what fever was, and keeping well ahead so as not to hear the grumbling of our men.

Nabora's classical Maya profile. Behind Nabora is Chan Bor.

One of the more pleasant moments of the journey—the expediti

ts for a while beside the peaceful waters of the Rio Euseba.

Harry makes a new shirt for the youngest Kayum. Kayum has a squint, which the Maya consider an aid to beauty.

At a distance it was sometimes difficult to tell men from women. This is the man Kayum. In the background, Ez and (*standing*) Nik'in.

Nine hours. Up and down; up and down. Finally more
down than up. Harry had vanished, miles away and out of
sight. Since midday we had not seen anything approaching
decent camp site. The mules ran like mad, stumbling along
like the bush Indians of Las Margaritas, but with heads nodding up and down instead of sunk. With their loads swaying
they ran as they had never run before because they were in a
strange, mysterious country, and because they were exhausted.
Time and time again we called for Harry. No Harry.

Nine and a half hours in the saddle.

We galloped ahead and came within calling distance of
Harry.

"Only ten minutes more!" Harry shouted back. Ten
more minutes to his wonderful jungle home. Everything
would be all right there. But we did not reach his home in
ten, or twenty, minutes. He must have lost his way. He was
nervous. He said he had not lost his way, but we did not
believe him. The animals were on the point of collapse and
night was falling. Night is a dangerous time for animals that
are exhausted, and even after an hour we still had not
reached Harry's, or anybody else's place.

We had to spend the night where the jungle was thickest.
My wife said afterwards that it had been quite a tragedy for
Harry. My wife is very emotional, and she sometimes exag-
gerates. I do not think it was a tragedy for Harry. Actually,
compared with what was to become our everyday life in the
jungle, it was more like a comedy. It was sheer bad luck that
we had to camp in the jungle a quarter of an hour away from
Harry's home. Night was falling and Harry had not lost his
way, but in a quarter of an hour everything would be pitch
dark. Incensed, I had galloped off again to ask Harry what
the hell he was doing, but when I caught up with him he had
already dismounted and was laying wildly about him with his
machete. On the right there was a still pond with reasonably
clear water.

"What are you doing, Harry?"

"Jesus!" Harry cried. "Night's practically on us and this bloody fool is asking me what I'm doing. I'm only clearing some ground for your damned tents."

I was overwhelmed by his kindness and jumped down and helped him.

"Leave it to me, Harry. Look after the others."

Kliesing and the others came up, and Kliesing grinned nervously at Harry.

"Don't stand there like a B.F." Harry told him. Kliesing grinned, turned away and started using his machete. Paulchen quietly found a place for his stove. Timber made himself useful.

"Is this water all right to drink?"

"Why ever not?" Offended, Harry took a six-foot leap over to the pond and with a sweeping movement scooped up a handful of water and drank it, his head thrown back, an ecstatic look on his face. Nearly all the water spilled on to his shirt.

The Mexicans arrived with the mules and hurriedly unloaded the animals. Aveckle and I slung our tent over the tree trunks and branches of the little clearing. Kliesing managed to put up his tent, too. Paulchen and Timber joined the Mexicans at their fire. We were very cramped. We fell over roots, baggage, boxes and over one another; and when it got dark and before the fire was lit we bumped into the horses' bellies and the mules' warm mouths. The horses and mules stood about in the darkness and smelt warm and wet. They had done an eleven-hour trek and were exhausted. Now they had not even enough room to lie on their backs and roll. Later on some of them trotted off down the track but they soon turned round and came back to the comfort of the fire and their fellows. They knew they were in strange country and they were afraid. It was a paradise for horses and mules, every bush offering them new delicacies, but it

was also a country of jaguars and snakes and they had to be
led to the pond one by one. Our Mexicans, too, were afraid,
although they did not show it and covered it up by joking.
Earlier on they had grumbled but they did not grumble now.
Like all of us they were pretty tired, and they capped one
another's jokes. They made a fire which lit up our roof of
trees and the maze of lianas: a green unbroken roof, which
covered hills, gorges and plains. What went on beneath this
roof? What secret life did it enclose? Who could have told
us?

Harry joined us and said he was glad that we were not
terrified or panicky. He had rather old-fashioned ideas about
women in the jungle. My wife found this charming, whereas
I was more charmed by the thought of a good Knorr pea-
soup with bits of bacon in it, something plain and honest and
suitable for a late camp. We asked Harry to dinner, offering
him pea soup without bacon. He only had to fish it out.
Harry said he would be glad to fish it out. He said he was fed
up to the back teeth, but he soon perked up and got over it.
Then we fired off the rockets and life became fun again.

With a hiss, the first rocket shot up into the treetops a
hundred and eighty feet above our heads and then we heard
it explode in the air above the green roof. The second rocket
only hissed and, making a semicircular trail of sparks, came
down somewhere in the jungle.

The third rocket went off properly like the first one. That
was enough. The Lacandones were sure to have heard us,
said Harry. If they were anywhere near they were bound to
have heard both rockets. It was a moving thought to imagine
the Lacandones listening to our rockets in the middle of their
jungle.

After that we all went to bed. We did not sleep much, for
the men by the fire talked the whole night through. Everything smelt of mould, wet horses and smoke. Our Mexicans
must have discovered a mighty interesting topic to keep them

going all night. None of the horses and none of the mules left the camp. All night long we could hear them snorting, pawing and stamping close to our tent. They stumbled over the guy ropes, and we heard them munching: hrrropp-hrrropp; hrrropp-hrrropp. We soon learnt to distinguish between the hrrropp-hrrropp of a horse and the h-h of a mule. None of them knocked the tent over; they merely spent the night stumbling to and fro over the ropes, without once pulling the tent down. They were intelligent animals.

That was our first night in the forest—a quarter of an hour away from Harry's hut.

Everybody will ask why we did not go on through the darkness for that last quarter of an hour. (Actually it was nineteen minutes: we timed it for fun the next morning.) The answer is: Heaven preserve anyone from ever wanting to try it! It would have ended badly for two or three—to say nothing of a caravan of nineteen animals and ten people. While the people would probably have survived it— although they would not have liked it much—at least two of the animals would have been lost.

The fact is that in the jungle you can only travel by day, even if you are a native. That is why the most important piece of equipment in the jungle is a compass. The machete comes second. Then waterproof matches, a gun, salt, suitable provisions. Then, a long way behind, come a few basic medicaments which, except for quinine, are no good if you are in a really bad way. In spite of this excellent equipment, however, it would be quite wrong to consider the jungle your friend. It is your enemy. There is only one other sort of country as deadly as a tropical jungle—that is a waterless desert. The latter has become more manageable, due to better traffic conditions, but these are non-existent in the jungle, which is now the greater, more inimical wilderness. And more fascinating, of course, if you can get your enemy to tolerate your presence.

I am not exaggerating. Our promptness in dropping everything and staying put at the onset of the brief tropical dusk was an action in keeping with the iron law of the wilds. Would the mules and horses otherwise have stayed with us instead of going for their usual evening stroll? Would Harry, experienced in bush travel, otherwise have given the desperate signal to camp a mere nineteen minutes from his house?

The jungle track, hardly recognizable even in the clear morning light, came to an end in a clearing—a jungle clearing, with a babbling brook, dark trees and curtains of lianas, flowering bougainvilleas and orchids, butterflies and humming birds. Harry's house! In fact the house was no more than a roof. A huge, low roof of leaves, a solid piece of native workmanship, resting on eight pillars made out of tree trunks. A typical Lacandones house, as Harry explained, open on all sides. Later on we saw that the Lacandones have two types of houses: the large, rectangular, open kind like Harry's, and a smaller, round type with walls made from the bark of the *mahagua* tree. This bark is also used for making clothes.

A large stone hearth. A box filled with books which served both as table and desk. A few smaller provision boxes which served as seats. The firmly trodden floor covered with dried palm leaves. Some mats. Lots of large tins with beans, rice, sugar and other stores. Of course, everything could be left lying about in a place like this; things only had to be protected against animals and insects. Half-way between floor and roof was a platform, reached by a tree trunk in which footholds had been cut. There, below the mosquito net, was where the hermit slept.

The clearing was beautiful.

My wife was at a loss for words.

I could not think of anything to say, either.

* * *

Harry was going to accompany us to the Jataté; our Mexicans had never gone as far as that. He was the only one who knew the way, and he wanted to take us to the Lacandones. So we only stopped in Harry's clearing for a short time. Harry stowed away the stores and then we let off two more rockets high into the blue, sparkling morning above the clearing.

We were very anxious to get to the river Jataté where we hoped we would really meet the Lacandones. We rode off into the forest, which later changed to a savannah. We rode across it in the flaming noonday heat. It was open country with six-foot high *alang-alang* grass and groups of trees and distant mountains and without so much as a sign of a rancho or a settlement or any human presence. It was infinitely lonely country wrapped in a yellow heat haze, and it was very noble of Harry to have left his cool forest for this heat. We were almost glad of the change, of being able to let our eyes rove and see something other than trees. We finally reached a wood; and behind it was the river Jataté, flowing broad and milky-green.

No canoe. No Lacandones.

It soon became clear that the Mexicans and the arrieros wanted to stop. We wanted to cross the Jataté with the caravan, then cross the Perlas and cut straight through the forest to the Lacandones' lake. Each crossing would take a day. A Swedish "Viking Fund" expedition had been here five years ago. They had built a landing strip for small aircraft on the peninsula between the two rivers and had been supplied by air from Las Casas. After them Don Pepe, one of the local mahogany-kings, had the strip cleared once or twice and used it for a time. From the river Perlas the Swedish expedition had cut a trail to the lake. Then, a year ago, a Danish expedition had come. They had discovered traces of the trail and had cleared it again. Harry had accompanied the Danish expedition right to the lake. That is why he was so well informed. They had not taken boats, and they had only been able to look at the mysterious islands in the lake, but Harry had been living here for five years and it was his greatest wish to take a boat on the lake. So far he had not had a chance to do so. Now there was a chance. We had collapsible canoes and we invited Harry to come on the lake with us—if we could persuade our men to take us and our kit right through to the lake.

It soon became clear that our Mexicans thoroughly disliked the idea. They had never penetrated that far into the jungle. They were afraid of the strange country, of the forest, of the large, swift rivers which had to be crossed. Everything seemed sinister to them—the vastness and the emptiness of the country and the size of the rivers. Even the caribes seemed sinister. One of the arrieros with the Danish expedition had been drowned while crossing the Jataté and everybody in the highlands knew about it. They distrusted the two rivers we had to cross and they distrusted the trail beyond, although Harry, who knew it, assured them that it was like a promenade. They said we should never find the trail, that we should lose a lot of animals crossing the Jataté, and a lot more on the Perlas. They had something there. Neither persuasion nor offers of money helped in the least, and so we set up a huge camp between the wood and the savannah. It could have been anywhere in Africa, except that here everything was empty and sinister and there were no gay negro crowds.

Down by the river, at the place where we would have to make the crossing (if we ever were to make it) our men discovered an old abandoned hut. It was not, however, a Lacandones hut. It was the hut of a Mexican who had chosen this delightful spot to start a maize plantation with a hand-operated mill. All that remained of the plantation were a few banana bushes. We later discovered a few old rusty bits of iron from the mill, lying about like corpses. The planter had died here ages ago of yellow fever or some other disease, but nobody knew where his body was.

At the place where we were to make a crossing (if ever) we saw a green, thin snake, four and a half feet long. The snake hurriedly slithered away at our approach. It was a maize snake, which is second only to the red *coralina*, or coral snake, as the most poisonous snake in Guatemala and tropical Mexico. It is much more poisonous than the innumerable rattlesnakes. The maize snake takes second place to the coralina because death follows one or two minutes later than after the bite of the coralina. There is no antidote. Both the maize snake and the coralina are ugly, thin snakes, four and a half feet long and vivid green or bright red. Every time we went to this spot we saw the maize snake, and the maize snake saw us. It did not attack us: that would have been a pretty silly thing to do, because it would then have lost the use of its poison teeth for quite a while. We did not attack it either, mainly because we could not get near it. The snake was far too canny. And we were jolly canny, too, whenever we went down there.

If the crossing were ever to be made it could obviously only be attempted with the help of the Lacandones. It would mean transferring the big loads into the large canoes which they (according to Harry) owned. Each animal would have to be swum across on a lead, above a whirlpool where the muleteer had drowned the previous year. For all this we needed the Lacandones.

But not a single one was to be seen.

In spite of the old hut and the landing-strip the country was wild and completely uninhabited.

Suddenly we heard confused cries from the river.

Our arrieros were down there. The short tropical dusk had just begun, when we heard our arrieros shout:

"*Los caribes!*" The savages are coming!

"*Los Lacandones!*"

For our two honest highland Indians it must have been like the Martians landing. The two muleteers had suddenly found themselves face to face with two strange apparitions. It had been a great shock. They had not seen the canoe until its two occupants had already glided into the bank. From there they disappeared along the track leading to the savannah.

It was on this track that we caught our first sight of them —followed at some distance by our gesticulating arrieros. They approached us slowly through the tall alang-alang grass.

In the last dim light of dusk, against the backcloth of the silent wood, they made an extraordinarily impressive entrance.

We got to our feet. Harry walked towards them with outstretched hands. We were all tense.

I was grateful to Harry for leading us to the Lacandones and because we seemed to have reached our goal so quickly —that is to say, as far as one can talk about a goal at all, what with the shifting horizons and the motives underlying such a journey.

It was the most impressive meeting with a primitive people I have ever experienced. We said to Timber, "Don't laugh", but Timber would not have laughed anyway. Not even our two Mexicans laughed. They did not laugh until later. Only a fool could have called the two small, beautiful, delicate people who solemnly walked up to us in antique-looking gowns "savages".

The two beautiful, solemn figures in the dusk were the last members of an ancient people. They stepped out of the dark wall of the wood from the ancient myths of archaic times, into our crushing, wholesome aura of tin and flash-light. A man and a young woman.

The young woman was holding a small dog against her breast. Her hair hung in plaits. She seemed to be pregnant.

The man, about twenty-five, with the noble profile of the Maya, wore his blue-black hair down to his shoulders.

"*Utzim putzikal!*" Harry cried with considerable emphasis. It was Maya and meant: My heart is pure. It was the greeting of the Lacandones.

"Don En-ri-h-que." The visitor spoke solemnly, in a strange, guttural, singing voice.

The young woman remained silent. The dog barked.

"This is Chan Bor," Harry said to us, "and that is Nabora, his wife."

"*Chan* means small," Harry explained. He was little Bor, the son of big Bor. "And this is Timber," Harry said to Chan Bor. Timber happened to be standing nearest to him.

"Tim-b-e-e-h," replied Chan Bor.

"Glad to meet you," said Timber.

The dog barked furiously at Timber.

"This is Mariana," said Harry.

"Mari-a-n-ah," said Chan Bor.

My wife shook his hand. We all shook hands with them. The dog barked like a small, wild devil.

"Don Er-b-e-hr-to," Chan Bor called out gutturally.

"*Utzim putzikal,*" I said.

Chan Bor took both my hands. Nabora swept the small dog under her blouse.

Harry told Chan Bor that we were all his, Harry's, friends, and therefore the Lacandones' friends too. Harry said all this in a mixture of Maya and baby-Spanish. Chan Bor and Nabora knew about ten words of Spanish, which they jerked out in their deep guttural voices as if they found all speech infinitely difficult, or as if they were imbeciles just about to have a lesson in speaking. But when they spoke to one another, their Maya flowed from their lips in a pleasant, melodious stream of sound. We did not tire of listening to them, although, of course, we didn't understand a word.

Harry said we were their friends because we, too, were pure of heart. When Timber asked Harry to translate this, Timber, the wretch, began to laugh like a drain, although he probably had the purest heart of us all—excepting perhaps my wife, who was furious at Timber's laughing. Timber's laughter infected everybody. Even the Mexicans stopped grinning and began to laugh; and our highland Indians, who never laughed, were seized by an irrepressible urge to laugh and our two visitors from the depths of the forest joined in. Even so they retained their archaic dignity.

We had a very merry time by the camp fire with our new friends. Kliesing and I photographed them from the back, from the front, from the side and from every other possible angle. They were not in the least put out. They were both gay and graceful. We kept on photographing them because we did not know how long they would stay, or whether we should meet any other Lacandones.

Harry learned that they had heard our two morning rockets, but not the two we had sent up the night before. He did not find out whether Bor, the casique, had also heard the rockets and would be coming down the river with the rest of his band. They were semi-nomads, who all lived by themselves, somewhere out of sight along the river bank. Chan Bor's settlement was the nearest.

We wanted to ask Chan Bor and Nabora to dinner. They only took a little of our tea, perhaps out of politeness; but they smoked our cigarettes and licked the lollipops which had really been meant for their children. Making my deductions as a serious explorer—I am very conscientious about such things—I was forced to the conclusion that the Lacandones' favourite diet was cigarettes and lollipops.

Chan Bor and Nabora lay down for the night in front of our tent. I stole a look out of the tent a number of times, but of course nothing happened "with a joke and a laugh" wherever they happened to be and oblivious of everyone, as

Harry had told us. It seemed that the Lacandones were perfectly aware of us—or rather of me.

They lay close together under our tent porch in their shirt-like garments, the little dog at Nabora's breast under her blouse. I pretended to look away over their sleeping forms into the distance. Two strange, graceful creatures of the forest . . . but they were not asleep. They were watching me, two strange, graceful creatures from an almost forbidden dream-land.

*   *   *

Next morning a whole flotilla of Lacandones came down the river. Four cayugis, two large ones and two small ones. Ten people altogether.

The last group of an ancient, astonishing people as yet untouched by civilization.

With their garments and their long hair, all of them—except the children—could easily have been taken for women. It was a splendid sight to see them all coming down the green jungle river in their cayugis.

"Hallo—Bor!" Harry cried.

"En-ri-h-que!" answered a deep, guttural voice.

The casique was the first to disembark. We shook hands. We had become expert hand-shakers.

Bor—what a character! A patriarch from mythical prehistory. Stately and clean, between fifty-two and fifty-six years of age. (Amazing this "between"—for the astronomers of the Old Maya Empire had worked out an extremely accurate calendar, one of 365.2420 days instead of 365.2422. But it had been a highly complicated calendar, and therefore they started a new era every fifty-two years. Every bit of crockery was smashed, and all fires were extinguished. The new fire was carried across the country from the temple and new crockery was made.)

But back to Bor. Leader of the last few specimens of a

doomed and dying people which had never been defeated and never inter-married with another race! Once he had gone the story would be ended. He accepted the fact with despair and sadness in his heart. A man and leader, who carried in himself all the traditions and myths of his people—a tragic and forlorn figure.

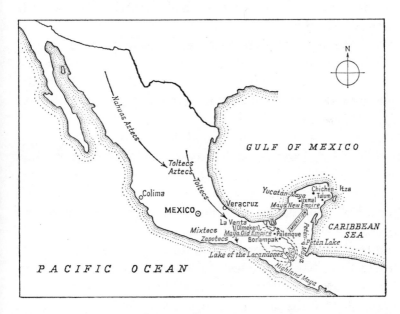

Since Harry's god-like appearance Bor knew that they had become "interesting" to the outside world. Foreigners came who were different from the Mexican mahogany-cutters, the brutal chicle collectors or the crocodile hunters. Learned white men came who pursued unfathomable, but obviously harmless, hobbies. Fair men from Sweden, Danes, a lady from Switzerland with a venerable professor, a writer from Germany. . . .

Bor and his Lacandones did not know these details, of course, but they soon found out that they need not hide away from these harmless people. Just the opposite! All learned, but harmless, men brought valuable presents.

On these rare occasions the Lacandones always acquired things which would otherwise have been beyond their reach.

Naturally they had no means of judging the value of the products of our glorious civilization. The leader of the Swedish expedition asked one of them what he would like in payment for some services he had rendered. He left the choice to the Swede:

"Give me your flying machine," he said, "or a dog."

They love dogs more than anything else. Their dogs are the most extraordinary mongrels, small, fat, cowardly, yelping creatures absolutely useless except for smelling out the occasional armadillo. But where do you get a dog if every one you see already belongs to somebody?

The Swede had almost decided on the aircraft, Harry told us, because the under-carriage had been smashed on landing. It did not look as if they would ever get the thing out again, but after a few weeks they managed to get it out, and they brought a small dog back from the highlands.

The Lacandones expected us to turn out to be specially learned and harmless. Our camp became a picturesque fair. Harry, happy and gay, behaved like a cheapjack: "Look here, Bor! Look at the things I've brought you! Now, here's . . ."

The usual useful articles.

The greatest (and most deserved) success was an immense enamelled cooking-pot with handles and a lid, brand-new and bright blue.

We, too, unpacked our boxes of gifts: white cotton for shirts for the men, red for blouses for the women. Needles, cotton, lollipops, salt, quinine, waterproof matches. Machetes. For the children, necklaces and balls.

Jubilation, excitement, gales of laughter.

Jealousies flared up, quickly to die down. In the last instance Bor decided who was to have what—always to his own advantage, I must admit, but never without the wise moderation of the born leader.

"They like you," Harry said.

That was true, and it was not on account of the presents, for all their usefulness. It was because we did not make fun of them as our Mexicans did. I am referring to Don Oscar and Don Emilio, not to the two arrieros. Nothing would have been farther from our highland muleteers. The Lacandones, for their part, treated the muleteers with a polite indulgence—they probably looked on them as "savages". Don Oscar and Don Emilio were, of course, lordly gentlemen who despised the caribes from the bottom of their heart. In return, the Lacandones hated them intensely. Not that either party showed its feelings. The caballeros simply made a little fun of the caribes, while the caribes cut the caballeros dead. For our new friends the Mexicans simply did not exist.

They stayed with us the whole day—and they came back. We were to spend many happy hours with these strange people, who were rather like dying flowers in the midst of a murderous wilderness, but in their ordinary, everyday life they were creatures of the present. A gay people, expert canoeists, splendid athletes.

But they had no intention of taking us to their mysterious lake. There was nothing we could do about it.

*   *   *

The Lacandones are a deeply religious people who take their old myths seriously. They worship the sun and the moon, the fire and the underworld. They sacrifice to the river god: before every meal Bor goes to the water and offers the first bowl of maize with a broad, sweeping gesture. We watched him, and his prayers and his demeanour were so dignified that we had not the heart to take photographs. It was a mark of their affection for us that we were allowed to witness the sacrifice at all, for the Maya believe that man was created from maize, and they hold maize in greater reverence than we had ever held bread. The grain, a gift of the maize-god, must only be used for food. If it had been used as barter, or if it had been caught by our cameras, they would have felt that sacrilege had been committed.

Bor's sacrificial bowls

In his hut, two hours down-river by canoe, Bor had an altar with two or three *idolos*—sacrificial bowls carved with the face of an idol—fashioned by himself. Bor also had a larger idol, about ten inches high, which consisted mainly of a large nose and ears, with a small sacrificial bowl stuck into its thick neck. A monster, *Chac Mol*, the rain-god, whose elephant trunk provided an abundance of water.

Bor prayed and sacrificed every day before this image. In addition to incense he offered up maize, fruit, and, on

Graceful Margarita, Bor's eleven-year-old daughter, destined in all probability one day to become his wife.

Lacandones in their natural setting as children of the forest. *Above:* Two of the Maya with their dogs—much-prized possessions. The story is told of a Lacandone, when asked what he wanted as reward for services, chose "your aeroplane or your dog". *Left:* This is Nik'in.

Right : A Maya child with a bowl of *pozoli.*

Below : The Lacandones have a much greater sense of humour than any other Mexican Indians. These two girls enjoyed watching the explorers.

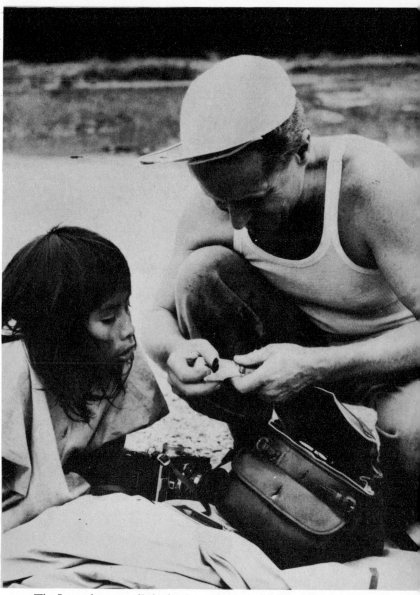

The Lacandones use little that is mechanical: this boy is fascinated by the cameras and the mysteries of the roll-film.

special occasions, the heart of a chicken. A domesticated god, and somewhat out of place in one of the world's rainiest jungles.

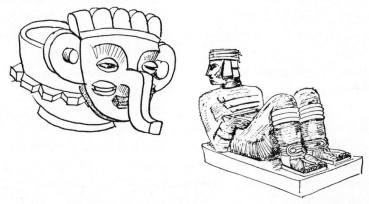

Left: Sacrificial bowl with the mask of the trunk-nosed rain god.
Right: The great *Chac Mol* from Chichen-Itza.

Chac Mol was the rain-god of the Yucatan Maya. After they had abandoned their Old Empire the Maya had moved from their rain forests to the barren, arid wilderness of the Yucatan peninsula, the northern part of which is without even a rivulet. The soil is chalk and the rain immediately seeps away. Settlements were only possible in places where *cenotes* had formed—well-like basins and subterranean lakes. There rain was vitally important and the rain-god was bound to play an important role. There he was not ten inches high, as in Bor's hut, but hewn out of a huge block of limestone and placed on the top of the pyramid of Chichen-Itza. Lying half-raised, his elbows and feet on the ground, his head held in an imperious attitude, he received his bloody tribute of bleeding human hearts which were torn from his victims' breasts and lowered into a carefully carved hollow of his stone body.

When the Spaniards came to Mexico twenty-seven years after the discovery of America, they found a warrior caste

97

who waged continual war on their neighbours instead of putting up any proper resistance against the invaders. They were forced into these wars by their terrible sacrificial cults, for which thousands of prisoners had to lose their lives each year. In all the towns through which Cortés' little band passed they found mounds of skulls and the wooden cages in which the victims were fattened, finally to be eaten—a fact which is generally omitted from glowing accounts of ancient Mexico.

It cannot be proved that there was a single race in America which did not practise cannibalism, although there are clues which suggest that the Incas were an exception. Cannibalism was a religious magic act, of course, and possibly not always unconnected with "economic considerations".

The civilizations of Mexico were nourished by death-wish cults. Not even the Maya were an exception, as is proved by the much-vaunted Bonampak murals. To call the Maya "the Greeks of Central America" and their culture "one of the most harmonious creations of man" is sheer nonsense.

*　　*　　*

When the Spaniards came to America, the Incas in Peru, with their collective agriculture and forced labour, were in the throes of revolution. In Mexico, the Aztec federation, enfeebled by constant wars with neighbours, was already past the peak of its power. In Central America, the second great period of Maya culture was in the process of dissolution. The cause of this is not yet fully known.

The great Aztec buildings, which had been used for religious and astrological purposes, were falling into ruin. In succeeding centuries they were not unknown, but simply out of use. The Maya buildings, on the other hand, remained unknown because the jungle overran them and destroyed them.

The Maya had come from the north, not as nomads but as farmers. The tribes which settled in the highlands of modern Guatemala remained ordinary peasants or became traders, but in the forest region of Petén in Guatemala, in Chiapas, and in what is now Tabasco, the Maya developed a highly individual State at the beginning of the Christian era. By the fourth century they possessed a script—hieroglyphs as yet undeciphered—and a calendar. They founded the towns of Palenque, Bonampak, Yaxchilan, Tikal and Cobán with their pyramids, temples and stelae. This was the Old Empire of the Maya.

Whether it was a single empire ruled by a single prince, or whether it was a federation of independent settlements is difficult to say, but it seems certain that the larger cities were governed independently by priests and priest-kings. For a long time it was considered a remarkably peaceful city-empire, for none of the cities were walled, and it was thought to be innocent of the practice of human sacrifice, too—till the discovery of Bonampak in 1946 disproved this theory. In Bonampak was found a temple whose walls were decorated with a series of magnificent paintings depicting a war against a strange race of darker, almost naked people and the sacrifice of prisoners on a pyramid.

The role of science in Maya civilization has been much discussed. It is safe to say that in the whole history of mankind there has never been a people to equal the Maya in mathematics and astronomy. Even before the founding of their Old Empire, roughly in the third or second century B.C., they made a fundamental discovery. They invented the number "o". A thousand years elapsed before the Indians made the same discovery, while the West still went on using Roman numerals. The decimal system, the basis of any form of higher mathematics, only reached Europe through the Arabs in the fifteen century.

All the same, the Maya with their highly-developed

mathematics and with their knowledge of the stars never developed any sort of technical science. Their technical achievements belonged to the late Stone Age: they could weave, make pottery and do feather-work; and, in the New Empire, they knew how to work a number of precious metals. They were ignorant of the wheel. They had no knowledge of the pulley. They did not know how to build an arch or a

Detail of a mural from Bonampak

vault. The building of countless pyramids never taught them anything except that every stone had to take the weight of the next one.

On the other hand there was their phenomenal mathematics, their calendar of 365.2420 days. But from all that we know of them today they appear to have had no desire for abstract knowledge. All their skill was used to organize their agriculture on a religious and magical basis. They were slaves to their calendar. But their achievements in painting, stuccoes and stelae were far superior to those of any other race in ancient America.

Then something inexplicable happened.

For some unknown reason this great civilization declined towards the seventh century A.D. The cities were abandoned by their inhabitants. Not slowly, after art and architecture had stagnated for several centuries, but "overnight", so to speak, within a mere fifty years.

What was the reason? Had there been pressure from Toltec groups in the north? Religious strife? Astrological signs prophesying disaster? Epidemics? Famine? Some catastrophe destroyed the Empire, and the great cities surrendered to the jungle.

One of the more satisfying theories is the climatic change which took place in Central America as a consequence of increased rainfall. With the antiquated agricultural implements it became impossible to hold the jungle at bay, and famine became a constant threat. . . .

The ruling classes turned their backs on the cities, leaving behind a huge treasure-house of temples, palaces, stelae, and the most beautiful paintings in ancient America. The jungle harvested the fruits of centuries of labour. The ruling classes emigrated to Yucatan and after an obscure nomadic period, during which they lost none of their mathematical or artistic skills, the Maya began to build the so-called New Empire from the beginning of the tenth century onwards. They built the monumental cities of Uxmal, Mayapan and Chichen-Itza, which display much the same magnificence as the buildings of the Old Empire, although the style became increasingly grotesque. This was due to the influence of the Toltecs with whom the Maya intermarried when they settled in Yucatan, an influence which grew stronger when Toltec mercenaries gained in political importance. Finally the three cities lived in a state of constant strife—till the Spaniards came.

In spite of this the Spaniards met—in contrast to Peru—a determined resistance which it took them twenty years to break. After the war against the Spaniards decline set in.

The cities were again abandoned. The priests and the ruling class, which alone had been engaged in politics and religion and had preserved the old traditions and the arts, lost their power and their hold over the people. With three exceptions the old Maya manuscripts, which might have provided modern scholars with the key to the hieroglyphs, fell into the hands of missionaries and were burnt.

The Maya became Catholics. Only in remote areas did a few tribes manage to remain undiscovered and preserve the simple fertility and other heathen rites which were part of the religion of the people.

The Lacandones managed to remain undiscovered to this very day.

While the ruling classes emigrated with the greater part of the people to the Yucatan peninsula when the Old Empire broke up, some people journeyed in the opposite direction, to the highlands. There they intermarried with the Maya who had settled there earlier. They now form the native Indian-Catholic population of Guatemala.

And so, round about A.D. 1000, we find the following three Maya groups: the Yucatan Maya of the New Empire; the highland Maya; and, finally, the jungle Maya.

It is obvious that a number of people must have remained behind during the great exodus. On the one hand the old and the infirm who could no longer stand the long trek; useless slaves; idle workers and other undesirable elements; on the other, tribes which had penetrated deep into the jungle; small communities which lived far away from the fabulous towns.

And lastly a tribe which had penetrated farther than any other into the shadowy realm of the jungle—the Lacandones.

The Conquistadores made only ineffectual attempts at subduing the warlike and elusive Lacandones. Cortés is said to have heard of them during his famous march to Honduras.

This march has been praised as a great military feat, which indeed it was. The most difficult part—roughly from the modern town of Tenosique on the Usumacinta to Lake Petén in the lowlands of Guatemala—would defeat an expedition today. A modern army equipped with bulldozers would take months to do it, but in those days the country was densely populated and well supplied with roads. The Spaniards, with an army of thousands of highland mercenaries, but without a medical service worth mentioning, marched unsuspectingly towards the miasmata and amoeba of the jungle. Before long they went down with dysentery, typhoid, malaria and the greatest scourge of these parts— yellow fever. Those who did not die of disease died of hunger. . . . For they had taken too little food, nearly all the natives had fled, and it was impossible to live off the country.

That Cortés had little desire to go searching for the fabled Lacandones is more than understandable.

It is possible that Las Casas, the Indians' only friend among the Spaniards, was the first who made contact with them.

Up to the sixteenth century the Spaniards sent punitive expeditions against the Lacandones. The accounts of them are few and full of contradictions. In one the *Laguna Miramar* is mentioned—but in mistake for Lake Petén in Guatemala. It is certain that the Lacandones attacked a number of Spanish settlements in the first decades after the Conquest. It is equally certain that after that period they sank into complete oblivion for a century and a half. So much so that their very existence became a legend among the highland Indians, who sometimes talked of a secret Maya empire deep in the heart of the jungle.

It is quite likely that the Lacandones founded some sort of "empire". They were a strong nation, capable of leading a self-sufficient existence in the jungle, hunting with bows and arrows, just as the last of them live now. There is plenty of game—deer, jaguar, tree bear, wild boar, armadillo and other animals. One of their delicacies—when they can get it —is howling monkey stewed in sauce: not as I once had it served by Indians on the Amazon, roasted over a fire, hairy and saltless, but really tasty. They also grow vegetables, as we discovered during a visit to Bor: maize, beans, *yucca*, sweet potatoes, sugar-cane. Their fields, or rather gardens, are small and the soil is soon exhausted. This may be the reason why they lead a semi-nomadic existence.

At one time, the focal point of the race was the great lake and a huge extinct volcano called Chamhuitz. On the islands of this great lake, surrounded by a volcanic jungle landscape of primeval immensity, they had their places of worship. There, in the old Maya tradition, untouched by the cruel Toltec influence of the New Empire, they sacrificed to the gods of the sun and the moon, of fire and the underworld.

The green empire of the Lacandones.

But it wasn't as idyllic as all that.

* * *

Life in the forests became more and more difficult for the last of the Maya. For instance, they had no salt, and without salt life is impossible. Since the Lacandones had neither mineral nor sea salt, they kept up a tenuous trade with the Maya of Guatemala, who extracted salt on the Pacific coast. The Lacandones grew—and still grow— excellent tobacco. They roll the tobacco leaves into ten-inch cigars which we ourselves smoked (that is to say, Paulchen and I) without passing out. These Lacandonian cigars may look a bit funny, but they were made of the best raw tobacco. Genuine Maya cigars!

These cigars they bartered for salt. The expeditions down to Guatemala, which took months, went along the Santo Domingo trail—which was then, of course, known by a different name. It was the same trail as the one we wanted to take but could not because it has become impassable.

It was through this sporadic trade that the Spaniards once more heard of the Lacandones, after a lapse of a century and a half. Meanwhile they had built colonial towns such as Comitán, Ciudad Real (the modern Las Casas) and Ciudad Guatemala. Towards the end of the seventeenth century three military expeditions were dispatched against the Lacandones—that mysterious jungle people, whose men looked like women because they wore their hair long. Two of the expeditions succumbed to the jungle bacilli and amoeba. Those who did not die from disease were killed by the Lacandones, for the Lacandones were savage fighters and courageously attacked the Spanish intruders with poisoned arrows.

The third expedition was a complete success—although only a few Spaniards and Indian mercenaries ever returned. This expedition started from the town of Ocosingo (from Comitán according to another source) and was commanded by a Spanish general by the name of Barrios Leal.

Barrios crossed the rivers Jataté and Perlas and succeeded in reaching the Miramar lake. He made contact with the Lacandones on its southern banks. After weeks of incredible hardship the Spaniards finally cornered this despairing people and slaughtered them by the thousand. History tells of the lake as being "red with Lacandonian blood and full of corpses". Since then, none of the Lacandones go near this terrible lake. The survivors fled to the Chamhuitz mountains and to the Sierra Caribe, or they settled on the most inaccessible banks of the Jataté, Perlas and Lacanja rivers. The lake was put under a curse. For more than two and a half centuries now this lake—the heart of the old country of the Lacandones—has lain under a taboo. Nobody even mentions its name. For more than two hundred and fifty years not one of the Lacandones has lived on its banks or in its many bays; no canoe crosses its mirror-like surface; nobody visits its islands where their temples, pyramids and altars lie lost beneath the jungle shroud.

The Spaniards did not have an easy journey back, and they had had enough of the Lacandones for ever.

Once again the Lacandones and their great lake fell into complete oblivion. The small, scattered groups lived undisturbed in their remote country. The centre of what is now Bor's group was the Chamhuitz mountains and the area round the confluence of the rivers Jataté and Santo Domingo. Undisturbed till the year 1941!

Strange as it may sound, the Second World War brought the final death-blow to the Lacandones.

During the war the United States needed the second-rate rubber from the jungles of Chiapas, the chicle which, until then, had been used only in the manufacture of chewing gum. The ill-famed, notorious Mexican chicleros came down the Santo Domingo trail. Some of them were convicts released on condition that they went and worked in the forests. They brought disease, rape and murder.

For many years Bor's group became completely demoralized and dispersed. As if that were not enough, in the middle of the 'forties they were stricken by a yellow-fever epidemic. Bor told us: first the monkeys died, then the people. . . .

Harry, who came very soon after this catastrophe, must have appeared as a saviour to them.

Today there are one hundred and sixty-seven Lacandones left, living in three groups.:

(1) A large group, comprising a hundred and thirty-two men, women and children, living closest to civilization and therefore the least "intact" of the three. Widely scattered, they live in the highlands near the old Spanish settlement of Ocosingo, the small villages of San Antonio and El Real, and in the vicinity of numerous lumber camps. This group was of no interest for our purpose.

(2) The Lacanja group of twenty-five members was also scattered and leaderless but still carried on the old traditions and regarded the ruins of Bonampak as their holy place. This was the group which Healey and Frey met in 1946 when they discovered Bonampak, and it was due to them that the Lacandones were rescued from ethnological oblivion. A number of members of this group work as lumberjacks for the Mexicans.

(3) Bor's group. This is the one that is least touched by civilization and, in spite of the havoc wrought by the chicleros, it is the group which is, ethnologically, the most intact. But it is also the smallest. It is outstanding because of the personality of its leader, and, in its cults and its rites, it is the most ancient Maya of them all.

Bor's and the Lacanja group probably speak the purest of the twenty Maya dialects known today. With their high, receding forehead which merges into the large, hooked and almost bridgeless nose, with their slightly protruding mouth and receding chin, they conform to the classic Maya ideal of beauty. They look like pure copies of the paintings and sculptures of the Maya empires.

*   *   *

Bor's group today consists of ten members. Their family relationship is quickly explained. Bor lives with his two youngest children, the boy Chan Kayūm who is six or seven years old, and "Margarita", a lovely daughter of eleven. Margarita, who keeps house for him, will one day be his wife —or is already.

Near Bor's settlement live Kayūm, who is about thirty, and his wife Nak'in, who is about twenty-five.

Kayūm and Nak'in (also one of Bor's daughters) were the only genuine married couple in this group. They had a five-year-old girl, Ez, whom they had adopted from dead relatives.

(As I was writing these lines I received a letter from Harry to say that Ez was no longer alive. She had been raped by her foster-father, Kayūm, and had died in Harry's arms. Kayūm had fled to escape Bor's wrath. But Nak'in, Kayūm's wife, was expecting a child . . .)

Bor's wrath, Harry wrote, would pass like smoke.

Also living with Kayūm and Nak'in were two boys: K'in ("Sun"), a sixteen-year-old son of Bor's, and "Pedro", aged twenty, whose real name was also Kayūm and whose parents had died some years before. Both were handsome lads—for whom there would be no wives. They were trying to get away from the group and had already made some contacts with the neighbouring Tolojabales.

Lastly there was Chan Bor, "small Bor", aged twenty-seven, with Nabora, his sister, aged twenty-five. Everybody hoped that they would have children. But they had had none. Our first impression of her had been an optical illusion. The swelling round her middle had not been a baby but her protruding tummy. Instead of children she kept dogs over which she doted like a spinster over a peke.

In his best days old Bor was said to have had three wives. This is comparatively harmless in view of the common and sanctioned incestuous marriages between brothers and sisters and fathers and daughters and the bestial rapes. It is quite impossible to apply our moral standards to this people, the last of an ancient race, living in their enchanted world. As we saw them, they were a morally "intact" group, deeply religious and with very high ethical standards.

Curiously, in spite of their inbreeding, they were perfectly healthy. They did not even suffer from venereal diseases, because they had expelled the women who had been raped by the chicleros. There was not the slightest signs of cretinism. Little Kayūm squinted, but he was an alert and highly intelligent boy. Later we learnt that the Maya consider a squint beautiful.

Except for yellow fever they seemed to enjoy a certain immunity from the usual tropical fevers. Dysentery they cured with ancient herbal remedies, but in the highlands the first cold would lay them low.

The Mexican lumberjacks are daily penetrating farther into the Usumacinta and Lacanja areas. These lumberjacks cannot be compared, of course, to the chicleros, but they do bring "progress". Today the Lacanja-Bonampak Lacandones all have Spanish names. They can only withstand the onslaught of civilization for a few more years. Even Bor's group on the remote Jataté will not be spared.

In a few years the Lacandones will have vanished from the face of the earth if Harry does not succeed, with the help of the State and UNESCO, in bringing the three groups together and settling them round the lake. It need not be round the lake, either, says Harry, since the Lacandones do not want to go anywhere near it.

But the world has other problems to solve. What, after all, is the importance of the last members of an old race who have become childishly pure in their last days and who stand as a solitary and rather strange reminder of the childhood of mankind?

CHAPTER THREE

The Invisible Bird

Back to our own story. Back to Kliesing, Paulchen
Timber, Aveckle, Harry, our Mexicans and yours-very-
truly.

We can say good-bye to our Mexicans very quickly. Fine
chaps, Don Emilio, Don Oscar and the two arrieros! But
they did not want to go any farther. I would not have wanted
to, either, if I had been in their shoes.

We were not sorry they did not want to go on. We were
not sorry because we had found the Lacandones, and because
we were carrying folding canoes and were on a river where
we could continue the journey under our own power.

To penetrate into the unexplored regions of the tropical
rain forest is only possible if one goes by water. However
difficult and dangerous the journey may be from having to
negotiate cataracts, waterfalls, rapids and other obstacles,
there are no other "roads" into the virgin jungle. That is
why even in jungle areas which have long been opened up
the native canoe—with or without auxiliary engine—is still
the most popular means of transport.

On expeditions into the unknown it is essential that one's
craft be adaptable and easy to handle. In the course of years
we have tried out a number of boats. We have found that it
is always a good idea to bring one's own and not to rely on
native canoes. Rapids in canyons, for instance, can be shot
quite easily in large rubber boats, provided they are
strengthened. (Not the seaside variety of course, but the
military, inflatable dinghy-type.) Dinghies with auxiliary

engines are useful for certain kinds of water—assuming, of course, that it is possible to get petrol—but in spite of all the tests we have made we have always gone back to folding, non-motorized, canoes. And this is not for sporting, but for purely practical reasons. I need not say more about this. An expert canoeist with a folding canoe, a tent and proper equipment is, militarily speaking, the smallest independent unit which can move through an unexplored wilderness and remain alive. That is why we were not sorry that our men did not want to go on. We were burning to "do it ourselves" and enjoy the grand sport of canoeing. . . .

It would have been more sensible to accept the considerable difficulties of crossing the two rivers and take the whole caravan up to the lake, a distance of some eight miles as the crow flies . . . but we were not able to put much conviction into our efforts to persuade the Lacandones to act as guides and carriers, and so the attempt failed.

We made a new and final plan. We had first-class maps of the area. Apart from a photostat of a map drawn by an archaeologist—the man must have been a practical joker—they were all aerial survey maps.

An American map to a scale of 1:250,000. This was the most important and the most reliable map although, in the end, it led us astray and proved to be wrong.

The "Istmo de Tehuantepec" sheet of the International World Map (scale 1:1,000,000) also printed in the United States. This was our second most important map.

Then, a Mexican military map (scale 1:500,000), a piece of mainly blank white paper, with here and there a blue river, the straight line of the frontier with Guatemala and a few equally straight lines of latitude violating its virgin purity. A map as honest as it was useless.

The next, a Mexican map (scale 1:250,000) distinguished itself by its wealth of imaginary—and obviously untrustworthy—detail.

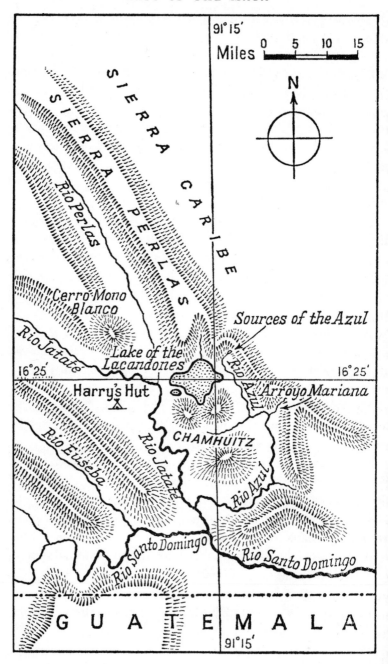

Finally there was a National Geographic Society map. It was a beautiful map, but unfortunately only to a scale of 1:3,500,000.

Of course these maps, valuable as they were, could not in the nature of things make any pretensions to detailed accuracy for purposes such as ours. It was our own fault that we relied upon them too much. All the same, it was disconcerting, to say the least, to find sometimes that mountains, rivers or plains either did not exist at all, or if they did were not where they were supposed to be.

However, the useful American maps showed that the Rio Jataté runs in a great southerly arc round one or two of the main ranges of the Cordillera, which slopes towards the south-west.

It looked as if the Cordillera had dropped to between three thousand and three thousand six hundred feet here, although we were later to discover that there were some surprisingly high jungle mountains rising between the various arms of the river. Inside the arc of the Jataté the Cordillera had broken up into a number of smaller mountain ranges, with scattered groups of volcanoes in its south-westerly folds.

One of these isolated ranges of volcanic origin was the Chamhuitz range. It was only two thousand one hundred feet high, but seen from our camp at the edge of the savannah it looked dark and mysterious. Behind it, invisible to us, the so-called Sierra Caribe stretched away to the bend of the Jataté.

Between the Chamhuitz and the foothills of the Sierra Caribe the Jataté was joined, on the left bank, by a river which was called Rio Azul (blue river) on our maps. According to all these maps this Rio Azul could only be the efflux of the Lake of the Lacandones! According to our prophetic maps the Rio Azul flowed out of the Lake of the Lacandones in a westerly direction, was joined above the lake by another river coming from the Sierra Caribe, and then ran due south through an area which was explicitly marked *Zona inexplorada*, unexplored region. After this it was joined, on the right bank, by an *arroyo* (small river) rushing down from the Chamhuitz range and finally turned east to terminate its long, almost circular course round the Chamhuitz in the river Jataté.

The confluence of the two rivers was, according to our calculations, about forty miles south-west of our camp. If we did not miss it—all too easy in the jungle—we need only travel down this river to get to the lake. (What travelling down an unknown jungle river actually meant I will explain later.)

According to our two Mexican maps the distance from the confluence of the rivers Azul and Jataté to the lake was about fifteen miles. On one of the American maps it was given as thirty, on the other as fifty. Kliesing thought fifteen miles seemed "reasonable". Kliesing was blessed with a happy, optimistic nature.

We compromised at forty miles.

Forty miles down the Jataté, then a maximum of forty miles up the Rio Azul, made a total of eighty miles to the lake. An enormous circular journey—ten times the distance the overland trip with the caravan would have been!

Nothing could have been more absurd; but nothing was more practical, practicable and logical, either. It still remained magnificently logical when we realized that our calculations had been entirely wrong—and not only because the eighty miles turned out to be nearly a hundred and twenty. But I must not anticipate.

Another question was what difficulties we should encounter on the journey. Of the Jataté, a big river, we expected few unpleasant surprises up to the point where it joined the Rio Azul. This part of the journey we should do fairly rapidly. On the journey upstream to the lake we might meet with rapids, cataracts and all kinds of natural obstacles, or even just a very fast current.

Kliesing thought the journey from the Jataté to the lake should not take more than three days. I said I should be satisfied if it took no more than six, but perhaps it would take ten days, or perhaps we should never reach the lake at all.

That is how we talked.

Our plan now was to paddle forty miles downstream to the confluence of the Jataté and the Rio Azul, then try to paddle upstream as far as we could—if possible to our main objective, the lake. After that we meant to go back down the Rio Azul and join the Jataté-Usumacinta at Tenosique. If, after two or three days, the Rio Azul proved too difficult, we would abandon the idea of making our lake and turn back. Even Paulchen said it was pointless not to turn back if the obstacles became impossible.

Well, we found the mouth of the Rio Azul. We really did find it, although for days we weren't at all sure that we were not on the wrong river . . . I may also admit straight away that after the first two or three days the going was so tough that it would have seemed silly to have gone through all this just to sound the retreat!

Come what might, we told one another, it would be a shame and quite irresponsible to abandon our great objective after all our sweat and toil merely because we could not face Kliesing's last three, or my six, days!

We stuck to the figures three and six with remarkable, and totally unjustified, tenacity. In our imagination the blood-stained lake became a paradise. The longing for this paradise gave us superhuman strength. Even Paulchen, who by now had grasped that we were going to a lake, said it would be pointless to turn back and forgo the paradise because of three or six days of sweat and toil.

But we did not make it in three, or six, days. Not even in ten. We very nearly failed to make it at all.

Thirty-two days on that river were enough almost to put paid to one of us. After thirty-two days on that river we were bang in the middle of nowhere.

But I must not anticipate.

*　　　*　　　*

After the final plan had been agreed on we became very active. With the help of the Lacandones, who were well-disposed towards us and very willing (except in the matter of the lake) and the Mexicans, whose animals needed another day's rest before they started back, we moved our camp from the steep bank between the forest and the savannah across the rocks and sandbanks of the right arm of the river to the large island in the middle.

It was an ideal camp. Here, although still surrounded by the Lacandones, we were at last free men (and one free woman), no longer hemmed in by baggage and porters. Here we could chuck our goods and chattels down just where we liked, prise open the numbered crates, unpack the bags and happily begin to think about assembling our boats. We allowed two days for resting, thinking, and sorting out and packing our supplies into the boats. The Lacandones stood or sat round and watched us with curiosity. In the general chaos they could have robbed us to their hearts' content and we should never have noticed, but it never even occurred to them. They were keen to pick up anything we did not want, and we gave them a lot of useless stuff. They accepted our largesse as a matter of course, but they did not beg or steal. In this respect they were the most gentlemanly aborigines I have ever met. I apologize for always using superlatives about them, but when I think of them I always think in superlatives. Even in connection with such monstrous things as incest and child-rape.

In the evening they always paddled off quietly in their canoes, each group separately, without saying good-bye to us or to one another. Saying good-bye is a ceremony which is unknown to primitive races.

On this, our first evening on the island, we settled our account with the Mexicans. To begin with they had taken us for gringo millionaires, but when Paulchen assured them that the idea was absurd and would get them nowhere—as he had never spoken to them before this was very effective—the accounts were settled without any great difficulties.

We paid 1,649 pesos for everything—horses, mules, arrieros, Don Oscar and Don Emilio. That was $133.73. By the time they got back home, Don Oscar would have spent altogether eighteen days in the saddle, Don Emilio twenty-three or twenty-four.

The next day the caravan went home. With them went Harry, who, as usual, had slung his hammock between two trees and spent the nights by the Jataté. Now he went home with the caravan. The caravan would pass his house, where he would remain alone for several months: alone in his house full of exotic birds and lurking snakes, surrounded by an over-lush vegetation, the stench of fecundity and rampant decomposition.

He came down again to say good-bye. In all probability we should never see him again. To him we owed contact with the Lacandones and many more things—but that was not the reason why we had come to appreciate him more and more. He was more sensible, more normal, more human than any of us. We loved him.

We watched him as he went back across the rocks and sandbanks, a tall, lean figure with a lemon-coloured topee, the author of a book about life in Sing-Sing. When he reached the other side he turned again, took off his topee and waved. Then he disappeared into the darkness of the forest.

I suddenly remembered that we had never asked him how he was getting on with his "worm". Heaven knows why I remembered that just then.

We heard the caravan leave and the cries of the muleteers. Some time later we heard Don Oscar blowing his horn. He blew a long, gay blast on his horn. He blew again and again, the notes sounding each time fainter and more distant. It was the last sound linking us with civilization—with civilization in the shape of two smart Mexicans and two simple *muchachos* and a wistful American hermit who had become our friend.

*　　*　　*

We had suddenly achieved what we had been looking forward to during the whole journey—since Mexico City, since Europe: we were alone on an ideal island in a perfect, wild river, which came green and roaring towards us from far away . . .

We were alone in the wilderness. Nobody to worry us. Except, perhaps, the *je-jenes*.

They attacked us the moment we threw off our clothes in the damp heat. Je-jenes are black flies, tiny *piúm* flies, much smaller than mosquitoes, anopheles, or yellow-fever flies. They are not as dangerous as those, but their immediate effect on one is much more devilish. They swoop down on you in their thousands, and every single one leaves behind a minute, but painful red pimple. For weeks you look like someone with measles. If you yield to the almost irresistible urge to scratch (irritation is so great that it is all too easy) your limbs swell and go dead, as if you had had an injection. It takes some time for the swelling to go down. After a fortnight you become immune to the swelling—but nobody ever grows immune to the immediate pain from the little devils' stings, not even the natives.

Even on the Jataté it became clear why the Lacandones do

not run about naked in their forest paradise, as, for instance, most of the Indians along the Amazon still do. In most reaches of the Amazon, particularly on the "black-water" rivers, there are no piúm flies, but here, and particularly in the Maya forests, they were everywhere. It is only the insects with their stubborn spite that turn the jungle into a kind of hell. Those je-jenes are a greater scourge than all other wild animals put together. Wherever they appear you are forced —in spite of the heat—to wrap yourself up from head to foot.

In this connection the long shirt of the Lacandones was a very practical garment. True, it left the feet uncovered; but this allowed a certain amount of air to circulate, which was absolutely essential. Nudism, as far as the Jataté was concerned, was out.

It was not such an ideal camp, after all, but fortunately even the almost invisible je-jenes had their favourite pitches, hours, and even days. On the less overgrown river banks, on sandbanks and rock islands we were sometimes free of them. On the water always. This was fortunate, for later on the narrow jungle rivers we had to travel stark naked. On close thundery days, or after rain, or just about sunset they made their sorties.

When we rested in camp we covered ourselves from head to foot with an American repellent of which we had taken a large supply. That gave protection for at least two hours, unless you went into the water in between whiles. I am told that taking two hundred milligrams of Vitamin B_1 tablets every day is a great help against mosquitoes and the like. The wretches still come and settle on you, but they do not sting. For the tents we had a DDT spray.

During the whole journey we never met any "normal" mosquitoes. Only je-jenes and that was quite enough! The wild cañons of the Blue Nile, with their dry heat, had been like a sanatorium compared with the Maya hell-forest.

But back to our first camp on the island in the Jataté. We were still not absolutely alone.

The Lacandones returned. Kayūm, and Nak'in, Chan Bor and Nabora, K'in and Pedro were curious about us, and did not seem to regard us as intruders. They did not exactly invite us to return their visits—although we did; they simply took a lively interest in us and watched our feverish activity. They had a great sense of humour and they thought we were wildly funny people.

Once, when Chan Bor and Nabora caught us emerging naked from the river after a bathe (at an hour when the je-jenes were kindly disposed towards us!) they did not laugh, but behaved as if it were the most natural thing in the world. But when Kliesing came unexpectedly on Kayūm and Nak'in bathing near their hut they were embarrassed; but for religious, not moral, reasons. The daily bathe is one of their religious rites.

The Lacandones have a much greater sense of humour than any other Mexican Indians. I should be telling an untruth if I said there was an air of tragedy and finality about them. It would have been unfair of us to pity these healthy-looking, cigar-sucking youngsters as being a "lost" and "unhappy" people. Our relationship was a very cordial one. They were no longer shy with us. After we had all been introduced the conversation had continued, even after Harry's departure. Using our five words of Maya and a childish Spanish—Aveckle talked in a kind of baby-German and Timber in fluent English—we held the strangest discussions. We had revised the impression, gained at the first evening's camp fire, that they spoke only with great difficulty when we realized that they spoke baby-Maya to us. But we soon forgot all about these obstacles to our strangely hilarious conversations. Once or twice, just to remind myself how strange they were, I imagined them taking place in Mexico City, or in a street in Munich or New York.

They were different from all other primitives. They were not "primitive" at all. They were an ancient people still living close to Mother Nature and all lost in their own strange, intact but doomed world.

We left the Lacandones—the living Lacandones—after various complicated preparations, at ten-forty-five on a sunny morning. We left the Lacandones behind with another rich load of treasures—empty boxes, tins, bits of string, bent nails, old shirts and trousers, and shoes which had split at the seams during the long march. We had asked them to take the old trousers, shirts and shoes to Harry. It was depressing to think of these noble people wearing trousers and broken-down shoes.

We called firmly out to them not to forget to take the trousers and shoes to Harry. They stared at us incredulously.

The boats—three single-seaters and one two-seater—lay deep, up to their rims, in the water, As usual they were overloaded. With all the experience in the world you will still overestimate the capacity of a folding canoe before every journey. A folding canoe can hold a great deal, but the right balance between what is necessary and what is possible is extremely difficult to strike, particularly on journeys into the unknown. Before us lay completely unknown country. It might be over a month before we struck a native settlement and stocked up again with maize, beans, sugar and other basic necessities. (We were optimists then.) Now work out what you need in the way of food for four weeks, quite apart from tents, air-mattresses, cameras and films, toilet requisites, books (which I refuse to go without) and medicines, and you will arrive at some staggering figures. One has no idea of the amount of food you consume in the course of four weeks. You could fill a small grocer's shop with the stuff.

Aveckle had put everything she could not stow away into waterproof bags and lashed them down on top. This made her elegant single-seater rather top-heavy. Well, one could only wait and see . . .

Paulchen, who shared the large two-seater with Timber, found him a great help, for Timber's motto was: Force will fix anything. Timber lay down on the hatch over the seat and stuffed the last-but-one tin of porridge oats into the last bit of empty space.

The reader will ask why we did not travel lighter. My answer to this is that, compared with other expeditions, we did travel light. The disadvantages of taking too little luggage become apparent at the most inconvenient moments even on ordinary journeys. Here, where we were pushing into a country about which nobody had any exact knowledge, to sacrifice this or that piece of equipment which appeared to be sheer luxury—air-mattresses, sleeping-bags, mosquito-nets, clean pyjamas, spare clothes, night-light and fuel for it, toilet things, manicure sets, medicines and instruments, or even the odd book (pocket edition, of course)—would have been not only rash but downright stupid as well.

There was obviously a limit to the amount of food we could take. That is why I was so anxious to live off the country—which meant fishing and hunting, and which to our vegetarian friends meant eating, or rather not eating, meat. To Kliesing this would be of secondary importance, but for Paulchen it would be out of the question, even if it were a matter of life and death, and I could foresee some interesting developments. Just to be on the safe side I had packed a number of spare fishing hooks and boxes of ammunition.

I had not yet shaken off the suspicion that Paulchen was still hoping to find (at suitable intervals) Indios who would sell him tortillas, or that he and his group would be able to live off the fruits of the forest. In this respect Paulchen was of a single-mindedness which was as admirable as it was frightening.

All the same, he had done his best for the party for which he acted as chef. Their canoe lay on the water like a frying-pan. It was a long, very broad boat, and they had packed it so full that Timber could find no room for his legs. Timber, who was a novice at canoeing, thought that a huge joke. He became very annoyed when we all got out of our boats again and forced his legs down inside, and he became even more annoyed when we told him that he would have to be able to get them out again very quickly if the boat started to sink.

We just hoped that we would not meet rough water. As long as the river stayed fairly normal we could manage, but in rough water Paulchen and Timber's canoe would be so unwieldy that it would sink like a stone. If we met rough water we should have to get out and tow the big two-seater or even carry it (if that was possible).

With its deep draught and its beam the big canoe floated very well (as long as the water was smooth) but Aveckle's top-heavy single canoe, which was less buoyant, bobbed about alarmingly. I shouted: "Get out at the next sandbank. We'll have to repack . . ." And that is what we did, after having gone a mere five hundred yards.

We had just reached the point where the Rio Perlas joins the Jataté at right angles. The whole mass of water shot down a rocky bar, surged against the right bank of the Jataté, forming, on the left, a mighty whirlpool. It was the very whirlpool in which the Indian had drowned. The Lacandones said a crocodile had dragged him under, but we did not believe in crocodiles. At least we did not believe in Central and South American crocodiles. The only crocodiles we believed in were the crocodiles of the Blue Nile cañons, the last specimen of *Crocodilus niloticus*.

From the canoeing point of view the thing was very simple: all you had to do was to take the strip of river between the huge, grinding whirlpool and the barrier set up by the rapids on the right. There was a wild tangle of dead trees where the Perlas came pouring into the Jataté, but all the same it was quite easy. Kliesing and I had already got through when I looked back and saw my wife capsize.

The way she capsized was very funny. It was a case of *force majeure*. She tried to steady the boat with her paddle, but it could not be done. The waters of the Perlas had got hold of the top-heavy boat, which was spinning slowly round and round. My wife tried to straighten out with her paddle, but the heavy load inside and on top of the boat was stronger and there was my wife in the water!

Suddenly she and the boat disappeared completely, leaving only her hat circling quietly on the water . . . Then she popped up and grabbed her sombrero, as if a gust of wind had swept it off her head. It looked terribly funny. Then, making another grab, she seized the boat which came shooting up out of the whirlpool. She called out: "I've got it!" By that time I was alongside and got hold of her and the boat, which was now drifting upside down away from the whirlpool and on to a large bed of rocks near the left bank. It was all perfectly easy. Aveckle got out, dripping and very cross. Then Kliesing came up, and we lifted the boat out of the water. With all the water inside it was pretty heavy. We shouted out to the big canoe to heave-to. The two men found this a pretty tough job in the fast river, but they managed it without capsizing. They had seen the whole incident from behind and had been struck dumb. It was a comical start to a journey.

"Damn!" said my wife.

"Well, I never!" said Paulchen who was still sitting in the back of the canoe. He was full of genuine admiration. "That was a smart bit of work, Marianne! And you've got the boat out already! Wonderful . . ."

"Yes," said my wife, "but damn it all the same."

"It's all part of canoeing," said Timber. "Before any big journey you ought to practise capsizing, to find out whether everything has been properly strapped on and stowed away."

"Shut up and help me," my wife snapped. But we were already helping her, although there was not much we could do. It was rather hard on my wife, after all the unpacking, repacking and careful stowing away she had already done, to have to take every blessed thing out of the boat again, and (in so far as it was not in sealed tins or rubber bags) dry it and stow it away a second time. As it happened, nothing had been lost. Everything had been stowed away so beautifully that the boat itself would have had to disintegrate before a button would have been lost. In this respect it was a faultless performance. It was just a bore having to re-distribute things, and we discussed whether we could not simply leave something behind. We could only think of the sleeping-bags. They were wonderful "Dralon" sleeping-bags, made by Klepper, and we had needed them in the highlands, but now we were only one thousand two hundred feet above sea-level and in the hot jungle. Even the nights were hot and close, and all that we needed was perhaps a bit of thin white ticking, or nothing at all. The sleeping-bags together weighed only eight pounds, but every ounce counted. Above all, they took up a lot of space in my boat—space which I could now use for some stores from the food boat. That meant that Aveckle's single canoe was now lying properly in the water, and the rapids were no longer a problem.

We could have given the sleeping-bags to the Lacandones or to Harry. For a moment I considered paddling back the five hundred yards upstream, but I immediately rejected the idea. We had finished with the Lacandones. They probably had left our island already. They could not have seen our sudden accident, and probably they had gone back to their forest hideouts. Five hundred yards had sufficed to take us out of their world as though it had never existed.

We thought of hanging the sleeping-bags up in the trees,

in case the Lacandones ever came down this far, but that was unlikely because the return trip across the whirlpool and the rapids would be difficult in their hollowed-out canoes.

In their inexperience Paul and Timber protested against leaving so much valuable equipment behind, so we told Paul and Timber that we would not leave so much valuable equipment behind, but we did—hiding it secretly in two parcels in the trees. The first contained one of the sleeping-bags together with an old ground-sheet, surplus tent-pegs, a pair of bellows with a thirty-two-inch piece of tubing; the second held the other, a pair of warm socks, three copies of *Reader's Digest* and a roll of toilet paper that had become too soggy for use. (Another roll of toilet paper which had not got so wet we unrolled—all three hundred and sixty feet of it—on the rocks and rolled it up again when it was dry.)

All this took place in a tropical landscape of unique splendour. To the north we looked across the dazzling white beds of boulders, across the confluence of the two rivers, and across the forests up to the mountains of this lonely country. Beneath white clouds sailing in an azure sky we saw the Monto Blanco, the Mountain of the White Monkeys, and, in the opposite direction, east of the Perlas behind the jungle fringe we saw heat vapours rising from more distant jungles. Somewhere out there the jungle came down to the mirror of the mysterious lake. . . .

When I think back to that hot noonday under the glorious blue sky life seems to have been perfect, unalloyed happiness. Indeed we were all happy, even Aveckle, although she was distressed at having capsized. But I said: "Don't worry, darling," and her misery slowly vanished.

We lay down in the shadow of tall trees at the edge of the bank, while the wet things dried. From time to time Paul-chen and Timber got up and turned the things over, so that they would dry more quickly, but suddenly we were not in any hurry for them to dry. It was pleasant in the hot sun, and it was pleasant in the shade. For the first time we were not being stung by je-jenes. Some *zopilotes* were circling high up in the blue, and now and again a pair of parrots flew screeching over our heads. Then a wonderful blue bird with a long beak and a crest came down the Perlas. I saw at once that it was an enormous Amazon kingfisher, and I got very excited, because next to the paradise bird of New Guinea it is one of the most beautiful birds in the world. Even my wife jumped up and walked across the bank. She pointed the kingfisher out to Paulchen and Timber and all of them walked down to the river. The fabulous bird had alighted on one of the trees in the river. There it stayed, and looked at my wife, Paulchen and Timber. Timber, by the way, was stark naked. No, sorry, that is not quite right: he was wearing his yellow hat. But although he was wearing his yellow hat he looked like a young god. My wife was naked too. Paulchen was the only one who was wearing anything: a short, grey, crumpled shirt which covered only half his behind. For practical reasons he did not wear trousers, either. In his fantastic get-up Paulchen, moving between the two stark-naked figures, looked an earthly, goblin-like creature. I do not want to carry the comparison too far, and give the wrong impression of our dear Paul, for I liked him, and when I saw him get excited about the bird, I liked him even more. I liked Timber, too, and, most of all, my wife and the kingfisher, and I asked Kliesing, who was standing by me and fiddling about with his ciné camera, whether he liked them all as much as I did. Kliesing looked at me with surprise and said: "*Como no? Of course.*"

We all felt something of the perfect beauty of this earthly paradise. Although we had hardly travelled an inch that day and had been delayed by a most annoying mishap we were all overcome with an overwhelming sense of beauty. This was a new experience. The last few days we had been too busy, what with the Lacandones and the excessive amount of sheer drudgery. And just as we were beginning to remember that we were in an earthly paradise, the je-jenes had come on silent wings. . . .

The kingfisher flew off, skimming away over the rapids and the whirlpools. Then it shot off over the Perlas to vanish finally in the stillness between river and jungle. Paulchen returned to lend a hand with the drying, and Timber and my wife came over and sat down in the shade with Kliesing and me.

"Do you think there are crocodiles here?" Timber asked.

"Of course," I said. "Alligators. But they run away."

"You and your runaway crocodiles," said my wife; "that's just hooey."

"I know they will. Especially when they see Timber in his yellow hat."

"I can take it off," said Timber.

"Keep it on or you'll catch cold," said my wife.

"The alligators here are just ornaments."

"Was the crocodile in the Blue Nile an ornament, too?"

"No," said my wife. "That was a real one and it had had bad luck. A lot of bad luck. It was an unhappy crocodile."

"What happens when an unhappy crocodile grabs you?"

"It's very simple," I explained to Timber. "You just don't get away. It pulls you down and hides you in the mud by the river bank. Every self-respecting crocodile has a larder there. You're put on a carving dish. When you've gone nice and mouldy you're eaten slowly. Slowly, and with the relish of a gourmet eating a good cheese slice by slice."

"Stop it," said my wife.

"It's true. I read it somewhere and it's right."

"All the same, you can stop."

"But it doesn't apply here. There aren't any unhappy crocodiles here."

A rest on the river that never seems to end: Aveckle, clothed for once, wipes off the perspiration.

On the River Jatate—a wonderful, lonely river flowing between the high walls of the jungle. *Above:* The canoes heavily loaded. *Below:* Hauling a canoe past one of the many obstructions.

Kliesing turned out to be the best fisherman.

Above : The melancholy figure is young Timber. *Below :* Aveckle pushes her canoe under one of the last of the fallen trees—keeping a sharp lookout for snakes as she does so.

"Since that crocodile business," my wife said to Timber and Kliesing, "the crocodile has become my totem animal. Well, would you talk about your totem animal like that?"

"There are only happy crocodiles here," I said, "and every man jack of them is a vegetarian."

"You've got it at last," said Kliesing. "I suggest we freshen ourselves up again and then move on."

We went to the river and bathed, keeping a weather-eye open for alligators. There were none in sight, although, of course, they existed. I should have liked at least one alligator to have approached just to prove that Central and South American alligators are perfectly harmless, but none came. Throughout the whole journey we saw only two live crocodiles (one of them will appear right away); apart from these we saw only track marks. I suppose they were hiding in the mud by the river banks, or in the pools at the bottom, anxiously watching in case we trod on them. After our experience in Africa we had painted the rudders of our canoes black, so that they would not act as reflectors and invite attack, as they had on the Nile. It was an unnecessary precaution. Here danger came from another quarter. For instance, we saw an unusual number of snakes. The most beautiful snakes, nearly all of them exceptionally poisonous. Nearly all the snakes fled at our approach, thank God, or were simply puzzled.

After a refreshing bathe we packed up and prepared to continue our journey. Everything that had got wet had dried beautifully. My wife was able to put on again the white blouse which she wore in the boat to protect her from the sun. Her boat now lay perfectly balanced in the water.

About two o'clock, just as we were ready to go after a delightful stop of three hours, Paulchen came running up excitedly.

"Stop!" cried Paulchen. "Your sleeping-bag!"

He had discovered one of the parcels, containing a

sleeping-bag, socks, and *Reader's Digests*. Dear, helpful Paulchen cried: "You nearly left this behind!"

"Yes," my wife said weakly.

"You know, Paulchen," I said, "I think we must leave it here. We don't need it; it's only a nuisance. The value of everything is purely relative. The Lacandones are sure to pick it up."

"You're mad," Paulchen protested.

"All right, we'll give it to you."

"I can't accept it."

"Then just put it back where you found it."

Timber roared with laughter.

Perplexed, Paulchen accepted the present. We had an awful lot of trouble persuading him to throw away at least the warm socks. (He kept the *Reader's Digests*.) When packing up our boats in the mornings we saw, with a mixture of despair and *schadenfreude*, how Paulchen tried to fit in the bulky sleeping-bag, first in one place, then in another, and always with the greatest difficulty. Till one day he had to leave it behind somewhere in the forest . . .

*   *   *

That day we travelled twelve miles down-river.

It was an enchanting river, swift-flowing, lonely and green between the high walls of jungle. Every couple of miles or so the jungle retreated, leaving open spaces where the river split up among a maze of sand, boulders and small islands. Rapids appeared, all of them easy to navigate. We had only to be careful not to take the wrong turning and lose ourselves, and to watch that the powerful current did not sweep us under the giant trees which had fallen into the river. And wherever the river divided up we had to be careful not to miss the mouth of the Rio Azul.

The Rio Azul was marked on all our maps, but we did not know how far we could trust them; or rather, we knew that they could only offer us clues—valuable clues, of course. Even on the first day we passed a number of tributaries. One, which looked a likely candidate, we followed for quite a distance, but the river finished up in a muddy swamp and soon began to look so foul that we were sure it could not be the Rio Azul.

In the middle of one of the Jataté's main arms we saw the first of the two crocodiles mentioned above. It was an extremely nimble alligator, not more than six feet long, which reacted in a most sensible fashion: it ran away. In the sun it looked yellow, like a canary. It rushed down into the water from a high sandbank when I paddled up to within sixty feet of it. At first I took it for an iguana, one of those Mexican lizards which can grow to the same size, but it had fairly long legs and a broad body, and before it dived out of sight it turned its head and looked at me again. Kliesing saw it too. We stopped at the spot where it had disappeared and looked for it, but in vain.

Shortly before sunset we set up camp on a small bed of rocks. It was close to the bank, except that the shore was not a shore, but an impenetrable thicket. It was a shore and it was not. It is very hard to describe. Imagine a river without any banks, a green, bankless and utterly noiseless river. Silent-flowing and green—greener than the forest, which here was so dark that it looked almost black. Only at high noon did it look a little less black; but even then it was still dark and forbidding. Even when the last, slanting rays of light suddenly struck it, and clouds of tiny violet and pink butterfles came billowing out of the forest the scene did not become idyllic. . . .

But let us console ourselves with the two toucans.

They ceased their hoarse quarrelling when they saw us get out of our boats. Distracted, they flapped away over the clouds of violet and pink butterflies. On the other side a tree trunk collapsed silently under their weight, puffing out a cloud of black butterflies, which seemed to throw the toucans even higher, right up to the topmost branches of a mighty tree, where there was already another bird amusing himself by turning somersaults. The toucans disappeared, the black cloud of butterflies spread out over the river together with the other clouds, and all the butterflies turned into millions of tiny dancing specks.

As to the bird that turned somersaults, I am sorry I cannot tell you what it was. It was not a toucan, it certainly was not a goatsucker, and it was not a parrot. He was just an amusing chap with a large beak and magnificent plumage. His colouring was indefinable, even through binoculars—the only living thing in this dark forest who was always delighted to see us. Wherever we saw one of these unprejudiced birds, he did his best to try and attract our attention. He would hang head down from a branch and call us. He called and called till we took notice and showed that we were watching him. Then, completing the circle, he would swing back up on his branch. When he was sure we were watching him attentively, he would turn one somersault after another. He was the most amusing bird we had the pleasure of meeting.

This acrobatic bird, this aerial clown high above everything, brought us back to earth. He gave a complete performance before the colours of sky and forest faded, the light dimmed, the je-jenes came and night fell. The camp fire blazed and the smoke drifted peacefully across the river, till the first motor-cyclist appeared; and then all the motor-cyclists appeared, about a thousand of them. The whole forest was their race-track. Judging from the noise they made they were riding round and round in a frenzy of despair.

They were frogs, of course. Bull frogs, roughly speaking, or perhaps one size smaller. They were dear little things which sometimes jumped into our tents. There they were quiet and only looked at us in a bemused fashion. They were half the size of a bucket, and they seemed to have complete confidence in us, looking trustingly at us with their golden eyes. One evening when we were sitting by the camp fire a frog jumped on to my back, and I gave a bigger leap than I had ever given before from a sitting position. Everybody became helpless with laughter, but just imagine yourself sitting peacefully and happily in the jungle at night, and then, all of a sudden, something large, sticky and wet jumps on your back. You'd leap, too.

On the whole they were nice. Later, when there were no more of them, we even missed them. The noise they made was like the noise cicadas make on a moonlit night, only amplified by a hundred loudspeakers. Two hours after sunset they ran out of breath, and perhaps despair, and the thousand or more motor-cyclists stopped their machines. Peace returned to the woods, till it was shattered by new excitements. But I will not reveal everything at one fell swoop. We wanted to go to bed and so we sprayed our tents with DDT . . .

In this part of the world none of the insects had ever heard of DDT and were therefore not immune to it. When the tents were clear we quickly brought in the lamp, closed the mosquito-nets, undressed, lay down naked on our air-beds and wrote up our diaries or read. It was all very cosy. It was always the same at this hour of the day, even when everything else had become anything but cosy.

The days on the Jataté were days of rushing water, trees and bird-song, if you want to put it romantically. It was a shining, living river. You will understand our feelings when I say that the world seemed to offer no greater bliss than to linger awhile by this river, soaking in impressions and making ourselves at home in paradise.

That was our intention. But then, on the second day, we discovered the mouth of the river Azul . . .

At least, we never doubted that it was the Azul: a narrow,

but deep and beautifully clear river which rushed down between steep banks into the Jataté as if it were in a hurry to escape from something dark and boundless . . .

Its much-longed-for discovery, which came far too soon for our liking, cut short our stay in paradise. With stupid cries of joy we steered our boats into the pools between the steep banks. In the deep, crystal-clear water beneath us we saw a lot of huge, strange fish: perch as long as a man's arm, broad thornback, fish with protruding teeth. All of them moved infinitely slowly. Some looked up and turned away again. Sheat-fish lay on the bottom and waggled their beards. They all moved as if they were in an aquarium and accustomed to strange spectators from another world. Our hearts beat faster at the thought of the fishing as we glided lightly over the clear whirlpools, the light became dim, the world sank into darkness, the smell of the tiger grew stronger and the patient wilderness closed in on us like a wave over a stone cast into the sea.

*   *   *

On the first day we managed to penetrate a few miles up this river.

We did not then know that it sprang from the depths of darkness. We had a foretaste of things to come: now a small rapid, now a barrier of rock, now something else . . .

Towing the boats through the rapids was not too bad; lifting them fully loaded over the rocks was not so good. The third rapid was a job for athletes.

The stretches between the rapids and the barriers of rock were easy. All the same, we downed paddles at three o'clock in the afternoon. A small island came into view, where we could clear a good place for our tents. For *playas*, proper beaches, beds of boulders or sandbanks, could no longer be expected. The jungle no longer kept its distance as it did on the wide, and useful, open spaces along the Jataté. It closed in on us from both sides in all its impenetrable glory. I began to worry about the camping because I saw that from now on we should be lucky to find anywhere to bed down.

The island was like the answer to my prayer. Momentous things happened on this island: we reorganized ourselves.

The boats were far too heavy for the journey upstream. Since we were coming back down the Azul after exploring the Lake of the Lacandones, the most logical thing to do was to leave some of our tinned food here. We should need it later. It was senseless to drag it there and back. We considered everything very carefully, made an excellent plan, and at this camp (which Kliesing called "the camp of happy certainty") we established a supply dump.

Earlier on I mentioned the figures on which we based our calculations: from this point Kliesing reckoned on three days' travel to the lake, and I reckoned on six. These were optimistic figures, based on sheer speculation and wishful thinking—that no bend in the river would reveal an unsurmountable obstacle . . .

After ten days we had reached the point of no return. We were stuck in this dark inferno like a mountaineer lost on a vertical rockface—only more so, since a mountaineer may still have a chance of making his presence known to somebody, and he can look out for a helicopter or a rescue team.

That was not the worst of it. When, a fortnight later, I found out that, in their crazy optimism, our friends had taken food for only two instead of four weeks as I had ordered them to, I went off into a tropical rage.

My reasoning had been perfectly sound: one week (at the very most) to get there, one week on the lake, one week to get back, one week in reserve.

Paulchen had mumbled his agreement. It would never for one moment have occurred to me that I could not trust him. In fact, their canoe remained overloaded, although Kliesing's boat looked suspiciously light.

It was a good thing that they had Timber. For Timber, in his eagerness to do us a good turn, had handed out twenty-five iron rations, giving us five each. Timber regarded these beautiful golden tins with a mixture of respect and romance. He solemnly handed them over and murmured something about "a matter of life and death". On the journey it was touching to see how jealously he watched to see that nobody degraded his gift by eating it before it became a matter of "life and death".

The rations contained great delicacies such as chocolate, toffee, Coca-Cola tablets, and vitamins; small biscuits which swelled up, thereby satisfying us as well as tasting good; dextrose, halazone tablets, tin openers, waterproof matches and a few other things. We paid Timber's gifts great honour. We stowed them away and guarded them carefully against the hour of need.

We filled a hammock with tins and other provisions wrapped up in waterproof bags, wound a ground-sheet round it and slung it up between trees where neither animals nor the elements were likely to get at it. Then we tied on a label in English and Spanish bearing our signatures and explaining that we were an expedition on the way to the Lake of the Lacandones and that we intended to be back by the beginning of March. (It was then 24 February.)

*   *   *

The journey upstream might have been very pleasant if, every thousand or fifteen hundred yards, we had not had to surmount a total of fourteen cataracts, both large and small, on the first day after the camp where we had left the dump. They were rock barriers with rapids bristling with the debris of mahogany and ironwood trees. Had we been going downstream we could have shot them without endangering our lives and our boats. In some places we were able to paddle very close to the backwash from the rapids, and had to carry the boats only a few yards over the rocks. Those were the bright spots, but there were other cataracts, snarling and brutal. Sometimes it took us half an hour just to get near them, and another half an hour to find the only possible place where we could get over them. To carry the boats round the shore part was nearly always impossible. We had usually to start below the rapids—wading up to our necks in the water and pushing the boats, or swimming through whirlpools and pulling them—till finally we got a foothold on a rock. Then all five of us would push and pull the boats, generally across a vertical fall of water. Above the cataract the water would be dammed up like a weir and rather deep. It was normally Aveckle's job to get up and find a firm foothold. There she would stand, up to her neck in some unknown water swarming with tropical fauna. With a great heave we pushed one boat after another over the top for her to grab and then secure. When we had got the last boat up, we would swim across the current and get in. It was a strange kind of amphibious locomotion in an intimate yet extravagant world of damp heat and suffocating decomposition.

It was a grinding sweat.

"After all this," we said on the third day, "it would be sheer madness to turn back and give up our great goal!"

Even Paulchen said that to have gone through all this for nothing would be pointless.

After a time we developed a certain routine, but we stopped saying we could think ourselves lucky that it was not much worse . . .

Our greatest worry was that we might be brought to a halt. Our next great worry was whether we were on the right river. Perhaps we had turned off too soon—and followed a completely false river, one not marked on any map!

Going upstream from the river mouth our course had been east-north-east. Then, in spite of a multitude of complicated twists and turns, the river had taken a clear easterly direction which filled us with confidence because it tallied with our calculations. We were now approaching a mountain range. It lay ahead on our right, and was so high that we sometimes saw it even through the jungle. For a long time we took this range for some of the Chamhuitz foothills although, according to our theory, we had to pass them on the left. Instead of making a definite turn to the south, the Azul finally ran right along this range, taking a lot of rock barriers in its stride. The rock barriers followed each other in increasingly close succession—all the fault of this damned range. Instead of passing the range on the left we were passing it on the right. It could only be foothills of the Sierra Caribe, which were not marked on our maps—unless, of course, we were on the wrong river.

Perhaps we should have taken the earlier river, which was swallowed up in an impenetrable thicket . . . Or else the mouth of the Rio Azul was farther down the Jataté.

In camp at night we suppressed our doubts, drawing geographical conclusions which were much applauded by Paulchen and Timber. My wife was the only one to make any inconvenient remarks. Although, as all the world knows, women know nothing about geography, my wife invariably exposed the weak points in our strictly scientific wishful thinking. We took the maps away from her.

This happened, by the way, in a camp on a dangerously small island where we had found the pale skull of a small crocodile. We christened it "crocodile camp", and we were glad to have found the island—although it was far too small and would have been threatened by the slightest rise in the water.

That day we had not only done fourteen cataracts, but we had also been visited by je-jenes. This was particularly annoying because, due to our mode of travelling, we had no means of protecting ourselves against them. The only way of protecting ourselves was to immerse ourselves in the water up to our noses. The moment we got into the boats we put shirts on; but since we had to keep on getting out of the boats and into the water, it became impossible to take adequate precautions. We could only rub insecticide on our swollen limbs in "crocodile camp".

It may sound odd, but in spite of all this it was a cosy camp that evening. It may have stood on a very dubious site, but for the time being we ignored that. Kliesing had put up his tent with the double doors, the two smaller tents of Paulchen and Timber were close together, and our fine Klepper tent with all home comforts stood in the middle, while we ourselves were recovering from the day and were in fine form. Even before we were properly installed Paulchen had made a glorious fire and was busy making waffles, brewing tea and cooking the vegetarian bean soup. Aveckle was cooking beans too, but with bacon, and when Paulchen had finished she borrowed his Swedish waffle-iron and made crisp waffles on which she spread a thick layer of jam. It was all very harmonious and the wilderness held its breath.

Then, suddenly, we noticed that there were no more motor-cyclists. It is not an important point, but we noticed it. The evening before we had still heard one, just one. He must have lost his way. From now on, along the whole of the Azul, there was not a single one of those desperate motor-cyclists in evidence. Oddly enough, even the je-jenes had disappeared.

Timber began to tell stories, and everything would have become even more harmonious, when suddenly, at eight-thirty p.m., the earth was shaken to its foundations and a clap of thunder tore across the wilderness while lightning struck the river right in front of us.

At the same time we heard the cloudburst roaring towards us. We scattered hurriedly, made the tents fast, and waited in terror.

Then it started. Thunderclap followed thunderclap with a deluge of rain that threatened to drown us. Several times lightning struck again right by us. Thunder, torrential rain and crashing trees united in a crescendo fit to herald in the world's end. It was unbelievable that nature would take all this trouble just to annihilate us, but this thought brought us no consolation. The large tent stood the strain very well; the others would probably stand the strain equally well, if they had not already collapsed. We were all thrown back on our own resources. Aveckle and I were probably better off being together. We were also the only ones who had the right kind of lighting, a petrol lamp. It shed its cosy glow, with the result that we did not see the darkness but only knew that there was darkness outside, and that it was probably rent continually by lightning for we could hear it crackle and strike in the midst of the downpour that was shaking the foundations of our home.

"My home is my castle, isn't it?"

"Yes," said my wife, "that's right."

"Well, well," I said. But then the rain became so loud that my words were drowned. Although the rain tore and shook for all it was worth, the tent stood as firm and water-tight as a diving-bell and the cosy little lamp swung thoughtfully. Aveckle was squatting on her air-mattress reading a book, one which I had meant to read but did not feel like reading because I was too nervous. I listened in every possible direction, and then came more thunder, reverberating in the mountains which we had passed on the right instead of on the left. They were to blame for the storm getting stuck here instead of passing on.

"I only hope that a tree doesn't fall on the roof."

"Blast! I always forget to look out for the damned trees which might fall on our roof. But I think we'll be O.K. here. I think there are only little trees on the river bank."

My wife put the book down. It was terribly hot in the

tent, although we had left the door to the outer room open. The flap of the outer room we had made fast. The tent was completely sealed. It was a super tent.

We were sweating profusely. All the same, it was nice in the tent. We would have liked to run about naked in the rain —if the rain had been nice rain. But it was not nice rain. Outside it was a wild world, a wild and furious world.

"I'm afraid we'll be swept away by the water," I said.

"Good night," said my wife.

"Yes," I said. "It'll be good night and good-bye."

"I'm hot," said my wife.

"It would be still less funny if it were cold on top of everything else."

"I'm satisfied," my wife said.

"Try and go to sleep."

Crash . . .

We had a number of things packed ready: the suitcase in a rubber bag; the cameras and the films also in waterproof bags; and the gun. All the same, there were still a lot of things lying about. The boats were firmly moored and quite safe, but there would be one hell of a mess. The river would almost certainly rise and wash us away if it went on raining like this. We had once been flooded on the Tagliamento and we knew what it was like, but on that occasion the nearest village had been only four miles away.

I went into the outer room and tried to see what the rain was like, but in the wild fury all I could make out was the roaring mass of water which was coming down. When I undid the zip-fastener a bit I could at least see Kliesing's tent. Of the two small tents not a sign. Kliesing had lit a candle and I called: "Kliesing! Hey there!" My shouts were drowned by the rain, and then there was more thunder and lightning. The thunderstorm lasted from half past eight till eleven o'clock. Then, and only then, could we emerge from our tents to review the situation.

The clouds parted. The forest steamed ghostlike in the moonlight, for all at once there was a moon. No je-jenes. Of course! It was the stifling heat before the thunderstorm that had goaded the je-jenes into such a fury throughout the whole day.

The river had not risen an inch. That meant nothing. It all depended on the amount of rain that had fallen near its source, and it might well descend on us like a deluge in the next few hours.

Paulchen and Timber crawled from their tents.

"I'm all wet," said Timber. "My tent leaks somewhere. Quite a show, eh?"

Paulchen got busy on the fire. The fire had gone out. But, God knows how, all at once it was roaring again. I believe Paulchen had simply looked hard at it.

"I was quite frightened," Timber said.

"Never be frightened," Paulchen said kindly, "it's pointless. If your vibrations are harmonious you never need be frightened."

"Yes," Timber said. "I'm sure you're right. Only I got wet and a little disheartened."

We stared in despair at the jungle, glistening wet in the moonlight. We were only twenty inches above the water and the river would soon overflow. We faced the delightful prospect of striking camp and spending the rest of the night in the wet swamp.

"Do you think harmonious vibrations are any good against floods?"

"I don't know what you mean," Paulchen said indulgently. "All nature is full of vibrations, harmonious ones and others. One must try to attract the harmonious ones, that's all. Then there won't be any flood."

"All right, let's try."

All through the night I had horribly unharmonious vibrations. I could not sleep and went outside every half-hour or so to look at the level of the water. Even at dawn, shortly before six, the river had not risen half an inch. Paulchen and his theory would have enjoyed a great triumph if he had bothered to gloat about it, but I think he was far too kind a man even to gloat.

From a geohydrological point of view the fact that the river had not risen was something of a phenomenon. What it meant was this: because of the mountain range opposite us, we had been the centre of a regional thunderstorm; further, that the river did not receive the bulk of its water from this range but from a remoter area, an area with a balanced in-and-out flow—in other words, the lake! And lastly it meant that, beyond a shadow of doubt, we were on the right river.

The chalky nature of the range also had something to do with it, of course. The thing that was really wrong was the thunderstorm itself—in the middle of the dry season!

*   *   *

Unfortunately this was not an isolated event.

When we continued our journey the next morning (a Tuesday) it did not rain (there was even a spell of sunshine) but later on it began to rain. And how! We had spent the day getting over twelve tough, rocky cataracts, one after another on this delightful river: out of the boats, into the water. Barefoot, across rock and stones, and often up to your chest in mud and creeper, in the warm water of a tropical river and its churned-up mud—but, thank God, no je-jenes! The absence of je-jenes was a great relief, for even if we *had* been fanatical anti-nudists we should have had no choice but to travel completely naked. How my wife and I had laughed over Peter Fleming's description of the search for Colonel Fawcett— how they all travelled up a river in the Matto Grosso pulling their canoe along by a string: Roger, Peter and the Brazilian, Queiroz. Naked, without even bathing trunks, but in the grandest style, and the whole grotesque situation recorded in photographs. We had been tickled to death by this way of journeying into the unknown, and now, to our astonishment, we found ourselves in exactly the same grotesque situation.

And then, as I said, it began to rain, while ahead of us loomed the thirteenth cataract . . .

Normally, rain in the tropics has not the same importance for a camper going by canoe as, let us say, a rainy Whitsun holiday on Lake Garda has. It remains warm, and if you have only your own skin to put between you and the wet, the moist heat does not greatly affect your physical well-being. This steamy moisture is very good for the skin. It is even a first-class cosmetic! The skin gets tight, smooth and shiny, and by going to the Chiapas or any other handy rain forest ladies could save themselves an expensive course of treatment with anti-wrinkle-recreation cream, or whatever it is called.

There is, however, a limit to everything, and not without reason, I had sworn never, never again to travel in a tropical rain forest, mainly for photographic reasons. So long as you do not put it right in the sun an exposed film can stand a temperature of a hundred and twenty degrees or more for months on end—provided it is a dry heat. In the moist heat of no more than ninety degrees that occurs in the wet tropics the material runs the gravest dangers.

In such a climate, a film goes sticky and glues up if it has been taken out of its tin and been in the camera a few hours. The emulsion swells up like a pudding from the all-penetrating steam. A veritable army of bacteria hurls itself on this delectable mush and settles in organized colonies. The results are negatives which are only interesting to a bacteriologist. That there exist special "tropicalized" emulsions is a widespread myth which is neither denied nor encouraged by film manufacturers.

There are certain ways of protecting one's material against

destruction. There are even splendid instruction leaflets on how to use cameras and films in the tropics. These instruction leaflets are well-meaning. They have all been written by well-meaning, but somewhat unworldly, specialists. What, in the jungle, was one to make of the suggestion to "solder exposed films into a tin canister in dry air"? Using "preserving jars filled with moisture-absorbing substances, sealed with rubber rings and fastened with a steel spring" seemed sensible enough, but not altogether practicable. The strict admonition to send the exposed film "as soon as possible by air" for development filled us with profound melancholy.

However, I had brought a pound of silica gel. It is an absorbent—blue when dry and pink when wet—which can be regenerated endlessly by drying it in the sun or roasting it by a camp fire. You have no idea how we regenerated!

My dear wife had sewn up the silica gel in small, porous linen bags, rather like the small lavender-bags which are sold at church bazaars. In the evening, while my wife prepared game at the camp fire, I regenerated. That is to say, I put the small bags by the camp fire and turned them over and over; or even, when the fire had gone down sufficiently, laid them on Paulchen's waffle-iron (silica gel has no evil vibrations) till it was blue again instead of pink. It was a dreary occupation, but the result was that this time—in contrast to earlier lengthy trips in the tropics—I got all my films home intact, despite the most unfavourable climatic conditions. Even the colour films. They were all Agfa CN films.

Another thing is that green and jungle-darkness are technically the most unfavourable things possible. Every amateur knows about the difficulty with green. Yet this time, from the earth's most inimical rain forest, I brought back colour pictures which had not only withstood the greatest vicissitudes, but on which the green had actually "come out". And so no photographer will smile at me if I say a heartfelt "Thank you, gentlemen!" to the emulsion scientists (whom I imagine as they are pictured in advertisements: standing over their microscopes in white overalls, looking benignly at you, while dropping valuable hints).

The cameras themselves are usually liable to disintegrate. In a hot-house temperature, in which no article of clothing ever dries out, not only does the leather grow a layer of mould but everything else soon develops a musty smell. The colour comes off leather carrying straps, and this can cause eczema. Iron rusts within a few hours. Modern alloys corrode. Everything comes apart and falls to pieces. When loading with film and when taking it out you have to be careful that no drops of sweat fall into the camera from your face and hands. Where the parts of the lenses are cemented together a fungus begins to grow whose white spawn makes fascinating patterns. Once it gets inside your lens, you have had it.

All this my cameras took in their stride. Their leather cases survived. The Tessar and Sonnar lenses stayed clear and free of fungi. Nothing came apart or corroded. Of course, I watched my equipment carefully and from time to time put a minute drop of paraffin on the more sensitive parts. My natural pedantry paid dividends. The cameras— all three of them Zeiss Ikon—were exposed to the climate only for short spells at a time. Otherwise they stayed in their waterproof rubber bags, together with some of the small bags of silica gel, so that the inside of the rubber bags should stay as dry as possible and the films should not disintegrate in the cameras. From the technical point of view everything went off without a hitch.

I did not know all this then, that afternoon before the thirteenth cataract . . . Then I only saw that we were up against it good and proper. We had come to a bank of unparalleled unfriendliness. There were lianas, rotting wood, wetness and mud. Mud above, mud below, mud everywhere. None of us had ever landed on a more un-friendly bank. We could not even land, because the bank was high and steep and matted, without climbing up the lianas from our tossing boats (which we did eventually, in sheer despair). We had only stopped there, each at a different spot, because the rain had become too solid and because the thirteenth cataract was too much for us in such solid rain. Without even discussing it very much we conceived the strange idea that we must wait till the rain was "over". By then the rain was no longer as nice and commendable as I said two or three pages back. It became an absolutely filthy rain. It degenerated into a proper rainy-season-rain; and when it rains in the rainy season, then, in the tropics, it rains differently from anywhere else, three or four times differently, so to speak.

Finally we did disembark, I suppose really out of des-peration. I climbed up a liana, made the boat fast and, lying with my belly in the mud, helped my wife to get out. She kept sliding back, but I finally succeeded in pulling her up and then we lay for a few moments naked and wet and sheepish in the jungle, comparable to those strange amphibi-ous creatures who climbed from the primeval ocean slime on to dry land.

The forest was lighter here and the trees more slender. The others had climbed out of their boats too, and then we all stood there naked and sheepish in the tearful, weeping forest and stared at the thirteenth cataract which we should never be able to master, at least, not today, and then we all went very cold. We should, of course, have got back into the water up to our necks, for the water was warm, about eighty-three degrees; but the river and its water suddenly began to look sinister. We heard the echo of successive cloudbursts, we looked at the turbulent water and preferred to freeze. . . .

The thing I remembered, as we all stood there naked and

cold, was that I had sworn never to go to the rain forests again. I had said to Aveckle, let us go to some pleasant sub-tropical place, some dry place where everything does not fall to bits, including the soul, where bacteria do not settle on the films nor fungi in the lenses. A place like the Gojjam on the Blue Nile—a paradise where even at night the temperature never drops below a hundred. And at the same time so dry that you do not mind the heat. Where there are neither mosquitoes, nor je-jenes, at least not during the dry season. Did I say paradise just now? Well, ninety-nine per cent had been paradise. Only the crocodiles had caught us a bit off balance. They had even frightened us a little . . .

Before we set out for the forests of the Lacandones we had calculated that we should arrive there at the height of the dry season—"some time between January and April"—and we would spend not more than one or two months there. During that time even the rainiest of rain forests must be bearable.

Well, here we were, at the "height of the dry season", shivering and listening to the echo of one cloudburst after another and the wilderness was shaking with mirth. Mother Nature was splitting her sides with laughter.

I went back to the boat and got out the machete. Simply to get warm I started working like a madman, clearing a camping place in the middle of the forest. It was not too bad when you had found a place where the trees were not too thick. I said we must build an emergency camp, and Timber, with his sense of life-and-death, went and fetched his lumberman's axe, and we laid madly about us to get warm. Then our cutting sobered down, and when we had got warm —which did not take long—we cut with great accuracy. Suddenly everybody became extremely busy. Suddenly it seemed the most logical thing in the world to make oneself comfortable in the middle of Nature's great joke; amid the spongy bolsters of algae and moss, in the dripping maze of ferns, lianas and orchids, we made ourselves comfortable enough to await the end of the world if need be. No jungle has more palm trees than the jungle of tropical America. It is quite easy to fell a palm tree, even right at the base. So we felled a few palm trees and within half an hour we had a proper site for our tents.

In spite of my ample experience of jungles in all parts of the world, I would not have believed that it could be so easy. One never stops learning. Admittedly I had generally been on my own, and if you are on your own you do not need much space, not even in the jungle. It was more from habit than anything else that I had always looked for some kind of beach or a less overgrown river bank, and that is why on this trip I had looked out for similar places up to now. This time we had landed not only on the most inhospitable bank imaginable, but also at the most unsuitable camping place in the heart of the wilderness. And didn't we make ourselves comfortable! From now on we camped wherever exhaustion compelled us to land. Having to clear the forest before we could put up our tents did not become one of our favourite habits, it is true, but it became a habit pretty quickly.

We cut the leaves off the palm trees. They were several yards long, and we laid them carefully over our camp site to keep out the mud. The only thing we should have to do without was a fire . . .

But look at Paulchen! There he was, building a fire, for all the world as though the rain were not teeming down nor the wind howling through the trees . . .

"Ha, ha," we said. "Forget it, Paulchen! It's a cold buffet today, and we'll make the tea on the cooker."

Paulchen was not to be put off, and suddenly a thin wisp of smoke was rising. It was a brilliant achievement. Timber raced off and collected the right kind of wood, only wet on the outside but seasoned inside. While we were still erecting our tents in the rain and struggling to unload the boats, with everything becoming wetter and heavier every second, Paulchen and Timber had built a roaring fire by the stove. This formed a globe of heat all round us, keeping us dry and warm and protected from the wet like a stuffed bird in a glass case. We were in an expansive mood and in splendid form. We even remained in splendid form when we thought of the thirteenth cataract and the last stage of the journey to the lake, which could not be far now. (We were wrong.) I never had wanted to go into the rain forest again—but if somebody came to me now and said: "Here's two thousand pounds. Take it and fly over the ocean to Mexico, and from Mexico City fly to Chiapas, and then fly as far as you can, and then take a look at that jungle and see if it's still raining" —well, neither your author nor his wife would hesitate for one minute. In spite of everything that still happened to us, we should start out again at once for six months in the jungle.

During the night the rain stopped. We guessed this, judging by the different dripping sound, for it was still dripping off the trees. It dripped all the time. Not a single animal sound could be heard, not even the faint sigh of a snake in a neighbouring hollow tree. Only the dripping, and occasionally, sometimes quite close, sometimes some distance off, the collapse of a giant tree. We had been too busy being in splendid form to watch out for trees! We always forgot this when we set up camp, so great was our desire to make ourselves comfortable. It just did not occur to us to look on trees several feet thick as epileptics, but the whole of this forest was epileptic. Every night we heard trees falling, sometimes only half falling, because other trees were in the way. It is easy to grasp that, after a heavy rain, no soil can hold trees which grow as tall as a church steeple but whose shallow roots extend over an area no bigger than a modern one-and-a-half-room flat. But we heard trees collapse during quiet nights when it had not rained for days. Sometimes, in the daytime, we saw trees simply crumple up without a sound because they were hollow and rotten. A great wave of insects would surge out of the trunk, and the snakes which had been living in it would be too scared to hiss and would dart out like lightning in all directions, and then disappear within a matter of seconds.

* * *

It did not rain the next morning, either. It was grey and warm. Our great good humour of the night before gave way to sober, everyday routine. It was a nasty job pushing the boats down from the high mud bank into the water and getting into them and going off and then getting out again after a hundred yards because of the cataract. It was a tough cataract. We took about an hour to get across it.

Shortly afterwards we came to a tributary which joined our river on the right in beautiful cascades. We were badly shaken. We thought we had—at last—reached the arroyo which comes down from the Chamhuitz range into the Rio Azul.

This "first" arroyo which was to join the Azul on the left, looking upstream, was our second most important landmark. It was marked on all our maps.

This "first" arroyo was supposed to be on our left. On no account must we take it. Once we had reached it and left it behind, it could not be very far to our other, even more important, landmark: the "second" arroyo.

This "second" one was to join us on the right. It was supposed to come from the Sierra Caribe. We should have passed left of it and carried on for another three or six miles along the Rio Azul to reach the lake.

We were shaken, because we thought the river which came down in cascades was the Azul, while the arroyo came from the left. Quite clearly the Azul came from the left, broad and stately—much broader and statelier than at the point where it joined the Jataté—past the romantic cascades which were fed by an unimportant rivulet which disappeared above them in the depths of the forest. This was quite obvious, and the direction was right, too. We had got a little worried that the Azul had swung too far east and even south, but it now became increasingly clear that it came from the north.

Then it seemed as if there were fewer cataracts. We advanced more rapidly.

That day we saw a large turtle shooting down a cataract. The current drove it hard against Kliesing's boat. Kliesing was still in his boat, and in the excitement the turtle failed to dive quickly enough. Kliesing tried to stop it with his paddle, but it was too big and heavy. Kliesing struck it on the back with his paddle. It did not seem to mind, and disappeared in some whirlpool. Later one of us saw an alligator. The frightened animal must have retreated in undignified haste. Nobody else saw it. None of us got excited about such a despicable reptile. We were ashamed that we had painted our rudders black against "furious attacks by crocodiles". That was the last crocodile we met.

Shortly after half past three we landed on a jungle bank, not as steep and muddy as the one at the rain camp and easy for hauling up the boats. We found a suitable spot for the tents in the middle of the forest, and within half an hour we had cleared it. If I am not mistaken we even made sure that there were no trees that were likely to crash down near us, only nice healthy specimens in the prime of life.

From now on our camps began to lose their identity. I remember this one mainly because my wife caught a large fish before dinner. She set up a proper hullabaloo. She yelled partly because she had no knife. Grabbing knives and machetes we raced to the river, to find my wife battling with the fish and trying to get it under her knee. It tore itself free from her and off the hook and then sprang back into the river with a mighty leap. We looked ruefully after it. We should have enjoyed a change of diet.

We remembered this camp also because in the middle of the night a sharp, pungent smell woke us up. A typical cat smell. Then we heard Timber—his tent was next to ours—moving about. All at once he shouted:

"Hi!"

Spitting and snapping in the undergrowth. Silence.

We ran out flashing our torches. The smell had gone.

A distracted Timber crept into the beam from our torches.

"There's been a jaguar here . . ." Timber said.

Some distance off monkeys screamed. Then silence again.

"Only an inch from my nose!"

Timber had heard something, had awakened with a start and had picked up his torch. Timber and Paulchen had a strange kind of ventilating tube at the back of their tropical American Army tents. The large, soft tube of rubberized material, thirty inches above the ground was there to prevent the rain coming in through the open mosquito window. The jaguar had stuck its head into the tube and had shoved its nose right down against the mosquito window when Timber looked out and switched on the torch . . .

Timber and the jaguar stared at one another, literally nose to nose. They were both scared out of their wits. Timber said afterwards that he did not know which of them had been the more scared.

From that night on we often smelt the sharp, pungent smell. It was so sharp and unmistakable that it always woke us up. It never stayed on the air for more than three or four seconds—then it was gone as though it had never been. A penetrating smell like the feline house in the zoo, but always very brief. A sudden burst of sweat, from fright or fear or anger, such as any house-cat will have, only in a much weaker form—or a man with the fear of death upon him.

From spending so many days and nights in the wilderness

our senses became so acute that we began to notice many mysterious smells. We were soon able to distinguish between them, from the stench of monkeys' piss to the dried-green-tea smell of leaf-cutter ants, and the musk smell of many orchids. But the ones stamped deepest on our memory will always be the short, strong smell of the jaguar's anger, and the heavy, slimy smell of snakes' holes in the sun.

The thin fabric of our tents was all that separated us from the jaguars' hot breath. For many nights they prowled round our camp and we could hear them breathing. In spite of their curiosity they were intelligent, powerful beasts, which wanted no truck with us. They only upset our cooking equipment by accident if they were disturbed by screaming monkeys or screeching parrots. *We* did not want to have any truck with them, either. We got on very well with the jaguars.

* * *

The farther we forged our way up the Azul, the more frequent became our encounters with animals—a sign that we were penetrating farther and farther into virgin country. There were still some natives on the Jataté, and according to the Lacandones even the lower Azul was occasionally visited by crocodile hunters, but now we were coming to a country of breathtaking, paradise-like innocence.

Various species of iguana are to be found throughout tropical America. We saw a lot the day after Timber's adventure with the jaguar. Iguanas are absolutely primeval. Not one under three feet long, often four and a half, with impressive-looking spikes on their ugly bodies. They used to crouch on the nipa palms and bamboos on the river bank and stare at us stupidly.

Kliesing tried to film them, but every time he had his camera ready and his boat in position they jumped into the water from a height of nine or twelve feet making a great splash. Without the cameras we got much closer.

Iguanas have white flesh and are much relished by native gourmets, but one is supposed to throw them alive into boiling water so that they expel their excrement and are clean inside. A difficult procedure, for where would you find a pot large enough to hold them? Iguanas that will fit into the normal cooking-pot hardly exist. Nor do they come quietly. They lash out and treat you to many a hefty blow from their powerful tails; and they can make a nice mess of you with their sharp teeth and their claws.

Paulchen, of course, had the recipe. After the first part of the operation is over, you cut off the creature's head, slit open its belly and take out its innards, chop off its claws and its spikes, skin it and stick it back in the pot, with fresh water, of course. Then you add chilli, garlic, pimpernel, ginger, saffron and some port and let it all stew for a time. It is said to be a very good dish, particularly the broth. Paulchen had never eaten it himself, needless to say, for vibration reasons.

We left the iguanas in peace. The difficulty of preparing them daunted even Aveckle, and later on there were no iguanas, even if we had wanted to eat them.

At this stage of our journey we had only begun to look out for *pavos* (turkeys) because we wanted to conserve our dwindling stocks. The first arroyo was still not in sight. Once we had reached it we should feel much better, but the first arroyo did not intend being reached by us.

Just when we had begun to get really worried about it I shot the first turkey. It was a large turkey with a beautiful speckled comb and a yellow hump on its beak.

Kliesing had seen it alight, and Kliesing himself was quite wild with excitement. He put his finger to his mouth and pointed upwards, and I saw nothing, but I quickly steered my boat on to a minute mud bank, got out, sank up to my thighs in the mud, unwrapped the gun, scrambled up the bank and ran barefoot and naked through the forest; and the great hulking lump of a turkey perched high above me, and looked down at me, black and yellow, from a height of a hundred and twenty feet, till it fell through the trees and I called "I've got it!" and ran up to it. Then, in spite of the noise, the hen came flying high across the river to see what was up and I got her with a second shot. She, too, came crashing down through the trees and the lianas. They were so heavy that I could hardly carry them, and I was filled with foolish pride, particularly over the second shot. It must have looked very funny, the way I ran barefoot and naked through the forest, only carrying a gun.

The turkeys had the most beautiful plumage and they were as heavy as fattened geese, only not so unnaturally fat, and their flesh was tender and delicate. They were the first of eighteen that we shot. Timber shot four; I shot fourteen. Although always we had to eat them up each time within a day, they kept us going. More than that: they saved our lives. Only Paulchen failed to realize this; and to this very day he has not realized it. Right up to the end Paulchen never realized that we must hunt for food.

More about that later.

We called all our turkeys pavos, but they belonged to very different species. In addition to the first one with the beautiful comb and the hump on his nose we had proper turkeys, but without the domestic turkey's warty neck and lobed beak. One could hear them in the undergrowth: an odd murmuring, a slightly asthmatic wheezing. There was no great skill in getting close to them, although they were not stupid, and sensed their danger. On the ground they were quick. They lived in strict monogamy, and their preference for an orderly life spelt disaster to many a couple. If we stayed in a camp for two days and found a couple but failed to bag them, we only needed to go to the same place again at the same time on the following day and we were sure to get them. Altogether it was rather humiliating for a sportsman, but soon we needed them desperately.

Twice we bagged a pair of birds quite different from anything else, but equally beautiful, with brilliant long tail feathers, the hen no less colourful than the cock. It was only at the end of our journey that we discovered that they had been some of the rarest creatures on this earth: *Domococcyx phasinellus rufigularis*. According to our scientific source, the species only occurs now in the Maya forests, "in the extreme south of Mexico and in Guatemala". We devoured those four "cuckoo pheasants" without being even remotely aware that we were eating a meal that was scientifically unique. Later, Timber and I saw another pair flying high up in the blue sky across a clearing. We following them with longing eyes. We were hungry, but we were not carrying a gun.

So much about our turkeys.

Apart from fish and small, partridge-like birds and pigeons, they were the game nearest to hand for our immediate needs. Aveckle implored me not to bring in any quadrupeds! That was what she said at the beginning . . .

A large quadruped, a wild boar for instance, is quite a headache for the housewife. Aveckle's arms were already aching after plucking the first turkey. She was soon using Timber and Kliesing for this job, and later Timber and she plucked the birds as soon as they had been shot, even if they were in the boat and it was morning and hours to go till the next camp and a fire. Plucking was much easier when the birds were still warm.

We could have shot more, of course, but we had other things to occupy our minds. New worries about pushing on ahead, about fresh cataracts which appeared in increasing numbers. Worries about an arroyo which simply refused to appear.

Pushing on ahead took all our strength; hunting also took time and strength and meant delay. We dare not shoot more than we could consume straight away because everything went bad immediately. Two twelve-pound turkeys were all that four people—Paulchen remained a vegetarian—could eat in a day and a half.

Pitch camp, cook, sleep. Strike camp—push on.

More cataracts.

The first couple of turkeys were just what we wanted to justify a break. We did not go much farther that day, firstly because Aveckle would have her hands full with the game; secondly because we were all pretty exhausted. There were more cataracts; and there were more trees in the water, enormous trees which blocked up the whole width of the river.

Of the arroyo, not a trace.

We landed in a beautiful bay. The river was clear and green. The bank was fifteen feet high, and twenty yards farther on, across on the other side, was another, equally broad river.

General rejoicing: the arroyo!

Our rejoicing was premature. On the side where the much-longed for arroyo should have been the river merely turned into a bend that ran from south to north-west. Then it disappeared in the forest—to come out again, after heaven knows what loops, on the right-hand side and on its old course—that is to say, towards us. A long way ahead, on the "left-hand side", roared a mighty cataract. I don't know how we had tumbled so quickly to the fact that the water on the left was the Azul again and not the arroyo, but unfortunately, it *was* the Azul, that meandering river, although it took us some days to be quite certain about it . . .

We made a fine camp at the narrowest part of the bend and called it the "turkey camp". Aveckle got to work right away, Paulchen built his hearth and made a fire, and Timber collected wood: and Timber and I looked forward to the roast which would give everybody all the food they could possibly want. Meanwhile Kliesing was fishing, using the turkey giblets as bait, and within five minutes he had caught three fish, two bream and one perch.

Kliesing turned out to be the best fisherman among us. He said he would like to try a bit of the fish. My wife said: "What is there to try, Kliesing? But you must cook them yourself, I have my hands full with the roast." Kliesing said he would quite like to try that as well.

It was the first time in fifteen years that he had wanted to try a roast. For a vegetarian, I explained to Aveckle, that must be tantamount to sacrilege, but my dear wife was far too busy with the roast to take it in. Kliesing said he only wanted to try it to get used to the taste, in case it became a matter of life and death. Kliesing got used to the taste all right, that evening. I had never been taken in much by his "trying". That is why I had already told Paulchen in the afternoon: "Just cook for yourself, and *save* the rest! Because we must begin to go very carefully now."

But Paulchen must have been temporarily deaf that moment.

"All right," said Paulchen.

"No, Paulchen," I said. "Having to go carefully now is not 'all right'."

"I've still got a lot of stuff," said Paulchen.

"I don't believe you," I said.

"It's true," Paulchen said quietly, but with a certain gentle finality. So I shut up. I stretched out under the tent and began to read. Whenever I looked up I saw Aveckle, her hair tied up in a scarf, busy with the cooking. A little farther on I saw Paulchen busy with the large kettle, the large pot and the waffle-iron. On the ground between lay the three fish —still untouched. A beautiful, but slightly enervating scene, and evidence of senseless extravagance.

It would have been equally senseless to explain to a man like Paulchen that fresh food was always to be preferred, and that beans, rice, maize and powdered milk could be saved up, and that I would not be able to shoot a turkey every day, nor Kliesing catch fish. Paulchen would not have understood because he was far too mad to understand why I should shoot turkeys at all and Kliesing catch fish. I found it hard to admit to myself that Paulchen—who was so tough, nice and ready to help—could be a fool. But if he was a fool, then he was one of those who are never left completely high and dry, even though it is due to other people's charity.

He finished his cooking an hour and a half before Aveckle, and he called his flock to dinner. Kliesing and Timber were jubilant. They filled their bellies with his superb bean soup, followed by milk pudding made from powdered milk, rice, sugar and cinnamon, and finished up with crisp waffles and honey. They had to drink a lot of herbal tea to wash it down. After that Kliesing and Timber could not budge an inch. By always eating vast quantities they suffered from chronic distension of the stomach.

Then Aveckle got going and served, as an *hors-d'œuvre*, turkey liver and heart on toast. She had made the toast from stale tortillas. Then she produced a turkey consommé. We offered Kliesing and Timber some of this consommé. (They were just showing the first signs of recovery.) Timber did not refuse it. As well as having a distended stomach he had a lumberjack's appetite. Kliesing thanked us but politely refused the consommé. He was still embarrassed about the whole business. But by the time the turkey was ready an hour later, he had got used to the idea and had no scruples at all.

We ate one of the turkeys, and kept the other for breakfast. After the meal Kliesing and Timber lay prostrate for the second time that evening, and Aveckle and I for the first time. Even so, Aveckle later used up the fish in a savoury dish because she could not bear to waste it. Our guzzling lasted from seven to midnight (Paulchen's party had dined at five), often interrupted by conversational interludes and je-jene attacks which forced us to wrap ourselves up completely for three hours.

Thrusting through the dark green tunnel which became more and more difficult to penetrate. *Below:* Negotiating one of the innumerable cataracts which took so much time and energy.

The anaconda which gave the explorers a few uncomfortable minutes.
Even when decapitated the enormous snake still seemed to be alive.

The next morning we all woke up late and in a daze, as though we had been drinking. We were also rather knocked out, not from all the food, but from the previous day's exertions. We just pottered about; nobody felt like going on. It was grey and warm and there was a fine rain falling; and suddenly everybody was in favour of having a day's break instead of going on. Aveckle, Timber and I were all in favour of not going on because we still had the second turkey in the pot and it was not yet smelling. We were looking forward to it. What is more, we all badly needed a day's break. We had swollen feet and still looked as though we had measles. There were a lot of things to put right—the boats, the tents, and ourselves. We were fully occupied, but it was a happy day for all that, with no more than the usual number of je-jenes and a fresh catch of fish. That turkey camp on the bend was to be the last camp where we were able to eat our fill.

*   *   *

I nearly forgot the invisible bird although it gave this chapter its name! No bird in our colourful jungle world was as close yet at the same time as evasive and always behind one's back as the invisible bird. We saw toucans, parrots, the somersault-bird, red cardinals and blue kingfishers and a tremendous number of feathered creatures of every description. There were other birds which we never saw. Every morning we were awakened by the flute-bird. It sang such beautiful, clear, slow melodies that it warmed our hearts. We had heard it in Africa and had never seen it. We never saw it here.

The melancholy cry of the tropical goat-sucker kept us awake many a night. Sometimes it got so bad that we threw stones into the trees. We never saw it either. But we knew that it was the goat-sucker, because we had heard it when Harry was still with us, and Harry was a most knowledgeable ornithologist. But Harry had been unable to tell us anything about the invisible bird except that it was what the Lacan-dones called "the bird-you-don't-see-it". Even Harry had still swung round with a start whenever he heard the uncanny "Hush!" behind his back . . .

Imagine walking peacefully in a forest (in the forest of the Lacandones), and suddenly somebody saying: "Hush!" behind your back—one cannot help swinging round with a start.

There is nobody there, of course, nothing but the forest, and the forest is silent.

When you walk on it says "Hush!" again.

You sit in your tent at night, and right outside somebody says "Hush!" By then you think it is a message from some uncontrollable, evil powers; a message out of nowhere.

CHAPTER FOUR

Rivers into Nowhere

FROM the turkey camp on we could not go back without endangering our lives. The cataracts—each one pouring over difficult, needle-sharp, tree-spiked rock and impossible to shoot travelling downstream in a canoe as we had hoped— had, at first unnoticeably, but later all too clearly, slammed the door on us with a resounding crash; the door between us and our wonderful provision dump at the mouth of the Azul . . .

From here our only salvation lay in going on. We were not quite sure what would save us when we got there, or even help us ever to get out. All our thoughts revolved round the lake. What hopes we had of it!

We hoped for unknown Maya ruins, of course, but more, we hoped to find light and beauty and a paradise, and some great, ineffable experience after all our crawling in the darkness of the jungle.

We had not yet reached the first arroyo . . .

Kliesing said we were practically upon it.

He had called the turkey camp the "camp of decision". It was the second or third camp which he had called the "camp of decision". Nobody took it seriously, but Kliesing was not to be disheartened. Even when reality proved very different from his prophecies he was not to be disheartened. He simply invented a new theory of esoteric unreality. It was all so overwhelming that it sometimes took our breath away. And apart from the fact that Kliesing was a grand companion and friend with whom it was impossible to quarrel, his fatuous optimism that we had practically reached the arroyo was completely justified!

We had hardly got under way the morning after our day off when we heard my wife call out from beyond a bend in the river:

"The arroyo——!"

We quickly paddled up to her.

It was true. A stream came at considerable speed straight from the north through the jungle, while the main river came placidly and much broader in a great sweep from the west. We had imagined it the other way round, but the direction was correct. I told my wife to wait for the others, and paddled over the rapids and up the new river and waited for Kliesing.

"The outlet from the lake!" Kliesing said. "There's a definite smell of sulphur . . ."

There really was a smell of sulphur.

"Only nine or ten miles to the lake now!" Kliesing said.

Although the water smelt faintly of sulphur it was absolutely clear. It was sure to be lake-water, for the Lake of the Lacandones was said to have sulphur springs. Up to now we had never noticed any smell of sulphur in the water of the Azul.

"And the direction! When we were at the "camp of decision", did you notice where the river on the other side came from? From the south! It was coming down from the Chamhuitz, *it* was the arroyo!"

"Very likely," I agreed. I was longing to get to the damned lake soon. What is more, it was perfectly logical. In the flat forest country between the Chamhuitz range and the Azul the arroyo was bound to flow more slowly and to wind about.

We stared at the compass and at our utterly useless maps and at the water which came bubbling towards us, smelling and tasting slightly of sulphur. It all looked very much like the outflow from a volcanic lake. Aveckle came up and we whistled and called to the big two-seater, and Aveckle asked: "Well?"

"We'll get to the lake today," cried Kliesing.

"It would be nice," Aveckle said.

The big canoe came up. Paulchen said that sulphur water was very healthy, and we went on.

It was a good thing that we had followed all the twists and turns. For if, at the turkey camp, we had carried our boats straight over the narrow part of the bend, we should have continued along the wrong river the whole time. Our conscientiousness had paid the highest dividends.

*　　　*　　　*

The river became deeper, even, occasionally, broader. There were no more of the old-style cataracts. The river had become too small. The jungle had grown over it and we were held up by a maze of pale wood and lianas. Mahogany trees lay across the water, their trunks so immense that three men together could not have put their arms round them. Mahogany is the gold of the Chiapas, the Tabasco and the Petén rain forests. Mexican mahogany lumberjacks' camps are pushing deeper and deeper into the Maya forests, biting into them from all quarters—but here, in the heart of darkness and in the realm of giant spiders, enormous riches were just lying about on the ground. "Riches!" This country was out of reach of the bulldozer's voracious bite. This was no country for midgets, the giants fell of their own accord. After their demise, strange fungi settled on their bodies, flowers of the underworld that gave a blue light at night. Had any other eye beheld them before us? Every midget would have been frightened by their blue light, just as we were frightened. But we shall talk about the riches rather than the blue light. No eye had ever beheld them. Nobody would come here to fell mahogany or iron trees or drag away those that had fallen.

Finally, it was no longer worth getting into the boats at all. Wading, stumping, sometimes swimming, we pushed them in front of us or pulled them behind us. Good, clear gravel constantly alternated with sharp rock on the river bed, and there were always the spiky branches, the mud and the creepers. We had long got used to the strange river with its snakes, spiders, fish, thornbacks and electric eels. In our green prison we crawled along like worms in a pipe . . . We neither looked right nor left. We just pushed on, led by Timber. With his Canadian lumberjack's hatchet, his Canadian lumberjack's belt and his Canadian lumberjack's hat he looked like some Robin Hood out of a *Folies Bergères* review. He cleared the river for us and we followed with the boats.

Towards midday we made a short break on some tree trunks in the river. It was a narrow, uncomfortable stopping place, but it lay in a river bend where the trees were spaced out enough for the sunlight to reach the ground, and where we could see the sky.

We ate a few nuts and raisins. With them we drank the clear river water and Paulchen informed us that sulphur water was a healthy drink. It did taste good, by the way, and for dessert we ate a few cloves of garlic with salt. Timber was mad about salt and gobbled it up by the spoonful. Paulchen said garlic was healthy, but too much salt was not. It made no difference. Paulchen declared, however, that he was not his, Timber's, father; and we told Timber that Paulchen was absolutely right, although he was not his father. Garlic was healthy, too much salt was not. Particularly as he complained of his kidneys. Timber had acquired his kidneys when lumbering in Canada—from eating too much steak with bacon and eggs, Paulchen said. Perspiring a lot might also have had something to do with it, he added by way of consolation. Timber thought that it might have something to do with his once getting trapped underneath a tree. The tree had fallen right on top of him, and he had suffered a nasty back injury and bruised kidneys. Whatever the reason, Timber had to be careful about his kidneys.

Timber said he was going to be very careful and even stop lapping-up salt, if it really was bad for his kidneys. Wading in the water for hours and days on end could not be good for him either, said Aveckle. I am sure she was right. But how could we wrap Timber's kidneys up in cotton wool?

Timber said he was in a wonderful mood today for pushing on, and so we pushed on, Timber always on ahead.

Once Paulchen lost his foothold and hurt himself slightly. Some time later Aveckle fell flat on her back while lifting a canoe. It was no joke, for her spine hurt her for days afterwards. Later, in some rapids where we were forced to haul our boats, naked, black, razor-sharp lava appeared . . .

"It means we're getting close to the lake," said Paulchen.

"For heaven's sake!" cried my wife. "Are you getting nervous too?"

"I? Nervous?"

"No, you won't get nervous, will you, Paulchen?" said my wife.

"No," Paulchen said. "You're not getting nervous, are you?"

"I?" said my wife. "What on earth makes you think that?"

"I only meant it would be pointless."

"Quite right."

"You're easily the bravest woman I've ever met," said Paulchen.

"Oh, stop it. Or I'll tell my old man."

"What are you going to tell me?" I asked. I had only caught the tail end of the conversation.

Well, nothing. Only that Paulchen, who even on the Jataté had hardly begun to realize that we were trying to get to a rather mysterious lake, was no longer serenely unconcerned.

For the first time he expressed the wish (only as a hint, but a pretty insistent hint) to move to a more attractive neighbourhood (with a sprinkling of Indian women selling tortillas, I suppose).

We assured him we shared this wish with equal fervour.

"The river," said Paulchen, "smells and tastes more and more of sulphur."

"Yes, Paulchen. It must be very healthy. Bathing in sulphur springs!"

"It's getting warmer all the time, too."

Actually, the water was very warm, even for the tropics. Up till now, Aveckle and I had always imagined water containing sulphur to be yellow, but where it was not choked by creepers, weeds and mud, the water was blue and crystal clear. It was obvious that it must come from some perfectly fabulous lake. Perhaps even from some steaming sulphur lake—as large as Lake Zurich, the Chiemsee, the Lake of Lucerne or some such lake. But we hoped that it would not be too warm, because it might damage our canoes and weaken us.

Our idyllic daydreams were interrupted by the roar of powerful rapids. A real cataract . . .

So there were cataracts—here! And it was not a quietly murmuring, small-river cataract, it was a vicious, thundering cataract. Not very high. Just a diagonal bar of rock. But the cliffs were razor-sharp, yellow and corroded by sulphur. In between were shark's teeth of black lava.

Four of us worked for a solid hour on this cataract. Aveckle helped too, although I told her not to because of her back.

Timber had gone on, clearing the way. Whenever we stopped working we could hear him hacking away somewhere in front. We had to clear away blocks of lava and make a two-and-a-half-foot channel to get the boats through undamaged, particularly the big, double one.

"What would you do," I asked Kliesing, "if someone came and offered you this kind of job for a lot of money?"

"I'd decline," said Kliesing.

"I'd decline, too," I said. "And if he raised the pay I'd politely hit him on the nose."

Kliesing looked exhausted. I must have looked exhausted too. Paulchen looked his usual self. My wife did not look particularly exhausted, although her back was causing her pain. When we had got the boats up Timber arrived, looking as white as a sheet. He had cleared the river and had begun to worry why we had not come.

Timber had learnt massaging as a lumberjack -particularly foot and toe massage, but other sorts too—and he had a gift for it. He often massaged us in the evening, and he pulled out thorns before they turned poisonous. He was second to none at pulling out thorns. To have massaged Aveckle's back at random would, of course, have been sheer madness, but Timber went over it carefully to see whether a vertebra was dislocated. It was impossible to be absolutely sure about it and we hoped very much that this was not the case.

We got into our boats and paddled through the channel which Timber had cleared. We felt pretty well all-in. We had to get out again soon afterwards, and haul the boats; and we were looking at the compass the whole time because the river kept steadily towards the east, whereas the lake could only be in the west. We did not lose heart, thinking it must be just one of those bends.

After that we suddenly found ourselves in a narrow, precipitous valley, and the river was no wider than an average room. We had suddenly plunged into the narrow valley and right into a mountain range, or at least into steep hills. Only a short time before we had failed to notice the slightest change in the country. On a narrow jungle river you never get a view of your surroundings. You never see any distance into the forest, and you cannot see whether the treetops high above you are on a level or are beginning to climb. You only notice it when the land right by the river bank begins to rise.

Be that as it may: it was of course possible that the river, after it left the lake, broke through a range of hills or ran round one. This would even lend some sense to its irritating change of direction. We should see on the morrow.

It was impossible to get to the lake that day. We had to hurry and find a suitable, reasonably flat space in the wood and clear away the undergrowth and small trees. All this was done quickly, in accordance with our well-established routine. In the narrow jungle valley we made a homely, intimate camp, a place of safety and confidence, where we could forget the day's toil. While I was performing my evening toilet—I always shaved, and the gentle scent of after-shave lotion drifted pleasantly through the wood—well, during this and our evening bathe we realized that there were no je-jenes here.

"It's the sulphur," Paulchen said.

It was delightful, and it compensated—almost—for everything. A turkey would have provided just the finishing touch, but I had not had a chance to shoot one. We had seen a few turkeys, but we had been so busy that shooting had been quite out of the question. We had had precious little time to look out for animals or their tracks.

There were still some provisions left. Only sugar began to run low in both our groups. Sugar is deadly on the teeth, and taken in excessive quantities—as it is usual in civilized countries—it is just as harmful as too much salt. You cannot possibly imagine how little sugar we eat at home. Here—in the jungle—we could hardly imagine how we managed with so little at home . . . That evening all of us were sucking, with a greediness that was quite revolting, the boiled sweets we had taken along as presents for Indian children.

I think nostalgically back to that camp because it offered us, at the end of an unusually strenuous day, refuge, shelter and the kind of peace only to be found at the edge of the world.

Next morning we were attacked by thousands of large, repulsive gad-flies.

At a very early hour Timber and I tried to obtain a general view of the area. We climbed up steeply through the thick, matted wood. A complete waste of time! We gave up the idea when Paulchen and my wife, far below, called us down to breakfast.

Strike camp—on with the journey.

We did not even get into the boats, but hauled them along the shallow river. Timber went ahead. The valley turned northwards. General rejoicing.

After an hour Timber called back:

"Hi!"

"What's the matter, Timber? . . ."

"Nothing. Only the river's come to an end. . . ."

"You're joking."

"No. It's come to an end."

*   *   *

It was a fact.

We had come to the end.

We had waded up a river, and after a hard battle with the wilds we had not broken through to the lake in a blaze of triumph, but reached the end of some river in the back of beyond. The end of some unknown, unmapped stream. Or rather, its beginning. In itself very interesting. We did not even swear.

The river came out of a chalky hole in the middle of the wood. I had never seen such a handsome source. A small basin, surrounded by wild ferns, set in a framework of lianas and orchids, and, a long way down, the water shimmering with an incredible blue radiance. It was so unearthly, that blue radiance, that I was sure the gates of Hell lay immediately beyond.

The water was warm, soft and very sulphurous. The whole forest smelled of sulphur. Yet the water was blue and crystal clear, with fish of the strangest colours and shapes swimming about in it. None of us had ever seen such fish.

"It's like fairyland!" breathed Paulchen, voicing everybody's thoughts. Although we were all pretty exhausted physically, we still had reserves of the finer emotions.

Then we climbed up the hill at the head of the valley to see whether the river reappeared from somewhere underground, but the forest on the other side looked as though there had never been a river there. It was all too obvious. Although we could not obtain a general view of the terrain or escape from the forest, it was quite clear that we had come to a spur of the Sierra Caribe—in the opposite direction from the lake. We had gone up a brand-new, totally unknown tributary of the Azul . . .

We called our newly-discovered river "Rio Aveckle", because my wife had been the first to see it. For Latin American use we called it "Rio Mariana" because it was easier to pronounce and because that is her name, and because Kliesing wanted to have it registered in Mexico City. Kliesing had an idea that there was some kind of patent office for newly-discovered rivers. All in all it was an innocent pleasure—apart, alas, from the discovery itself.

The same morning, without wasting any more time, we started back. We wanted to reach the Azul—and the turkey camp—before evening. The prospect of reaching a familiar place in this country which was as alien as Mars gave us an inner glow.

At the shelf of rock with the razor-sharp, vicious, sulphur and lava cliffs we had to work just as long and hard as we had on the way up. It was a good thing that there was only this one cataract on the Rio Mariana. Although the trees blocking the water had been partly cleared, we found we could not get past them any quicker.

Half-way down I managed to shoot a couple of splendid turkeys. I was out of the boat and on the bank in a flash and had only to run ten yards before the cock fell heavily at my feet. But then the hen rose, and I had to pursue it quite a time till I finally brought it down from a hundred and twenty feet. When I ran to get it a sharp thorn pierced my navel. In this part of the forest there were a lot of palm trees which boasted thorns as sharp as a needle, four inches long and barbed. One of those daggers had stabbed into my navel. In my excitement I had again run barefoot into the forest— barefoot up to the chin, and rifle in hand. But at least I got the hen. It was really sad that marital fidelity should be thus rewarded, but I believe that a civilized jungle is a more suitable place to worry about ethics than an uncivilized one. Be that as it may, I pulled out the thorn, but the barb stayed inside and I bled profusely. At first I thought the blood came from the hen, but when I got back to the bank my wife drew my attention to the wound. The bleeding stopped soon afterwards, and the whole episode would not have been worth telling if my wife had not made such a fuss about it. But let that be.

Once more we had two fine turkeys.

Not long afterwards a fine herd of wild boar dashed through the undergrowth, among them some uncomfortably large animals. One made as if to attack Kliesing.

"As big as a donkey," said a pale Kliesing.

He was a little ahead of us and the boar charged him like a rhinoceros, but when it came to the water it braked hard, and almost slid down the bank. The stupid creature had not realized that it would be separated from Kliesing by a stretch of water. Perhaps it had been frightened by the water, and the boat, and even by Kliesing.

"I was wondering where a donkey could have appeared from round here," said Kliesing.

"Oh boy!" said Timber, looking round to see whether Paulchen was listening. "Leg of pork!"

"Don't shoot a wild boar, please," Aveckle said. "For one thing it's dangerous, and for another I simply couldn't cope."

Later, in a group of trees in a clearing not ninety feet from the bank, we saw a number of bears. Charming animals. They were the size of Malayan tree bears and very playful. They were not in the least afraid of us. At first we saw three, who looked at us and squealed with displeasure. Then we saw another one who stared at us and growled. Then we saw another, and another—the trees were full of bears. They lifted their heads and watched us. They climbed sedately up the trees and down again and studied us carefully. After a while they lost interest. Two stretched up their paws to pick some fruit and sat on their hind legs to eat it. All of them seemed to have decided that it was not worth while making closer acquaintance with us. Their loss of interest was so definite and final that we felt hurt.

Shortly before dusk we glided out of the Arroyo Mariana and on to the Azul. Behind our backs, a voice said: "Hush!"

Ahead lay the lovely bay marking the turkey camp.

Toucans looked down on us from the trees, their heads to one side. They have to put their heads to one side, otherwise they cannot see across their long beaks. They were very curious. When we reached the camp our old friend, the gayest and most charming of all the somersault-birds, greeted us with great excitement.

*   *   *

The next day we decided to have another "day of rest" This time it was not a spontaneous decision, unanimously acclaimed. It was an unspoken decision, unanimously

regretted but silently approved. We simply did not go on.
Everybody felt exhausted and Timber was depressed. He
had gone up the Arroyo Mariana like a fire engine, probably
overdoing it. Now he was rather depressed.

"I'm not depressed," he said. "I'm only a little bit
weary. Not depressed, only weary."

"Perhaps it's your kidneys."

"I hope not."

"Perhaps it's the quinine?"

"Quinine affects the liver and, possibly, the stomach. But
the quinine we're taking doesn't affect anything because
it's 'Resochin'. It's the latest sort."

We took "Resochin" regularly for malaria. Except
Paulchen. Paulchen was against all pills and drank herbal tea
for malaria. For anybody—except Paulchen—spending any
length of time on the coasts of tropical America or in the
Mexican *tierra cliente* it is absolutely essential to take some
form of quinine. You will not believe it: but none of us got
malaria because we looked after ourselves with the utmost
care, and Paulchen did not get malaria because he drank
herbal tea. In this connection we had nothing to complain
about.

"If I control myself in the matter of salt my kidneys will
get better," said Timber.

"You've overdone it in the last two days," said my wife.

"I'm only a little bit weary."

"You just pushed on too quickly!"

My wife looked splendid as she was getting breakfast.
She had recovered from her fall. She took a long time getting
breakfast because it was such a terrific breakfast: turkey.
When we had turkey, we had to eat turkey for breakfast,
lunch and dinner in case it went bad, but we never got tired
of it. The ones we had were the world's biggest and best
turkeys, and we were saving a lot of oatmeal that way. The
oatmeal was just as delicious as the turkeys. We made it into

porridge in the morning and into waffles in the evening. Heaven alone knows what else my wife made it into. It soon became our only food, apart from what we shot or fished. On top of that we had to give some of it to Paulchen, because he ate neither game nor fish and because we had to feed him somehow. That's why it was a good thing to save it whenever possible.

After breakfast we relaxed and amused ourselves watching our friend the somersault-bird. Then everybody set to work repairing the boats and other damaged equipment. Timber was not quite so weary then and began repairing me. A carbuncle had formed in my navel overnight. Other barbs from the thorn had become inflamed, and Timber got them out with the help of needles. We put the needles in disinfectant first. Timber was very good at taking out the bits of thorn, but one piece, which had gone in very deep, he failed to get out with the needle, so he used his Canadian bush knife, which was ground to a very sharp point and therefore admirable for the operation. We disinfected the knife, too.

Just as we were in the middle of the operation, and busily contemplating my navel, and Timber (who is really highly skilled at these things) had got his great Canadian knife ready and was about to carry on with the repair, my wife ran up screaming. She asked us whether we were right in the head.

We were taken completely aback.

"They've gone mad!" she exclaimed.

We told her not to talk nonsense.

"Come on, Timber," she said, "give him a penicillin injection."

We had taken two syringes with beautiful needles and an adequate supply of penicillin. We always carry syringes in the wilds, particularly for snake serum and—in case things get desperate—morphia. But we had never used them on ourselves. Personally I dislike injections on account of the prick. My wife regards this as cowardice.

Timber had never given an injection in his life, but he said he could do it. If it were absolutely necessary he would do it. He would do it right away.

Timber was a great coward, giving in to my wife like that. I did not give in. I stood firm. Would you let a Canadian lumberjack give you an injection? It was by no means necessary, at least not yet. I had never been healthier and in better shape. The ridiculous carbuncle and the other small sources of inflammation would clear up without penicillin. The whole idea in getting out the last bits of thorn was to prevent any new inflammation. There was no reason for injections. Perhaps penicillin would have some highly undesirable secondary effects in the jungle. But my wife said I was a coward over the prick, and Timber was a coward because he backed me up.

Timber, the coward, collapsed completely and said he would give an . . . But I kicked him so hard in the behind that he did not finish the sentence, and my wife said we were a couple of weaklings.

The following day we did fourteen cataracts and two trees. The day after that we did nine cataracts, one of which was particularly steep and tough, and one tree . . .

Up to now we have done fifty-nine cataracts and twelve trees, counting only the "trees" where we cannot get past either underneath or at the side; trees which need either a lot of work with the machete and/or where we have to lift the boats out of the water and carry them across to the other side, generally under the most dismal conditions.

During those days we saw squirrels. We saw wash bears and dear little otters. We saw lemurs, bats and horned owls. We saw snakes which hissed with fright, and we saw the strange armadillo. Jaguars padded again through the camp. We saw the forest and, on rare occasions, we saw the sky. We did not see the "Hush!" bird—and we did not see any arroyo either.

When we got fed up with seeing nothing, Timber climbed a tree. He took a lot of time and trouble selecting that tree. He found it fifty yards from the camp, and we heard him sawing and hacking at the tree; then we heard nothing for a while. Then we heard him again sawing and hacking high up in the tree; then we heard a great, thundering crash . . .

Our hearts stood still.

Now our cup was full.

After several anguished moments my wife called out in a strange, choking voice: "Tim-ber!"

"Yes," came back from above.

"You're the biggest fool I know," my wife called out, genuinely indignant.

"I thought I was that," I said.

"What did you say?" Timber called down.

"She says you're a bigger fool than me," I called up.

"Impossible," Timber shouted. "Why?"

"Because of the branch you sawed off."

"Oh, I see. Sorry."

In Canada, when some heavy tree is about to fall, the lumberjacks call out "Timber!" to warn their mates. That is why we had called Timber "Timber".

"But didn't it come down quite a way from you?" Timber called.

"Yes. Only we thought it was you."

"I?" called Timber. "What made you think that?"

It was hopeless. But it was a good thing we had him. None of us would have got more than twenty to thirty feet up the tree. Timber was an expert with rope, lumberjack's belt, hand-saw and hatchets. All the same, we watched his performance with mixed feelings. Ever since the Arroyo Mariana he had been weary, sometimes more, sometimes less, but we had to see where we were. Timber had suggested it himself, and he had not been weary when he was getting ready for the climb. He had gone up with compass, notebook, pencil and my Zeiss binoculars. I stood below, likewise with compass and notebook. We were going to do the thing scientifically. In situations like these we worked with military precision. The more it became a matter of life and death, the more military became our habits.

"I can see hardly anything but trees," roared Timber when he had climbed to the top.

"You don't say."

"From about north-north-west to—wait a minute— through north, north-east and east to east-south-east great mountains. High. A mighty arc. Between twelve and twenty miles away. Difficult to judge. Wooded right to the top."

"Can't you see a lake?"

"A lake? No."

"Roughly north-west?"

"Wait a minute. There are still some treetops in the way. I'll go a bit higher."

"Be careful."

"Not to worry."

He was then about a hundred and fifty feet above the ground.

"Wonderful view. Wait. I'll look through the binoculars."

I waited. The others had gone back to the camp, not thinking much of the whole business. My wife did not think much of it because she was afraid Timber might fall down and break his neck. The others did not think much of it because Paulchen was busy baking waffles and Kliesing was hungry, and because they, too, were afraid Timber might fall down and break his neck. Paulchen used white flour for the waffles. They had nothing else left for their main meal. For their other meals they still had nuts, raisins, garlic and salt. Aveckle was cooking, too. Our food was just as monotonous, because I had not been able to shoot anything during the past few days. Perhaps not quite as monotonous, because we still had the oatmeal and concentrated meat extract and

Erbswurst (dried green peameal), and even a little bacon. While Paulchen was baking his waffles and Timber was on top of the tree Kliesing quietly ate eight waffles. When Paulchen noticed this he got very angry. Paulchen said it was pointless to eat eight waffles at one sitting because he had been baking for tomorrow as well. We had never seen Paulchen so angry. For days Kliesing was a model of behaviour, trying his hardest to make it up again with Paulchen.

"West-south-west," Timber called down from the tree, "a long way off and in a haze I can see some strange-looking mountains . . ."

"The Chamhuitz?"

"Could be."

"But the *lake*, Timber!"

"No lake. Treetops, nothing but treetops. A lake of treetops."

"Not even a *haze* where a lake might be?"

"Haze? Everything is hazy to the west."

"Not a *thinner* haze in between?"

"No. It's all the same. Haze and trees."

"And the arroyo?"

He looked a long time through the binoculars. Not a sign of an arroyo.

"And our river—the Azul?"

"I can only see a bit of water a short distance ahead, north-west. Must be our river. A bend. Before and after that there's nothing. Except forest, of course."

Timber tried to see what he could. While he was up there he made a sketch. After a frugal dinner and with half-empty stomachs, we sat up half the night poring over the sketch. Timber's climb had been valuable—but we did not gain anything by it. The only thing of any interest was the high mountain range which ran in a semicircle from north-west to south-east—the unmapped and unexplored Sierra Caribe.

Far to the south another, smaller range seemed to approach it, the nameless range of the thunderstorm and the terrific rain.

Our spirits fell.

It was annoying that, after two weeks up from where the Azul joined the Jataté, we had not reached even the first arroyo.

The following day we did thirteen cataracts that were free of trees. The rock became even sharper. More lava.

To avoid any hold-up I let three easy turkeys go. A little later I missed two, because I sank up to the navel in the mud. The navel's unimportant, of course, but it was inflamed. The first carbuncle had broken. The wound would not heal and looked ugly. Next to it a largish abscess was forming. I apologize for remembering it in the mud. After that we landed on another mudbank which was not as deep, but the river bank above it was clean and pleasant, and a good spot for making a clean and pleasant camp. We just sent Paulchen and Timber round the corner in the big canoe to try to find a less muddy landing place. After they had gone twenty yards Paulchen suddenly shouted:

"But here's the other river . . ."

*   *   *

This time there was no doubt about it.

It was a proper confluence: on the left the arroyo from the Chamhuitz—an infinitely sombre, almost static, muddy stream nearly buried beneath an impenetrable thicket of trees: on the right the Rio Azul, which emerged from a weird, dark forest of tall trees, flowing fast on a north-south course. Our spirits rose.

They sank again quite quickly despite the discovery. However, we were glad not to have to go up through the muddy, infinitely depressing thicket on the left, but along the clear river Azul which came from the lake.

The lake could not be far now.

When we pushed off the next morning the voice said "Hush!" behind our backs.

A thin snake came shooting out from the muddy arroyo. It was four and a half feet long, very thin, very pink and very poisonous. It dived in front of our boats and was gone.

We went on our way with a doggedness worthy of a better cause.

What cause? I do not know. All we could think of was the lake. In some muddle-headed way we imagined the lake as bringing a kind of liberation, because we were slowly going to the dogs.

After the arroyo the character of the Azul began to change rapidly. The river bed became sandy, the river itself narrow, the current quicker. The cataracts were lower; they no longer had the full-throated roar they had had farther down. They began to rattle like the cataracts on the Arroyo Mariana. They were also farther apart. As a compensation there were more trees, the river became more choked, our advance more difficult. Even the lianas hanging down ninety or a hundred feet from the trees now gave us a lot of trouble. We often had to cut a way through them with our machetes, because our bow or stern got hopelessly entangled and the boat was driven against the bank by the strong current, or was whirled round and threatened to capsize.

On the first day past the arroyo, after the river had changed so much, I did not get a shot in. It was a strenuous day for all of us. Then Paulchen discovered a date palm with wonderful dates. Dates! Timber cut down the palm tree, which was over sixty feet high. It was the first time Paulchen had searched in the forest for food apart from his herbal teas. To our surprise Paulchen explained that they had only a week's food left . . .

It came as an unpleasant shock. Not the fact itself, but that he mentioned it at all. A week—living as carefully as possible, of course, and despite the fact that Timber, and Kliesing too, lived mainly off us whenever there was game. We still had enough food for a fortnight—but a good supply of fishing hooks and cartridges as well.

All of us still had the splendid iron rations presented by Timber. Each of us had five tins, but we were only going to open those when we were on our last legs. When it was "a matter of life and death", as Timber put it.

The date palm fell with a crash into the river. It was not a date palm. There *are* no date palms in Central America, and certainly no wild ones in the jungle, but Paulchen had been quite certain that it was a date palm. We wished it could have been one for his sake. We only remembered afterwards that date palms did not exist in Central America, and certainly not "wild" date palms. Seen from below the fruit had looked like dates, but in fact they were not. It was a *cocinella*, explained Paulchen, who knows a lot about botany —a kind of coconut palm with tiny coconuts. But the fruit turned out to be bitter, hard and uneatable.

It may sound strange: you cannot live off the fruits of the forest. To put it more harshly: a vegetarian purist is doomed in the jungle. True, for a few pence the markets of tropical America offer the most delicious fruit you can imagine. Half of them are unknown in Europe, or, if they are imported, they are far too expensive. But it is all culti-vated fruit, whether aubergine, avocado, papaya, pineapple, mango or a dozen other kinds. All these fruits exist in the jungle, too, but if you find them you find them in their wild state and quite inedible. Should some fruit suitable for human consumption ripen it will always—literally always— be gathered by the ubiquitous monkeys who are the greatest gourmets among fruit eaters.

"Paulchen simply *cannot* change now," Timber once said to me. "He once had a weak stomach. If he began to eat meat now it would be a matter of life and death."

We gave Paulchen some of our oatmeal so that he could survive. Later he lived on herbal tea and four hazelnuts a day. He survived magnificently. He collapsed once, but apart from that he survived magnificently.

*　　　*　　　*

The second day past the arroyo I failed again to get a shot in. Perhaps it was because of my stomach wound, which had got bigger. Part of it was suppurating. The larger part was hard and red. It was uncomfortable, but I did not mind, as it was bearable. It was merely a nuisance. My wife said I looked chalky-white, but Timber looked chalky, too. None of us looked like bronzed gods. Since being on this damned river and in this damned forest we had forgotten there was such a thing as the sun. True, it had shone sometimes, and sometimes the river had even been wide enough to reflect it —but at those times we had probably been far too busy hauling our boats over a cataract to notice it. Then clouds and thunderstorms had followed the sun, and when the clouds and thunderstorms became less frequent the river had become so narrow that the forest closed over it . . .

Of course, Timber looked particularly chalky, and he was not merely weary now, he was sick. We kept wondering what it was. We thought of his kidneys and debated what we could do about them.

It was much easier to see what was wrong with *me*. One glance at my belly was enough. It was a picture. But it would have been a mistake to assume that I was sick, as my wife did. It was just a nuisance, and I had made up my mind to get rid of the abscesses in the most natural way, that is to say, with hot poultices. In the evening I sat outside the tent on the air-mattress, reading and holding the hot poultice against my belly till it got cool and Aveckle took it away and heated it up again.

We had set up camp on a gravel bank on the left-hand

side of the river, and Timber crept into his tent straight after dinner. During the night there were flashes of lightning, and the next morning the barometer had fallen considerably.

That day we sighted a dry river bed on the western bank. It was a wide, shallow, sandy river bed twenty to thirty feet wide and absolutely dry. It looked very much like an over-flow from the lake. The country appeared to continue flat. According to our aerial maps we should now be on a level with the lake. According to our first-rate aerial maps the Azul had possibly been running parallel with the lake for the last seven miles. Therefore we must have almost reached the "second fork" in the river, the "second" arroyo which came in from the right while, looking upstream, the Azul swung left towards the lake . . .

What we should have done was to stop at the dried-up river and make a reconnaissance. Paulchen's group were not at all keen. Nor were we, although I was the one who suggested it. It would have cost us several days and probably only have led us to the conclusion that, in spite of everything, it was easier to get to the lake by water than to strike across-country with compass and machete.

After the dried-up river the soil became more and more gravelly. Since the muddy arroyo, the mouth of which had been teeming with fish, we had not seen a single one. I was lucky enough to shoot a heavy turkey from the boat. Un-fortunately I did not get the second one. It was grey and began to rain softly. Then it stopped raining. We hurriedly made camp. We ate the turkey, which Aveckle cooked to perfection. After that we felt a great desire for sweets.

Timber had recovered. I made hot poultices. Timber was furious with Kliesing, because he had discovered that Kliesing had secretly eaten one of his (Kliesing's) iron rations. Now Kliesing only had four left for an emergency. We all had a craving for sweets. We did not even have one left of the boiled sweets meant for the Indian children.

The next day we were not afloat till ten o'clock. (We suffered from many things, but our watches still worked.) We looked a pathetic lot.

That day we met no cataracts, but had to put in some hefty machete work to deal with the trees and lianas. Things got worse. In one place we had to hack away for an hour and a half to advance fifteen feet. After that we packed up for the day, although it was only early afternoon. A thunderstorm was threatening. We packed up because of the thunderstorm and because Timber was exhausted. He had hacked much harder than anybody else. Timber's weariness kept going up and down, and I began to think he was suffering from malaria. If so, it was a very queer kind. I myself wanted to pack up not only for that day but for the next one as well, because my inflammation was becoming troublesome. Another abscess had broken, but nothing much had come out. Everything round it was inflamed and looked horrible. It was a nuisance, because I had to keep getting into the water, and I said I must have hot poultices today and tomorrow, till everything had come out. I was quite determined.

We found a wonderful camping place. By now the river was no more than a stream, at most thirty feet wide, but still deep and clear, and overgrown by a super-jungle, if I may put it like that. However, the bank was pleasant, almost park-like. The tall trees stood farther apart and there was not so much undergrowth. We did not need to cut very much away. It was like a beautiful clearing, an oasis in the forest. It was camp number twenty-three, our third rest camp on the Azul. It was a camp to which Kliesing did not give a poetical name. Not that Kliesing was not as friendly as ever, but he was hungry and had lost some of his poetic *élan*. We were all hungry, even when we thought we had just had an ample meal. We certainly all suffered from a natural vitamin deficiency. Aveckle gave Kliesing and Timber some Vitamin C tablets and I took some for my inflammation. My wife prepared the poultice, and I sat down on the air-mattress and began to read. Then the sun broke through the trees—really and truly. We had completely forgotten the thunderstorm. It just had not come. It would have come if it had been the rainy season, but in the dry season the air above the rain forest needs to be only a little less humid than normal for a thunderstorm not to get through. The sun's rays clothed everything with an enchantting, flickering green, and when my poultice cooled off my wife took it away and heated it up. There was no peace for her and I felt a worm. At the last obstacle she had worked as hard as any of us. Now she was the only one who could not relax.

"It's asking a lot of a woman."

"Why?" she asked. "What's happened to you?"

"It's asking a lot of a woman, dragging her into all this."

"You're getting soft."

"All right," I said. "But I've been thinking."

"You look sweet when you're thinking," she said. "One can see it's hard work."

"Leave the damn poultices and make yourself comfortable."

"What next?" she said, in the irritating yet irresistible way of all wives in all countries and in all ages.

In the evening we secretly opened one of our iron rations. What a feast!

*　　*　　*

That night I slept better than I had the night before.

Timber, too, had one of his less-weary days. He and Kliesing went off in the empty two-seater at the crack of dawn. They were going to carry out a reconnaissance. They wanted to see "what was going on". They intended pushing on to the "second fork" and—if possible—getting to the lake and back. I gave Timber the gun and some cartridges and plenty of useful advice. It was vital for us to get more food.

They left before eight and we heard them hacking for about an hour. Another hour passed and we heard, far away, two shots. Then another one. Then we heard the "Hush" bird.

We could no longer hear Kliesing and Timber.

After the first poultice everything suddenly burst and something like a pound of pus came out.

"That must take a lot out of one," Paulchen said.

"You were absolutely green in the face yesterday," said my wife.

"But I didn't feel green."

"You looked it, though."

She cleaned the wound with disinfectant. It did not hurt much.

"Now you must be careful not to get gangrene. But it won't be so bad if you leave the dressing on and don't go into the water unnecessarily." (Yes, she said "unnecessarily!") "I was scared stiff that the inflammation would spread to the abdominal cavity. You were a fool, not taking that penicillin injection in time. I've never met a bigger fool in my life."

During the next four weeks I had sixteen more carbuncles in various places, all from the same source, but none of them attained the dimension and viciousness of the original one. They grew smaller as time went on, and to talk about the last ones would be absolutely pointless.

After eight hours' reconnaissance Kliesing and Timber came back—with two turkeys, thank God. Timber was in high spirits at having got them. They were not turkeys at all— they were the *Dromococcyx* pheasants I mentioned earlier. They were less plump than turkeys, but weighed almost the same. Their flesh was unbelievably tender. If we had realized the scientific importance of Timber's bag, Aveckle would have made a drawing and I a photograph of them before we cooked them, but as it was we behaved quite unscientifically and shouted for joy at the sight of them.

We were so overjoyed that we got hiccups and only took in the other message with half an ear—although, strictly speaking, it was a most depressing message:

NO LAKE! NO SECOND FORK!

The sole result of the reconnaissance was that Kliesing and Timber had cleared a large stretch of river and that to-morrow we should be able to advance more quickly.

We had the feeling that we *must* advance more quickly, that we should never make the lake, that we should never get out of the dark forest. Even if we advanced faster, we should merely get nowhere faster.

We knew where we were, and we did not know where we were—we knew that we were on a wooded plateau, on a small plateau or, maybe, on a large plateau. We were on a river which, for the time being, had become placid and cool. It might at any time start rushing again and get colder. A certain lake and a range of mountains might not be all that far away, and a small ray of light or a few fixed stars might be enough to help us get nearer to one or the other.

We advanced quickly—Kliesing and Timber had done their job well. Then the days merged into one another, and the camps were more and more alike, and everything became vague; and Timber did not tell any more stories or eat any more salt.

One day, after we had worked so hard levelling a site for a camp or carrying the boats that we were running with sweat, my wife said:

"I taste quite salty. I'm sweating like a bull and it tastes quite salty."

"I don't taste salty," Timber said. He stretched out his tongue and licked his left arm. "Not a bit salty!"

We all tried the experiment. We all tasted salty. Only Timber did not, and we dropped the subject.

We dropped nearly every subject, and we did not sit round the fire at night as we used to, but crept into our tents. My wife and I lay on our air-mattresses and read by candle-light—we had run out of petrol. We read for hours without needing to wear glasses. I mention this, because in "normal" life we both need them for reading and writing, but here we did not even need glasses to read by candlelight. There was practically nothing that we *did not* need—but glasses did not figure on the list. Weeks of jungle half-light and the floods of gentle green had strengthened our eyes to such an extent that we did not need glasses any more.

That cheered us up enormously. Not only could our ears hear the whispering of snakes and our noses smell the smell of jaguar and the sweat of the night birds, but even our eyesight was good again. To celebrate we allowed ourselves an extra spoonful of marmalade. This marmalade was nothing special, but to us it was a treasure. Each night Aveckle and I treated ourselves to a medium-heaped tea-spoonful. It was quite out of this world.

Later on we had thunder and lightning almost every afternoon. The thunder made a hollow sound, and the lightning was always directly overhead. We saw vaguely whole sheets of lightning over the forest. We saw in the way fish in an aquarium must see the outside world. We never had a drop of rain.

Once a thick tree lay across the river. Its fall had knocked a hole in the forest. Through this hole we saw a bit of the sky. We did not have to get out of our boats. We found we could get past by paddling to the far left-hand side of the tree, lying flat on the boat, and pulling ourselves through underneath.

Kliesing was the first to pull himself through. When he was half-way he got his back jammed under the tree. Kliesing tried to squeeze himself even flatter and lower. It looked very funny. I pushed his boat from behind and

Kliesing was free. Then I prepared myself to go through, but Kliesing leaped out of his boat on the other side and quickly clambered on to the tree, looking very pale. He did not even stop to recover his breath.

"Boy!" Kliesing said. "I passed a snake, *that* close!" He waved his hands about to show that the snake had been no more than two feet away. "*That* close! By my head . . ."

He had had a shock. Now I hurriedly climbed out of the boat and scrambled on to the tree from my side. The gun was with Timber in the big canoe. We called Timber, and Timber got out with the gun and came along through the thicket on the bank.

"Where?"

"There! And what a monster! An anaconda . . ."

Kliesing pointed to the bank where the tree had fallen, its roots sticking up in the air. The snake was supposed to be just below, in the narrow channel by the bank where we had to pull ourselves through lying flat on our stomachs and unable to look left or right.

That is where it had been. It was there no longer, but Kliesing swore that it had been there, and that it had looked him straight in the eye, not two feet away from him as he lay there stuck and unable to move either forward, backward or sideways.

When I pushed Kliesing's boat from behind—without knowing about the snake—he had made a last desperate effort and freed himself. The anaconda had been lying coiled, its head erect and poised for the attack. After that it could only have been a minute before both of us were on the tree looking for the snake, but it had gone.

The three of us searched as much of the bank below the fallen tree as we could. No snake. I got into my boat, glad that the snake had gone, and I pulled myself under the tree. My back grated against the tree. Ants, spiders and bark came tumbling down on top of me, but I got through. Then

I helped my wife through. She, too, was glad that the snake had gone.

The big, double canoe, lying deep in the water, came through best of all. Only Timber, who sat in the front seat, got slightly stuck. We waited to see whether he needed a helping hand. When Timber squeezed himself even flatter, Paulchen, still half outside and just starting to duck, called out:

"*But it's here!*"

Timber yelled: "Ouch!" Not because of the snake, but because, in his terror, he had raised his head and hit it on the tree. Paulchen, however, his head a foot away from the snake, hissed:

"Keep quiet. Just keep quiet."

He was speaking more to himself than to Timber. We saw Timber's arms come out from under the tree and reach upward—and giving a mighty heave he pushed the boat clear and released them both.

They sat in a daze in the drifting boat. The anaconda had been lying in exactly the same spot.

"*Caramba!*" Paulchen said and wiped the sweat from his forehead. "The way it looked at me! At least nine feet long and *that* thick! It must have had the shock of its life."

It had probably never moved. We must have crept right past it. We had not seen it from the tree because from there we could not get close enough to it, and because, subconsciously, we had assumed that it could not still be there. It was a good thing that anacondas—normally aggressive creatures—seemed to be a bit slow in sizing up novel situations. The boa must have been dumbfounded by all the canoeists and the appearance of a new sport on the Rio Azul.

Thoughtfully it glided into the water. Gratefully we watched it disappear.

After that the river became small, fast and increasingly colder, the trees darker and taller. In the afternoon the

Timber climbing hopefully to establish their position. All he could see on
most occasions were more trees . . .

After days of short rations fresh fish were very welcome.

thunder rumbled and the lightning flashed again without a drop of rain falling.

Then we came to a cataract. It was our one hundred and fourth. It was a rushing, tearing, shrill, vicious cataract. Out of the boats and up on to the steep bank and swing the machete! I had gone ahead and I had a good look at the cataract from the left bank—the real left bank, looking downstream. It was different in character from all previous cataracts, which had been wide cascades. This one was a narrow passage between low rocks, no more than six feet high. The rocks were smooth and round, no longer sharp and lava-like. The river with its icy water had become more and more like a mountain torrent. At the narrowest point the rocks were only five feet apart. There the water shot past: deep, smooth and shrill. At the end the water was white and deep.

That was where we had to get through. Two of us had to stand on the rocks and secure the boats with rope, while the others had to stand chest-high in the water and drag the boats up. To take the boats through the wood would have been a day's work.

The others crouched apathetically in their boats and waited for suggestions. They were so apathetic that they were willing to do anything.

"It would be a good thing," said my wife, "if you didn't go into the water with your dressing."

"It's all healed up."

"Not properly. You still look like chalk."

I was barefoot, the topee on my head and a huge dressing round my middle. I only wore the topee from habit and because it was difficult to stow it in the boat. My inflammation was subsiding, and I felt very well, but I did not really want to stay long in the water with my dressing. But then none of us wanted to. However, they would do everything that had to be done, of course.

I went down to my boat, fetched the compass, put on some trousers and a pair of plimsolls and took the gun.

"Listen," I said to Kliesing, "the river makes a definite turn east."

"Yes?" said Kliesing.

"And the ground rises on the other side. Here, too, only a bit more inland. I don't like it."

"No," said Kliesing. "But the lake can't be far away."

"That lake . . ."

"It's got to turn up, hasn't it?"

"I'll tell you what I'll do. I'll cut through the forest and have a look. I'll see if I can find it, and I'll look out for a camping place and something to eat, while you tackle this thing."

"Splendid," said Aveckle. "You'll have a look and find us something to eat. We'll tackle the cataract."

I went off with compass, gun and machete. Once or twice I had to cut through some lianas, and once or twice the gun got caught in some branches; but it was perfectly easy and I felt a coward. While the others were struggling to get the boats over the cataract—they all had to wade into the cold, rushing water, because the idea of pulling the boats up with ropes had proved impracticable—I was going for a walk in the woods. But perhaps I could make up for it by shooting something. Then I noticed that on the other side where the lake was supposed to be, the forest rose more and more steeply . . .

It was impossible, of course, to see how far it rose and whether it was merely undulating ground, or a small hill, or the foothills of a mountain range. The ground rose on my side, too. The forest became darker, the trees looked taller. Above the cataract the river flowed evenly for some distance, its bed cut deep into the dark forest, placid, clear and deep, and only about ten feet wide. I had never seen a river coming towards me so quietly and solemnly.

I pushed on farther and finally found a camping site on the far bank. A small river came tumbling down. The hill seemed to step back to allow us room for our tents.

I turned back, lost my way, found it again. On the far side I heard two pavos, or perhaps pheasants, take wing noisily. I did not see them. Then the forest became quiet again, and I failed to get a shot in. After an hour and a half I was back at the cataract. They were just about to haul the last boat up. They had all been standing up to their necks in the cold water and pulling for all their worth. The water was not all that cold, of course, but it seemed icy, and everybody was exhausted. I was not exhausted. I was in fine form, and no wonder. Only it was a nuisance that I had not shot anything.

We then travelled up the long, straight stretch to the camping site. Here the river again ran faster and shallower. We decided to call it a day and hacked out a camping site nine feet above the river.

It was high time to make a camp, for it was getting dark. When we stopped hacking, putting up tents and our other noisy activities we could hear the roar of the next cataract. We had not seen it when we landed. The river came towards us fast, clear and dark. But the cataract could not be far.

The darker it got, the louder grew the roar of the cataract. It was different from the usual sound.

"That'll be the bar of rock at the exit from the lake!" Kliesing said.

"Listen . . ." I said, but then stopped. During the last few days we had several times given way to fits of bad temper. Even our gentle Paulchen had become edgy. Only Kliesing had retained his sunny temperament.

There were other things to admire. When Kliesing and Paulchen began to feel hungry, they did diaphragm-exercises instead of eating a meal. We watched them open-mouthed. That was how they kept going.

River and forest had opened out to give us a bit of a view. Not a view of the sky—no fear!—but a view of a steep mountainside, completely wooded, and of a sombre cluster of rocks half-way up. We must be at the foot of a mountain. That was why the invisible cataract was making such a din.

The mountain stood at right-angles to the river. We had been unable to make out whether the river passed it on the left or on the right. According to the aerial map it must pass it on the left, on its western side. If the river continued on an easterly course the outlook for us was grim.

During the night a heavy thunderstorm broke immediately overhead. It could not escape from the narrow valley. But when the thunder stopped, the rain stopped too. Afterwards the air was heavy with the sweaty reek of wet night-birds.

The next morning the valley was filled with warm mist which invisible sunbeams tried to pierce. The palms and treetops on the far bank cast weird shadows on the white mist. Timber and I went off "to survey the situation". Timber had to come along because he was the only one who could climb tall trees.

The time for experiment was over. What we undertook from now on had to succeed. I had very little hope that we could manage the next cataract. Something devilish was cooking up there.

We went along the western bank. A hundred yards from our tents we came across a huge boar's skull. No domestic pig has a skull that size. It was quite clean and must have been there a long time. A little farther, on the other bank, was a watering place and a wallow with fresh track marks.

The warm, drifting patches of mist over the dark river melted away and the sunbeams came through a little stronger.

The roar of the cataract was deafening.

Far ahead light was streaming down. We could not see the

cataract, but the valley opened out wide to reveal the steep mountainside. Now, with the sun on it, it was light green, and the group of rocks which had looked so sombre the night before looked small and pleasant. The mountain rose twelve to fifteen hundred feet straight up from the river. The whole Azul valley wheeled round in front of the mountain.

It wheeled east.

Then we saw the cataract—it was a series of wild water cascades.

Three branches . . .

Beyond, the river came to an end.

*　　*　　*

Again we had come to the end of a river . . .

No, to its beginning, of course; to the source of the Rio Azul—if we were on the Azul at all.

(We were. Only our maps were all wrong.) We were the first men, or at least the first white men, to reach the source of the Rio Azul.

We were not overcome by the solemnity of the moment.

Two hundred and fifty yards from our present camp the Azul—a jungle river which comes out of nowhere and discharges itself into nowhere—originated in three strong springs at the foot of a steep mountain somewhere in the Sierra Caribe.

We had travelled for thirty-two days and seventy-five miles up an unknown river, we had done a hundred and four cataracts—to say nothing of the trip up the Arroyo Mariana —to reach the mysterious lake from which it was supposed to come.

Now, in spite of the cartographers, it turned out that there was no connection between the lake and the river.

We greeted this discovery not with dismay, but rather with the stupefaction which is experienced when a long-awaited event finally takes place.

Stupefaction gave way to a sad awakening. We could not go back. We were trapped.

"What next?" asked Timber.

"We must find out where we are."

"Yes," said Timber solemnly. "It's a matter of life and death."

"The lake's got to be somewhere. We must find out where. There's probably only the western range of hills which we passed between us and the lake. We *must* see it. We'll make straight for the ridge and you look for a good tree. You simply *must* see the lake."

We took a closer look at the springs. They were beautiful springs of clear mountain water. No wonder the water had been so cold the last few days. Cold and without a sign of fish. Just as we were looking particularly closely at the sources of the Azul, a murderous howling broke loose right over our heads. It sounded hollow and penetrating, like a lion. . . .

It was a howling monkey. An enormous fellow of a size I have seen only among baboon leaders on the Blue Nile. He was hanging down from all fours, hardly sixty feet above us, and was shaking with fury because we had taken the liberty of coming there.

After he had been howling for some time, he threw a branch at us with remarkable accuracy. After that he scratched himself under the armpit without taking his eyes off us for a moment. Suddenly there were three more devils, black and reddish-brown, almost as imposing as their leader. They joined in the howling chorus at the top of their voices and scratched their armpits. They howled more loudly than the jaguar ever does, that sweaty but unobtrusive gentleman who is the essence of noiselessness and who only seems to raise his voice when tormented by love. They howled shamelessly, and more and more came. Small and large howling monkeys, and females with their babies clinging on to their bellies or their backs, and everywhere the branches were alive with young monkeys hopping about and screaming, whilst the adults roared like elephants, but with a terribly hollow, not a trumpeting, sound. It was an incredible noise. Our friends in the camp heard it.

"What's the matter *now*?" my wife was reported to have said.

Well, you can imagine that it was all very entertaining and that we were very amused by the youngsters and the mothers with the infants, and that we said some pretty rude things to the elder males. Sometimes they answered by throwing themselves with all their force on to a large, hollow branch, and while they were getting a sound grip the branch fell on us. But it was not difficult to see through these manoeuvres and take cover. Also, since we had other matters to attend to, we could not spend too much time with the monkeys, so we hacked our way up the hill.

The long ridge, running mainly at right angles to the mountains, was not very steep. Its maximum height above the river below the springs could not have been more than a hundred and eighty to two hundred feet.

The troupe of monkeys, now consisting of seventy or eighty acrobats, followed us in the treetops at varying distances.

Howling monkeys are by far the noisiest creatures on earth. They seldom attack. They live in a group and have a great sense of responsibility: the speed of their movements is decided by the group's weakest member. (We could observe this as they followed us.) Fruit is their staple food, which means that they have to cover large areas in search of it, but they do not generally cover more than a mile a day.

So much for the monkeys that followed us and threw branches and hard green nuts on our heads when they were over us.

On the ridge we found a good, isolated tree, about a

hundred and fifty feet high. We ate our lunch, although it was not yet lunch-time.

"I'll have more strength," Timber said. He looked hollow and emaciated.

"Don't climb up . . ."

"No. It's a matter of life and death. But when I've nothing in my stomach I just collapse."

Timber's meal consisted of three hazelnuts and three slices of dried apple. At breakfast he and Paulchen had had the same, but for dinner Paulchen was going to bake them one more waffle—the last one.

"I must get something," I said, eyeing the monkeys. Timber followed my gaze.

"You think——"

"Only if there's nothing else," I said.

"Tastes a bit odd, doesn't it?"

"I ate some once," I said. "On the Amazon. The Indians had shot two with arrows."

"Interesting," said Timber.

"Isn't it. How I long for those happy days."

"Tell me more."

"It's not that I don't like the flavour," I said, "but they're too close to us here. They can finish us off. In Ethiopia the baboons will kill you if you fire at them by mistake. They're very nice otherwise. But they don't like you to shoot at them. Two old baboons can put paid to a leopard, and one baboon is a match for a man. Perhaps these fellows here will not do us in, but they look as if they could if they wanted to."

"All right," Timber said. "We'll only shoot if the shares hit rock-bottom."

I had taken a small tin of sardines for my lunch. Unfortunately they were not done in oil, but just in their own juice. They were Mexican sardines, and when we opened the tin they looked grey and unappetizing. I had bought those

tins in the face of my wife's protest in one of the romantic
tiendas at Las Margaritas, and I regarded them from the
start as iron rations. Earlier on we had opened two which
looked just as sad; so sad that Aveckle wanted to throw away
the other six. But now we were glad we had not thrown them
away. I shared the contents of the tin with Timber, secretly
giving him more than his share as he needed it more than I.
My wife still had some oatmeal, and even some Erbswurst,
so we could still breakfast after a fashion. If we managed to
bag some turkeys again she would have to give Paulchen
some more oatmeal so that he could survive. She had a
compassionate nature, whilst I nursed a considerable, but
unjust, anger against that determined vegetarian.

Timber tried to pacify me. "It's difficult for Paulchen,"
he said. "He's fifty-seven, twice my age . . ."

"Sure," I said. "As a fifty-seven-year-old vegetarian in
the jungle he's not a bad advertisement. Look how tough he
is! Look at his stamina! Look at his vibrations!"

"Yes," Timber said. "When I'm with Marianne I feel it
dreadfully that I'm not as tough as he is . . ."

"Oh, shut up," I cried. "I didn't mean it like that.
You've got your kidneys, and the tree which fell on you."

"All right. But what I was going to say was that, at his age,
Paulchen simply can't change. It would be the death of him."

"I appreciate that. I appreciate that more than his
vibrations."

"Perhaps he needs them."

"It's high time you were back among normal people," I
said.

"Yes. I'd be glad if we were at Harry's now."

"Yes," I said weakly.

I was touched by Timber's defence of Paulchen. We
picked out the last bits of squashed sardine, and, after first
politely refusing it and saying: "After you," Timber gulped
down the last spoonful of the sad-looking sauce. It had not

gone bad; it only looked as though it had because it was just salicyl-and-sardine-sauce without any oil. In spite of that it seemed to be a great delicacy, to judge by Timber's expression.

Then we ate some salt and a few garlic cloves, of which my wife had brought a large supply. After that we faced the future with more confidence.

In the course of the next days we shared the last five tins of sardines in the same way. Unfortunately Timber was careless enough to tell Paulchen about the treasure. On the strength of that Paulchen reduced Timber's rations by three hazelnuts and three slices of dried apple—which was the whole of his lunch. I was furious when I found out that we were now supposed to feed Timber, or else watch him exist on the three hazelnuts and three slices of dried apple which he had as breakfast. I was going to kick up a row about it, but Timber said it was pointless, and of course he was right. It would probably have been quite unjustified; but from that day on I did not like Paulchen as much as before—but let that be, since we are just about to face the future with more confidence and Timber is about to climb his tree. . . .

All at once the monkeys started up again.

We had almost forgotten about them. They were squatting all over the place, from dress circle to gallery, all eighty of them, whistling, cursing and howling so loudly that we had to put our fingers into our ears. They had never let us out of their sight, and when Timber began climbing, their leaders shook their fists—that's exactly what it looked like.

"Come down again!"

"I'm not up yet," Timber called from fifteen feet up. "Do you think they'll turn nasty?"

"I don't know—they may throw something at your head when you can't take cover."

"Their aim is not as good as all that."

"No."

"You couldn't fire your gun? I mean, only if one of them comes too close."

"You're out of your mind."

"All right."

A huge monkey, only his red head visible amongst the leaves of the nearest tree, accompanied our conversation with ghastly belching.

"Wait," Timber said. "I'll give you back the binoculars. They worry me when I'm climbing. When I'm at the top I'll let a line down and you tie them on."

"All right."

Timber tested some lianas on the tree and suddenly he was forty or fifty feet farther up.

The big monkeys quietened down. Only the young ones went on howling.

Timber climbed slowly and quietly higher. All the monkeys stopped. There was a rustling. I took the binoculars and saw some of the large monkeys swinging along the lianas and the branches of neighbouring trees and closing in on Timber. They looked nonplussed. I had never seen animals look so nonplussed.

"Hi!" Timber called. "There's one looking at me—twenty—no, fifteen feet away! You couldn't send up the camera?"

The camera! We had had to leave it behind in the camp, because the gun and the binoculars had been more important. I peered through the binoculars and saw nothing. Then I saw Timber's monkey. He was staring at Timber with a horrified expression. He was obviously the leader of the tribe. Horrified, he went back, hand over hand, watching Timber all the time . . .

Then I saw two other large monkeys. They, too, retreated without taking their eyes off Timber. They looked at him in sheer disbelief and retreated.

When Timber was on the ground the howling monkeys

had understood that we were men. They had behaved accordingly, showing utter contempt, hurling branches at us and feeling perfectly safe because they had never met men before. But now, because one of those men was climbing like a monkey, they realized that he could not be a man. What had gone up that tree must be another, higher form of life—a monkey like themselves. It said much for the wisdom and sense of responsibility of their leader that they had not attacked blindly but retreated.

All at once the monkeys disappeared, silently and quietly, like mice. So much for the monkeys.

The rest was not so funny. To cut a long story short, Timber saw from that tree only what he had already seen from the first tree—forest. The tree was a hundred and fifty feet high, stood on the crest of a hill and was comparatively isolated.

All the same, Timber saw nothing but forest. No glistening water, no lake . . . Only forest.

It was most discouraging. Nothing but treetops and treetops. No lake. Not even a lighter haze because there was haze everywhere. Hell!

Timber came down exhausted.

Although he had seen nothing but trees I could have kissed him for coming down again and not falling off in his exhaustion. We crept back in the depths of despair. We stopped many times en route and Timber asked what would happen now. I told him that we should have to climb the mountain. First thing tomorrow morning we must climb up to the group of rocks on the mountain. I told Timber we were bound to see the lake if we climbed up there, but Timber said we need not go that high. We only needed to get above the treetops. Then he would find a tree and climb it and have an uninterrupted view.

Meanwhile, our friends at the camp had been enjoying a nice rest, that is, as nice a rest as you could expect with diaphragm exercises having to take the place of meals. Paulchen was too busy cooking the last waffle to be disappointed about our finding not the lake but the end of the river. Kliesing did not show his disappointment, whilst my wife was mainly interested in all the noise we had raised in the wood, and in what was the matter *now*. We gave her a satisfactory explanation as far as the howling monkeys were concerned.

Then she asked whether we had brought anything to eat, but it was only a rhetorical question, and we said we were shattered that in all the excitement we had forgotten to bring anything to eat. So she dissolved the last piece of Erbswurst.

Then Timber went to bed so as to be fit for the next day, when we had to go off on another reconnaissance. Kliesing, Aveckle and I sat down to make an appreciation of the situation. We agreed that we had spent thirty-two days and covered seventy-five miles going up the Azul; that we had got up over a hundred and four cataracts and in doing so must have climbed eight hundred feet, which was a gradient of 2.3 in 1,000 . . .

We shirked drawing any further conclusions.

We knew only too well, and even Paulchen must have known it instinctively, that we were unlikely to survive if we went back by the same route. I do not mean that we would have starved. We were simply no longer fit enough to cope with the hundred and four cataracts. At least ninety of them were more dangerous going downstream than going upstream. Going downstream each one of the ninety could be the end of us . . .

The next morning Timber had somewhat recovered. We took watches, the compass, binoculars, rope, climbing belt, the machetes and the small Zeiss Ikon camera. The gun we had to leave behind. Aveckle was to try and shoot something from the camp.

At nine o'clock we were standing at the foot of the steep mountain. There were no monkeys to be seen or heard. The sun shone. The mountain rose almost vertically, but as it was thickly overgrown it was easy to climb. After an hour we reached a kind of ledge where there was a tangle of fallen trees, and Timber climbed one to have a look. He could not see much, and what little he saw was forest. He came back disappointed, hardly believing that even from the mountain it was impossible to get a view. We had to go up to the group of rocks after all.

Before that, although it was early, we ate our lunch—the little tin of sardines and garlic with salt.

"Tonight I'll open one of the iron rations," said Timber.

"Go right ahead."

"Do you mean it?"

"Yes."

"Kliesing's had two already."

"Really."

"But they were meant for extreme emergency. For instance, if we now had to abandon everything and make our way through the wood."

I did not dare tell the hungry and exasperated Timber that we, too, had opened one of our iron rations . . .

"I don't think it's right," said Timber. "I caught him secretly eating one in his tent. It's unfair."

"Why? It was his, wasn't it?"

"But all of us must have the same chance. And when one of us throws away his chance . . ."

"You mean, eats his chance up before the time's come?"

"Yes. The burden falls on the others."

"Listen, Timber. We've eaten one, too."

To my surprise Timber was inclined to judge our crime more lightly. After all, my wife was a woman. But we were all weak, myself included. I did not tell Timber about the spoonful of marmalade which we were having secretly every night. Aveckle and I had worked out that the jar must contain forty-eight medium-full teaspoons of marmalade, that there were fifteen left, and that therefore we had another seven and a half days, or rather evenings, in which to enjoy our secret dessert. I did not tell Timber. We were all hungry and suffering from lack of sugar. Timber was mad with anticipation of his first iron ration. I advised him not to eat it in public, but he was far too honest and open to do anything in secret.

We climbed on up.

We sweated profusely. Our shirts were soon wringing with sweat and swarms of ugly yellow flies came and settled on us. They ran over our faces and crept into the corners of our eyes. They got into our mouths when we had not a free hand to brush them away.

But I forgot our troubles when I reached the foot of the main rock which towered above us. Through a gap in the trees I could see across the forests. I saw a sea of white light over everything, and in this sea of white light, between the heat haze of distant jungles, I saw a shimmering, glistening surface in the far distance, and I shouted down to Timber.

"*The lake!*"

It was exactly eleven o'clock. I was quite certain it was the lake, but I did not stop. I went on climbing, for farther up the mountain there must be some way of getting on to the rock, and from the rock there must be a superb view. It was quite easy. It took no more than ten minutes, and when I had clambered right up to the top of the rock I almost forgot to breathe—for there, in all its glory, was our lake.

A vast lake in a breath-taking landscape of mountains and jungle. No settlements along its shores, no smoke rising from native huts, no human beings whatsoever . . .

In the southern part were two large islands and a few small ones.

The Lake of the Lacandones.

We looked down on the lake, its bays and its islands, down on the forests and the volcanic mountains, and the mountain ranges in the west beyond the valleys of the Jataté and the Perlas. How can I convey to you the feeling of that lonely country and that lake? You know how it is when you are overcome by something. Timber, too, was overcome. There were tears in his eyes.

We then very solemnly made a sketch on a triangular scrap of paper and noted down everything. The position of the lake; the position and direction of the mountain ranges; the shape of the lake.

On our 1:250,000 map the lake was shaped like an ink blot through which flowed the Rio Azul as a mighty, definitely navigable river. On the military map it was like an elongated lemon with a knob at the top and bottom. Again, through this lemon there flowed a great river—the Rio Azul. On the archaeological map it looked like a squashed kidney with a malignant growth out of which flowed the Rio Azul. On every map the Rio Azul came out of the lake at some spot or other. The archaeological map was remarkable for showing a long river coming from the north and passing the north-east shore of the lake—the "second" arroyo on which we had relied so much and which now turned out to be non-existent. The National Geographic Society's 1:3,500,000 map of Central America also showed a long river coming from the north. But on this map it both entered and left the north-east side of the lake from where, after making almost a complete circle, it joined the Jataté. The most accurate map was the 1:1,000,000 sheet of the International World Map. On this, too, the Rio Azul flowed through the lake and, in the north-east, a large river that came from the north-west skirted the lake. But the lake itself was fairly correctly mapped in the shape of a heart, and extending seven miles long from north to south and seven and a half or eight miles wide from east to west.

On the lake—at last

Above : No settlements on its shores, no smoke from native huts, no human beings whatsoever—the mysterious lake of the Lacandones.

Left: Back to some sort of civilization on route to Harry's hut.

Right: The author at the face of one of the Maya pyramids.

Above : The jungle is far behind.

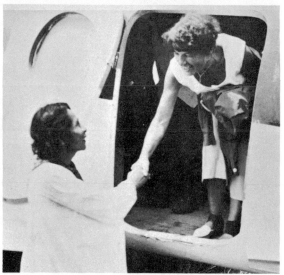

Left : Saying goodbye to Bor.

The map gave a height of much less than one thousand five hundred feet—on all the other maps it was given as one thousand seven hundred feet. The height of the Sierra Caribe was given at one thousand eight hundred to two thousand, two hundred and fifty feet. In reality those mountains rose almost sheer from the northern and north-eastern shore of the lake to a height of one thousand two hundred to one thousand five hundred feet above it, without leaving any room whatsoever for a river on the north-eastern shore. On the farthest northern shore, between the Sierra Caribe and the "Sierra Perlas", there was a valley. From where we were, however, we could see a large, funnel-shaped outflow on the eastern shore. That rather annoyed us. Could it be that we had simply travelled past this outflow?

I thought of the muddy, infinitely melancholy water from which the red snake had shot out, the water which we had taken to be an arroyo from the Chamhuitz. I thought of the dried-up river which we had seen in the dark thicket, which could only have been an overflow from the lake during the rainy season.

Whatever the answer was, this much was obvious: the funnel-shaped bay with its possible outflow was so clearly visible and must have looked so good on an aerial photograph that it was bound to fire the imagination of any cartographer in faraway Mexico or Washington.

"What will you do now?" asked Timber.

My stock had risen to dizzy heights. Of course I did nothing to shake his high opinion of my ability. He was still at an age when one is enthusiastic. To him it seemed miraculous that I had picked on the one tiny point from where we could see the lake, take our bearings and make a new appreciation of the situation.

Our situation still did not look too good. We had to get across to the lake, transporting our boats and tents. That done, we must cross the lake and find the "trail" which the

Danish expedition had cut and which Harry had recommended. Finding this trail, which must have long been overgrown, would be like trying to find a needle in a haystack.

If we found it, we should only have to do seven miles overland to the Jataté and the so-called Savannah of San Quintin where we had left the Lacandones. Thus we should have completed our grotesque, circular journey. All that was needed at the moment was a tiny circle . . . but that was the hardest task of all, as we were to discover. Only when we reached the lake should we discover whether we were trapped, as we had been at the source of the Azul.

Where we had pitched camp the river was between two and a half and three miles from the lake. Farther downstream it was only two miles away. After that the river turned abruptly east.

"I think we can use the camp as our base. From there we can cut a way through to the lake. There's no point getting into the boats and going back down the cataract just to look for a nearer and easier approach."

"Sure," said Timber.

We climbed down, sweated freely, encountered yellow flies, and got very thirsty. We drank the clear, bubbling water of the Azul springs, and it was the most delicious water imaginable. Our great thirst made us forget our hunger. Anyway, it is much better to be hungry and have nothing to eat than to be thirsty and have nothing to drink. At half past three, exhausted but elated, we were back in camp with the great news. My wife had not been able to shoot anything, and Timber did not wait till the evening to have his iron ration. He ate it in full view of everybody and crept into his tent at four o'clock.

I tried to shoot something that afternoon, but there was not a living creature about. There seemed to be nothing, not even fish. Kliesing and Paulchen had not been idle in our absence, but had cleared the camp of undergrowth, cut a fine path to the river and made a bathing place to which they had pulled up the boats. As I washed off the mountain sweat and bathed I saw a three-foot-long poisonous snake near my foot on the shingly river bed. A few minutes later I saw a smaller one. They were probably mates.

I warned the others to take care. We were careful, and we saw the pair of snakes nearly every day. The snakes seemed to get used to us, kept a safe distance and watched us. They did not disturb us in any way. There were no fish—the wonderful rushing mountain stream seemed too cold for those spoilt creatures—but snakes were plentiful. Unfortunately one could not eat them.

The food situation was grim. I thought of the wild boar wallow with the fresh track marks . . . True, for a big boar I would have preferred my heavy African rifle, but I had solid shot (besides some calibres not allowed in Europe) for my double-barrelled Belgian gun. This would do for a jaguar at close quarters, but my dear wife implored me to leave the boars alone. Neither she, nor Timber, nor even the converted Kliesing could cut up such a hulking great animal. It would make an unbelievable mess.

Then Paulchen, that first-class cook whose conversion to vegetarianism had inflicted an irreparable loss on the culinary world, Paulchen by the camp fire that evening said—we had long dropped the subject, but our stomachs were rumbling —Paulchen, and may he go to paradise for overcoming all his instincts, which a non-vegetarian who has no vibrations can never, never fully appreciate, said:

"Herbert, shoot a wild boar. *I'll cut it up for you* . . ."

That shows you the plight we were in.

At ten past ten that night such a terrible thunderstorm broke overhead that I feared for my life. The forest was in a turmoil. Branches crashed down and whole trees collapsed close to us.

"The barometer rose afterwards," my diary informs me.

The next morning my wife shook me awake. Whilst cleaning her teeth by the river she had seen two turkeys.

I stumbled sleepily outside with the gun. In the tropics I wear just a cummerbund at night—a woollen tube with open ends, very practical—everything was wet and damp and dreary outside. Barefoot, cummerbund round my middle, gun in hand, I shot the two turkeys practically from the tent.

On which day did God create the turkey?

*   *   *

We remained twelve days in that camp. Sultry days in the jungle twilight. Even the nights were sultry, and almost every night we heard the jaguar stalk through our camp and smelt his savage, pungent sweat. Often it rained all day and night.

Timber and I had left the morning after our climb to find the best way to the lake. We started along the right bank of the river, and asked Kliesing and Paulchen to begin cutting the trail there, because we had to take that way in any case. Next we came to a depression and then had to climb steeply. For three days we tried to find a good route to the lake—but in the end we did not even find the lake.

Although we now knew for a fact that the lake existed, it again eluded us. Although we now knew for certain that it *existed* and *where*, we could not find it. It was enough to drive one mad. Every time we thought we had found it we came up against a bamboo thicket, or a marsh, or an impenetrable belt of holly which barred the way. Tired and discouraged we stumbled back. Sometimes it took Timber an hour to get over his disappointment and on his feet again. No more funny stories! Sometimes he threw himself across a tree, sometimes he lay on the ground, pale and lifeless, before pulling himself up and slinking home so slowly that I got impatient and even my wife in the camp shouted at him: "Pull yourself together, Timber." Timber said: "I'm sorry,

Marianne. I'm terribly ashamed of myself," and it was obvious that he could not help himself.

It was not just weakness. It could not be. For during those few days I had shot some wonderful turkeys. Turkey in the morning and turkey at night, without anything else except spices is a monotonous but very nourishing food, and the broth is recommended for invalids.

Actually Timber always recovered a little, and on the fourth day after our return from the mountains he went off with Kliesing and they succeeded in getting through the thickets and finding the shore of the lake . . .

Heavens! What a shore! Inhospitable. Vicious. All the same, we now knew where we were. We knew where to cut the trail. A trail four miles long through the jungle, across hills and valleys . . .

We hacked away from morning till night. Kliesing and Paulchen started from the camp, Timber and I from half-way. Timber had to stop more and more frequently. One break was particularly long because we had had no breakfast. Half a turkey had disappeared from the pot during the night.

It was surprising and embarrassing. It was embarrassing because we suspected Kliesing. Then Aveckle and I thought it over and decided that it could have been an animal. Yet we had heard nothing, and the problem of how the animal had replaced the lid so carefully remained unsolved.

In spite of having turkey we were all hungry all the time because there was nothing else to supplement it with. Paulchen lived on one teaspoonful of oatmeal and three hazelnuts a day and diaphragm exercises.

Timber's power of recovery grew feebler and feebler and soon ceased altogether. It became evident that it was not just a case of malnutrition from monotony of diet. It was a kind of recurring malaria, complicated by his kidney trouble.

The day the turkey had disappeared from the pot Timber had hardly been able to work, but we still made quite good progress. Timber pulled himself together admirably. "You faint," he said, "and then it passes and your strength comes back and you start again." Going home in the evening I hoped that Paulchen and Kliesing had also made good progress. They might have finished the first half.

But we did not meet them on our way back. We met them a mere five hundred yards from the camp. In four days they had not cut more than the first five hundred yards of the trail. Except that it was not a trail. It was an avenue.

They had built a road six feet wide, cutting down dozens of trees and removing every trunk over which we might stumble when carrying the boats. They had more or less swept their road clean of any stray twig. Even Timber in his semi-conscious state stared fascinated at this first-class highway. No, ours could not compete with that, although it was four or eight times as long. Although it was several times longer, our stretch was crooked and untidy compared to this royal road built for eternity.

"Let's built an *autobahn*," Timber murmured vaguely.

"What do you mean?" Paulchen asked seriously.

"I just mean an *autobahn*," roared Timber.

"Leave him alone," I said to Paulchen and Kliesing. "You're going about it like a couple of road sweepers. Have you never seen a road sweeper at work, Paulchen?"

"I'm not a road sweeper," Paulchen said, hurt.

Timber stumbled away slowly. His vibrations were not harmonious.

"You shouldn't build for eternity," I said quietly. "The main thing is quantity, not quality. Just enough for us to cut the trail. Just enough for us to get the big canoe round the trees. If you insist on quality we'll be here come Christmas. And if we're only here a twentieth of the time till Christmas we've had it."

"Perhaps we've had it anyway," Kliesing said. "But as long as I don't know it I don't mind."

"You're a cheerful bloke, damn you," I said to Kliesing "But I like you more and more. It's a fact."

It was a fact.

In camp my wife came up to me and said:

"Six iron rations have gone."

I did not understand at first. Then I took it in. It was absurd.

"They've gone from my boat. They've been pinched."

"Perhaps you've mislaid them. Left them behind. Thrown them away . . ."

"Impossible. I'm quite sure, and it's made me feel awful."

Systematically we discussed every possibility. Had we left them in the food dump at the mouth of the Azul? No. Furthermore they had all been there a week ago.

"I feel awful," said my wife.

"Don't mention it to anybody . . ."

"No."

"We must make quite sure."

We made quite sure. The iron rations, ten golden tins, had been right up in the tip of Aveckle's boat. We had only eaten one of them secretly. After that there had been nine tins. No possibility of a mistake. Now there were only three left.

The boats lay out of sight a hundred and twenty feet away from the camp. We brought our detective faculties to bear. It seemed impossible for a jaguar to have taken them. Nothing had been missing when the boats were turned upside down. Timber could not have taken them because he had been with me all the time. This left only Kliesing—or Paulchen. It was a silly business. A short-circuit. It is even stupid to mention a silly thing like that. But when you remember how precarious our position was you can well understand how everything had got distorted and out of proportion—the value of small objects as well as the importance of human values. Hence our shock.

We did not mention it to anybody that day. The following days were lived in an atmosphere of ignored tension. I did tell Timber about it, in the forest. After all, the iron rations were his gift.

Timber was all for bashing the culprit's head in. It was a mercy we did not know who the culprit was.

I asked Timber not to do anything of the sort even if we found him. In the circumstances, I told Timber, we could not afford a culprit. The great thing in the tropics, I explained, was to keep one's temper.

"But when we've reached safety," Aveckle said later, "I'll say something about it. Nobody will stop me."

We kept our eyes open and gathered "evidence". It was grotesque—but please remember the circumstances! It was not until much later, when we had concrete evidence, that we mentioned it. We spoke about it in the casual but bitter way of people who have finally lost faith in humanity.

"Perhaps you pinched them yourselves," Kliesing said simply.

That took our breath away; so much so that we began to doubt ourselves. Our investigations and our conclusions became confused, and in the end we almost came to believe we had pinched the tins ourselves. I apologize to all our comrades I may have suspected.

Let's forget it.

* * *

Days and nights came with rain drumming down on the drowning earth, and again the wood smelt of the sweat of wet night-birds. We despaired of ever getting out of this sombre valley at the end of the earth . . . We were pale and emaciated. Each one of us had lost at least twenty pounds. Each one suffered from something—small things on the whole—and almost everyone had large worms under his skin.

They were worms with rings. Worms like meal-worms, only much fatter when they were fully grown. Whitish, ringed worms with black heads. They were the same kind as

Harry's—dear God, how long ago! But if you turn back the pages of this book you will see how we joked about Harry's worm, and how we refused to believe it was a worm and took it for a carbuncle. We had shuddered at it then. Now we did not have *one*, but two or three dozen. Now *we* had been attacked by the *Muscae gusanerae*, which had laid eggs under our skins. There they had grown into worms. Some grew just under the surface and remained small and we could squeeze them out, but some burrowed deep, becoming as thick as a thumb and very handsome with their rings and their black head. When they moved the sensation was unbearable, something between itching and pain. It was not advisable to cut them out because of the danger of complications; so we had to kill them off with tobacco juice—another scarcity—before we could squeeze them out or until they began to fester and come out of their own accord.

At the end Kliesing had sixteen. The last ones only saw the light of day long after his return to civilization. Timber had a lot, too. One he got out was a very fat one which he wrapped in his handkerchief and took back to Mexico as a trophy. It remained alive and he showed it to anybody who wanted to see it. Most people wanted to, but when they did they shuddered. The Mexicans call these worms *colmijotes*, which means "back teeth".

My wife did not have very many and I had only two or three small ones which were not very active. Perhaps they were affected by my furunculosis. The only one who did not get a single worm was Paulchen.

"Of course not," said Paulchen stolidly. "*You* got them from the turkeys' ticks."

My wife absolutely exploded. "He hasn't yet grasped that he's only still alive because of our turkeys, even if *he* never touches meat! Why doesn't he go and collect some food in the jungle? Why doesn't he gather some radishes or pick some dandelions? And I gave him the last of my oatmeal!"

We had to hunt every day. Swallows have to hunt for sixteen hours a day. While feeding their broods swallows spend sixteen hours a day just searching. If they went to the cinema in between, or read books, or had any other hobbies they would starve. We were like the swallows—Paulchen had become a cuckoo—but we had less than two hours a day to spare for hunting and therefore our stomachs were often painfully empty.

Once my wife missed a large turkey by inches. My wife is a good shot and we needed this turkey urgently. The fact that we had nothing to eat, and needed it desperately, over-excited her and she missed it. The heavy bird flew away much surprised. My wife was inconsolable.

The rest of us, working on our trail, had heard two shots and were delighted.

"Where did it happen?"

"On the *autobahn*. Not more than a hundred yards from the camp."

The next day I went there at the same time, and I had been waiting hardly half an hour when a very fine turkey strutted across Paulchen and Kliesing's avenue. Just at that moment I was not ready for him and he disappeared in the undergrowth, whence he eyed me with curiosity. All I saw of him was his head and comb. I fired . . . missed. The turkey flew away.

After him up the hill. Half an hour over hill and over dale. Then I got him in the air. Thoughtfully I made my way back to our trail. I could not get over missing him the first time. I went through the undergrowth at the place where I had missed and saw the hen—or rather the cock. The second one was the hen. I began to believe in miracles. Although the whole thing was quite logical I began to believe in miracles. Perhaps I had a temperature: but it was not a temperature, it was joy.

The day before we had managed to carry two of the boats

to the tangled shore of the lake. While we were cutting the trail we had carried the boats and some of our equipment part of the way towards the lake each day. Now the first boat was there, and the second one as well. Empty, of course. An empty single folding canoe weighs about forty pounds, but you would not believe what a job it is for two men to carry it four miles through the jungle, up and down, and in one place a hundred and fifty feet up a slippery slope.

It took us nearly all day because Timber had to put it down every five minutes and rest. Timber was in a sorry state. On the way back he crawled on all fours. Then he gobbled up an iron ration in full view of everybody and crept into his tent. He was hiding himself like a sick cat. It was heart-breaking. He slept right through the night and into the afternoon. It was then that I ran after the turkey because I thought I had missed it and thought he needed the broth and that the liver would do him good. In the end they did.

Aveckle started preparing them in the early afternoon although she had helped with the carrying, and Kliesing helped to pluck the birds. We were all at home that afternoon. Timber slept in his tent, and Kliesing and Paulchen had come back about noon because they were exhausted. Paulchen had gone quickly into his tent, too. Perhaps he did not feel well, or wanted to do his diaphragm exercises, or open another iron ration. Farewell, iron ration! Or perhaps he just wanted to sleep. When you sleep you do not have to eat. It is very practical.

Then there was lightning without thunder. I read outside my tent, my wife squatted by the river and cleaned out the turkeys, her arms covered with blood. The clear water washed everything clean again. Then she came back with a naked, clean turkey in each hand and went across to the fire.

I turned to my book again and, by sheer chance, glanced at the river. I saw a sight which made me jump to my feet. In the middle of the river, swimming against the swift current, was a huge snake. The snake was longer than the river was wide. It had raised its mighty head high out of the water and looked excitedly to the place on the bank where Aveckle had been cleaning out the turkeys. Its long body whipped to and fro. It looked like one of those sea monsters in old prints. I called my wife.

"Look at *that*!"

We stared at the snake.

"Shoot it," said my wife.

The whole atmosphere was one of great peace and intimacy: strange green twilight, motionless lianas, the river flowing silently, the forest holding its breath, the snake swimming against the current, but not appearing to move . . .

"It won't do you any harm."

"It smelt the turkeys. I do not think it will see the difference between seizing a turkey or my arm."

"Perhaps not."

"When you're all gone and I'm alone in the camp cooking the turkeys and knowing that this monster is around, and perhaps its mate also, I'll get nervous. I'm not usually nervous, but this would make me so."

"I don't think anything will happen. Snakes hunt at night."

"That's the last straw!"

So I went and shot the snake. At first I thought it was a boa-constrictor because of the beautiful marking on its back, but boas do not go into the water. It was an anaconda. I took careful aim and fired, carefully and sadly. I know it sounds banal. The first shot shattered a vertebra in the snake's neck and the four subsequent shots shattered more. It reared up in the water and its immense length sped downstream like lightning. A hundred yards away it crept up on the far bank. Kliesing and I went after it, and even Timber came out of his tent to see what was the matter. We climbed along a tree which had fallen across the river, saw the snake squirm quickly past a piece of rotting wood and vanish. Although we searched hard we did not see it for quite a time. Then suddenly I heard a hiss and leaped into the air. I had almost trodden on the anaconda. I would never have believed you could stand right by a giant snake fourteen feet in length without seeing it, and that it could hiss the way it did after being mortally wounded. I fired from a distance of two yards and blew off the whole of its head. The death of the wonderful snake was sheer butchery; but I do not know what else we could have done. We waited some time, although it was headless. Then we carried the remains across the tree and hung it up in the camp. It still moved although it was decapitated, but it shrank visibly. It was still alive even without its head and we were almost afraid of it. We did not know how to skin it to make a pair of high-heeled shoes or a handbag for madam, or any other pretty things. Timber assured me he would not have been able to skin it either, even if he had been in better shape. The snake went on squirming, its blood dripping on to the ground. Aveckle said the blood would attract all the other anacondas in the vicinity as well as other wild beasts, so we threw it into the river, where the current swept it away, but probably not very far. We sprinkled ashes from the camp fire on the many traces of blood.

*   *   *

The next day, in this darkest corner of the world, our friend collapsed and my wife cried out:

"Don't you see he's dying!"

Of course we saw, but we could not help him. We were scared stiff that he would die on our hands.

For the first time we began to doubt whether we would get Timber out of the forest alive. We had with us a large medicine chest, but you cannot experiment when you do not know what the trouble is and when there are not any symptoms that a layman can recognize. When you do not know what the matter is there is nothing you can do for your patient except keep constant watch, give him quinine and doses of Vitamin C and, if the worst comes to the worst, morphia. Despite all our medicines we lacked the one thing that Timber needed, but we did not know that then.

Later, in Mexico City, a specialist in tropical medicine explained to us what we should have done and what we should have carried with us.

It was a miracle that Timber did not die. It was a miracle that he rallied once again. And it was a very good thing that he kept alive, for his death would have created new difficulties and delayed our escape from that hell even longer.

After this almost fatal attack we gave Timber strong, but only partly suitable, medicaments, put him to bed as well as we could and left him. We spent the whole day carting as much stuff as possible to the lake, until only the barest necessities were left in the camp. On the twelfth day in that forest-tomb we struck camp at dawn and gave Timber a heart stimulant. He never spoke, but we were grateful he was able to move at all, although it was generally only crawling on all fours. We got Timber across the hill and to the lake. It was the only happy moment in that long, weary, difficult day.

It was far too much for a woman. I felt an utter swine when I shut my ears to her soft whimpering and my eyes to her distress as she forced herself to struggle on through mud and jungle There was nothing I could do to make things easier for her. Each of us had reached the final stages of exhaustion. Physical exhaustion is healthy up to a point, but we had long passed that point.

It was now or never. It was the very last moment for getting out of that murderous hole. Possibly just to run into another trap . . .

I do not think we even looked back at our camp, but we

gave an involuntary start when the voice suddenly said "Hush!" behind our backs.

By noon we had mastered the ridge between the sources of the Rio Azul and the Lake of the Lacandones. After twelve days of apathetic exhaustion and wild despair the will to live had carried us over this geographically unimportant obstacle . . .

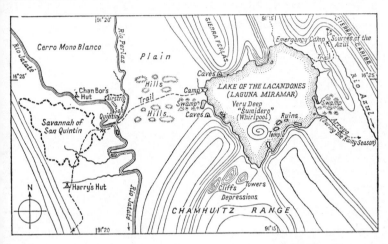

The boats were in the water. We had to pull them through the last barriers on the tangled shore. Then a flood of light broke over us. We were on the lake. Timber had been deposited in the front seat of the large canoe, where he sat slumped.

Kliesing filmed the great moment, the moment when we crept blinking into the sun after weeks of jungle twilight. Through darkness into light. Through battle to victory.

Kliesing had the novel idea that we should raise our arms towards the sun so that it would look right in his film.

Aveckle raised her arms to the sun. Paulchen did not.

The old vegetarian with his rampant-growing beard was angry because he had to paddle the apathetic Timber across the lake. He looked like a mixture of Mime and Alberich. During the last few weeks I had begun to love him a little less, but I mentally took off my hat to him as he, the oldest of us, was about to paddle the youngest across a lake of molten lead.

We shall take our hats off to Timber later. It would look too much like a funeral if we did so now.

How did I get on to this hat-raising business? Oh yes, because Kliesing, hollow-cheeked and exhausted like the rest of us, produced some outrageous cinematic ideas.

Paulchen and I did not raise our hands to the sun; we would have felt foolish. We ruined that bit of film for Kliesing. We were very annoyed with him; but we kept our mouths shut, thank God. Paulchen was furious and I was childish. It was extremely mean. We might just as well have granted Kliesing that little favour.

We glided across the molten lake.

But when you looked straight down the water was crystal clear. The surface gleamed like silver in the noonday heat and below us lay a green fairyland. Fish came darting up and followed us. Beautiful fish, big fish, barbaric fish, in colourful shoals. Far down swam bearded eels. They had never seen boats before. They came up from the depths and swam behind us.

We made course for the islands and passed some large rocks. We did not land, because our main concern was to find the trail and the little peninsula which the Danish expedition had reached. Looking through the binoculars at the southern shore and its volcanic formations we could see only two possibilities. I became confident that we should find the trail, or at least the Danes' camping place. But I did not think we should find it immediately.

In the burning tropical heat we travelled nearly ten miles across the lake.

We landed on the little peninsula, and discovered the trail, wild and overgrown. We felt much better.

We pitched our tents on the grass under tall trees—now welcome for their shade. Shortly after landing my wife almost collapsed. The journey across the lake and the effort of the last two days had been too much for her.

She recovered in an hour.

"Where's my hat?" I asked.

"What d'you want it for?"

"I want to take it off to you."

"Very funny."

"Not a bit funny," I said. "It's high time I took it off to you."

"You may take off your hat now, but you'll shout at me again later."

"Of course I won't. Never."

"Yes, you will. And you'll throw ashtrays at me."

Twelve years ago I had once thrown an ashtray at my wife. Odd that she should remember it. Especially as I had missed her, and the ashtray had not broken.

"What's for dinner?" I asked quietly.

There was nothing.

Kliesing had gone off a long time ago. Half an hour later he came back with a net full of fish.

He was wild with joy over his catch. All of us, except Timber, danced with glee like a bunch of madmen.

During the short dusk a turkey landed in one of the tall trees above our heads. Then lo and behold! Timber, seeing the turkey—in a nebulous dream I suppose—awoke from his apathy and had the gun in his hand in a split second.

We all stared at him. He acted like a man in a trance. He fired straight up into the air and fell forward, his face on the gun. The turkey crashed down, right in front of the cooking-pot.

Then even Timber laughed like a madman.

CHAPTER FIVE

We've Got to Get Airborne

WE had reached the lake, but not the end of our difficulties.

In all our misery we could hardly bring ourselves to think about the lake and its secrets.

The next day we were still weak, but confident. We had almost finished our round trip. The seven and a half miles across to the river Jataté—once, a long time ago, considered insuperable—seemed a mere nothing after all we had been through.

What now?

Food was the main problem. Paulchen was near the end of his tether, if in a different way from Timber. He suffered from hallucinations. He envisaged us watching him with a malicious delight as he lay at death's door and bit for the first time into a leg of turkey . . . It would probably never occur to him that such a sight would only fill us with pity. For at that moment the old vegetarian's world would collapse.

He had heard us speak of a trail and of "only seven and a half miles" to our starting-point on the Jataté. He was now dead-set on getting there, paddling down the fifty miles to the mouth of the Azul, recovering the food dump we had made there forty-five days ago, bringing it all up here and getting back to the vegetarian flesh-pots. His idea of the journey home was a steady progress through innumerable Indian villages where tortillas could be bought.

Kliesing supported Paulchen's urge to collect the food.

We, too, had quite a bit there: rice, beans, maize, oatmeal, Erbswurst and, above all, sugar. We were all in favour of their expedition, although it was not really necessary any more, except for Paulchen.

The question of provisions had become unimportant except for him. There was game in plenty on the shores of the lake, and particularly the fish we had been without for so long. Apart from our morbid craving for sugar we could have lived there happily for days, even weeks, and explored the lake thoroughly.

In reality everything depended on Timber's condition. Timber was better, by the way. A diet consisting of grilled liver, consommé, bouillabaisse, sole à la Lacandon and roast turkey had set him up to such an extent that he was able to walk again, though rather shakily.

We thought that Timber's collapse was connected with his kidneys, complicated by a tropical malaria, and brought on by malnutrition and physical exertion. We were right, up to a point. But Dr. Gonzalo of Mexico City, who took great interest in our expedition from the medical point of view and treated Timber on his return, gave us the full explanation.

"Mineral deficiency," he said. "You're very lucky to have got away with your life."

The exertion of weeks, the malnutrition, perhaps some liver trouble, his kidneys—all that had been enough to destroy the mineral balance in Timber's body.

After our return to Mexico City everything became clear . . . For instance Timber's excessive, but instinctively sound, desire for salt. Every cow needs to lick salt, but it can stay alive for some time without it. If it does not get cobalt, which it absorbs when licking stones and eating certain plants, it will die.

His strange statement that his sweat did not taste salty! He had started to go downhill after "pushing on" at the

Arroyo Mariana. The final blow had been climbing the hot mountain from which we saw the lake for the first time.

The mineral balance in the body, Dr. Gonzalo informed us, can generally be maintained by eating a few vegetables and drinking milk. Meat, on the other hand, is poor in minerals.

In normal circumstances it is rare for the body's mineral balance to be disturbed. But if it is disturbed the consequences soon become visible. For some reason Timber had had no reserves. It would have been a different matter if we had eaten the meat *raw* or had had the proper medicines, but we did not have them.

If it had taken us two or three days longer to reach the lake Timber would have been finished. The lake was his salvation, for from the day when Kliesing brought back the first catch of fresh fish Timber picked up.

We revelled in the fish. I apologize for talking so much about food, but my wife made a bouillabaisse of twenty kinds of fish . . . Kliesing and Timber were so impressed by the dish that they took their largest pot—which previously, for reasons of vibrations, had only been used for porridge, bean soup and suchlike, but had never been allowed to come into contact with fish or meat—and made a second bouillabaisse for supper. They did not make as good and appetizing a job of it as a canoeing wife would have done, they told me, but then they were men. They were quite pleased with the result. In fact, they were enthusiastic, and Timber invited me to be their guest.

I love fish. Timber raised the lid invitingly. What my eyes saw was indeed remarkable: fish heads with glassy eyes, fish bones, fish tails and scales in a muddy broth, probably fortified with dead tadpoles and fish spawn . . . I shuddered involuntarily.

"Aren't you going to help yourself?" asked Timber.

"No, thank you," I said. "Really not. It's revolting."

"Why?" asked Timber. He was squatting in front of the pot with a faraway look in his eyes. "Well, if *you* don't feel like it . . ."

He then lifted up the great pot and drank the whole broth. At least a gallon.

And that is what finally set Timber up. No exaggeration. Fish are rich in minerals and they had nearly everything that Timber needed, although he did not know it then. Timber blissfully lapped it all up, making a great deal of noise and never suspecting that he was taking his medicine. For hours he picked the bones, smacking his lips. The disgusting brew saved his life, just as the few spoonfuls of dirty salicyl-sauce from the sardine tins on the Sierra Caribe had prolonged it.

Timber's instincts were thoroughly healthy.

*　　　*　　　*

To cut a long story short, we left the lake in a hurry. My suggestion to explore the lake first and then make our way out of the forest fell on deaf ears. I did not mind, and Aveckle and I did not feel particularly bitter about hastening our departure.

Paulchen and Kliesing set off for the Jataté to secure the provisions. The rest of us thought only of Harry—Harry, a kind of shining guardian angel.

The lake? To hell with the lake!

We secured the boats and the tents and left everything behind except the big double canoe, which we had emptied because Paulchen and Kliesing needed it for their trip down the Jataté. Apart from machetes, compass, camera and other absolute necessities we only took Timber's American Air Force inflatable dinghy, a one-man affair we had brought with us as a life-boat.

Good-bye, lake! I had the feeling I would never see it again since we were leaving it with such haste, but my feeling deceived me.

We dragged the light—fifty pounds light!—two-seater folding canoe seven and a half miles to the Rio Perlas, a little way above the Jataté. We started at seven in the morning and got there before sunset. The carrying of the boat fell to Kliesing and myself, because Paulchen collapsed before we had covered a third of the way.

It was almost a repetition of our march from the Azul to the lake. Kliesing and I carried the big canoe on our shoulders. Fifty pounds distributed between two men should be a mere nothing, but it was anything but that going across hill and valley, through jungle and marsh. It took us eleven hours, although the trail was good and quite recognizable. The last hours were a race against night. We had no wish to be caught by darkness in the middle of the forest. We wanted to reach familiar ground and the river we knew before then, and we did it.

On arriving at the river Perlas we dumped the boat on the bank, and whilst Kliesing returned to fetch Paulchen the rest of us paddled across to the far bank. Then I swam back with the boat and when I got there the je-jenes swooped on me. We put on all the clothes we had and went to the ruined hut on the spit of land between the Perlas and the Jataté which had belonged to the planter who died of yellow fever and whose monument was the rusty parts of a maize mill and an overgrown banana plantation. That was the first sign in forty-seven days that there were, or at least that there must have been, other people in the world besides Kliesing, Paulchen, Timber, my wife and myself. As for Timber— weak as he was, and only partially alive after the gallon of fish broth—he disappeared immediately into the banana plantation and, with unerring instinct, discovered instantly several bunches of golden yellow bananas from amongst hundreds of green, unripe ones!

Timber ran down to the bank of the Perlas. On the far side Kliesing and Paulchen were just starting off. There was only half an hour left before sunset and they wanted to use it to get as far as they could. Timber hailed them, and as they came across he threw two bunches of about seventy or ninety bananas into Paulchen's lap. In his bad temper and his depression Paulchen had begun to look on Timber as his arch-enemy, just as he had looked on Harry—and still did. But Timber realized this as little as Harry had done—we had never pointed it out to him—and none of us could understand why Paulchen felt like that about Timber and never spoke to him. We had all kinds of theories but we could not find a reason. Even if Timber had known of Paulchen's enmity he would still have thrown those bananas into his lap. Paulchen needed the bananas more than anyone else.

The canoe quickly disappeared from sight.

The rest of us spent the night in the ruined hut. We were in excellent spirits because of the bananas which Timber had discovered, and the next morning we blew up the rubber dinghy, threw our stuff in and swam across the Jataté with the boat between us, just above the whirlpool where my wife had capsized. On the far side we dressed, moored the dinghy to the bank and saw a green snake about four and a half feet long which hissed at us and went away. It was probably the same snake that we had met before.

We climbed the steep bank and the snake appeared again as we looked back on the wild, lonely land on the far side, with the ruined hut and the landing-strip somewhere between the two rivers.

Not one of the Lacandones to be seen anywhere.

We saw the maize snake and all sorts of things, even the island where we had spent happy days with the Lacandones, but we did not see a single human being. The country looked as if no man other than the dead planter had ever been there.

We came to the edge of the savannah where we had camped and where Chan Bor and Nabora had made such an impression on us when they appeared the first time. Although we had camped there—how long ago!—with ten people and nineteen animals there was hardly a trace left. We looked for the trail by which we had come and found it—only to lose it again immediately. Although we had crossed the savannah with our big caravan we lost the trail and spent two hours trying to find it. We were desperate, because we had imagined that once we were out of the forest all our problems would be solved. Then my wife's voice rang across to us: "Here it is, you nitwits!" But we did not keep it for long, because all at once the savannah ceased—ceased completely. It had caught fire. It was charred right up to the forest on the far side.

When we reached the forest we did not have to search for more than an hour before we found the notches Don Oscar had cut in the trees coming down. After that it was easy. We had been going seven hours when we came to the part where Harry's hermitage was.

Doubts assailed us the nearer we approached. Would he still be there? If he were, would he take us in? Perhaps he was short of food himself! Perhaps he had his Indian girl friend with him . . . Despicable doubts!

We were firmly convinced that we should have to go on straight away, go on for many weary days to Porvenir in the highlands.

The nearer we got, the more unlikely it seemed that Harry's, or anybody's Robinson Crusoe house could ever have existed in that empty country. Then we saw Harry's brook and heard it murmuring. And as we stepped out of the dark forest and reached the spot where a tree lay across the brook we saw, on the slope in the clearing, Harry's house—and Harry.

With flowing hair, golden beard, and legs crossed, Harry sat enthroned in his house like a blond god of fire and heaven. After forty-eight days he was the first man we saw— if he were a man and not an angel with a flaming sword . . .

Half naked and in blue jeans.

"Where," the flaming angel called, "is Paulchen? Where is Klee-zing? Where are the others?"

He asked us as if we had killed, skinned and eaten them. For a second we were so frightened that we wondered whether we had done so, and if not, why not. Then I pulled myself together and called up:

"They're safe. *Safe* . . ."

"Thank God!" said Harry.

He came towards us with outstretched hands.

"What a story you could tell *now*!" Harry said.

"Yes," I said. I could not think of anything else to say.

"And the lake?" asked Harry.

"Oh, the lake . . ."

"I know the forest," Harry said. "When I saw you arrive, and only three of you, I feared the worst. When I heard the sound of voices I thought it was some Lacandones paying me a visit. But then I knew from the voices that it couldn't be Lacandones. But *only* Lacandones come from that side— never Mexicans or foreigners. That's why I was a little perturbed . . . Thank God you're all safe. Sit down. The way you look . . ."

"It isn't as bad as all that."

"Isn't it? *That's* what you look like," he said, sucking his cheeks into terrible hollows.

We looked at Harry. When we had come down to the forest with him he had had a fever for two days, and he hadn't looked well afterwards. Now he looked very well. He even looked splendid. He looked calm and balanced. He looked serene. There must be something in a hermit's existence for a man to look so calm and serene after two months' solitude.

Dear Harry! We were made to sit down and he did his utmost for us. The first thing he did was to prepare sweetened milk with raisins from dried milk which stood around in large tins, as our eyes had immediately noticed.

Today, as I write these lines, my wife disputes the fact that Harry gave us sweetened milk with raisins. That, she says, is something that would never, never have passed her lips. How short memory is! For it *was* sweetened milk with raisins.

(I have just told my wife that she threw herself upon it with the same shameless greed as the rest of us. I have told her that she knocked it back by the pint, this sweet—over-sweet—baby food which, in normal circumstances, would never have passed her lips. And as I spoke shreds of memory were reflected in her eyes, lending them a thoughtful look.)

After that Harry made us a drink from fresh oranges that he had grown himself. With it he placed before us a plate of dried tortillas and piloncillos, brown-black lumps of raw sugar the size of your fist . . .

We helped ourselves while Harry made up the fire and started to cook a large pan of beans. We waded in like ravening wolves.

Do you remember our first impressions of Harry's hut which, unfortunately, I wrote down earlier in the story?

Now, while we sat there silently stuffing, Harry asked us with a smile:

"How do you like my hut on second sight?"

"Harry," we said thickly, our mouths full of black sugar and stale tortillas, "it's the height of civilization!"

And it was. In Harry's hut we got in touch again with the world of men and its thousand-and-one things—with food from tins and fruit from the garden, and with food for the mind in the shape of books and Harry's conversation.

"You've got the worst behind you," Harry said. "But you're not out of the wood yet."

"No."

"What do you imagine as the next step?"

For the time being we could not imagine anything. We gorged ourselves with stale tortillas and piloncillos, with black beans in oil and tomato sauce, with rice-pudding and sultanas, with fried bananas and a lot of other things I've forgotten. Everything was vegetarian, everything was superb. Everything was full of vitamins and minerals.

"We thought we would go up to Porvenir. We can't leave all our cameras, films, boats, tents and equipment behind on the lake. Kliesing needs his films. I need my films, and the boats as well. Marianne and I are going on somewhere else from Mexico. That's why we must hire men and animals in Porvenir or elsewhere and come back again and fetch our stuff."

"You won't get animals in Porvenir. You won't get animals in La Realidad either."

"Didn't we see quite a lot when we passed through?"

"Not very many. They need them now for transporting the coffee. And then it'll be the maize harvest. I don't feel very optimistic about it. You may be able to get animals up in the highlands, but it will take you four to five weeks, going up, coming down, and going up again."

"Sure."

"An aeroplane would be much better."

"I thought of that, too. I thought of Don Gustavo's Cessna. But a Cessna can't take all of us and all our equipment. It would have to fly there and back ten times. We could never afford it."

"No. But there are one or two large twin-engined aircraft in Las Casas."

"Could they land on the strip the Swedish expedition made?"

"I don't know," said Harry. "In the States they wouldn't. But here they do. Here they land anywhere. Here nothing's impossible."

"What type?" asked Timber.

"I've no idea," said Harry. "I don't know much about aeroplanes. I once flew in one—twelve passengers, the two pilots and myself. And a lot of freight."

"It must cost the earth!"

"I shouldn't think so. It will take two or three hours and cost you a thousand pesos an hour."

"If we hire animals and men for five weeks it will cost about the same. Since there are five of us it won't be so bad."

"Listen. Some Tolojabales who came back from Las Casas told me Don Pepe is flying down here with a party at Easter. They're coming on a shooting trip. He told the Tolojabales to tell me."

Don José de Vilanueve-Bulnés—or Don Pepe for short—was one of the country's big forest owners, one of those fabulous *hidalgos* and *hacendados*. Practically all the timber in the forests of the Lacandones belongs to him.

"You only have to be on the airstrip when Don Pepe arrives with his guests. Then you can fix it up with the pilot."

We were relieved that we should not have to go on.

"And what about you, Harry? Didn't you want to go to the lake?"

Harry sighed. He had been in the country five years and in all that time he had only once seen the lake—the previous year with the Danish expedition and from the only accessible spot, where our tents now were. But they had not had boats. For years it had been Harry's dearest wish to go on the lake in a boat and explore the islands. We suggested to Harry that he should go to the lake with us and he accepted. But first we stayed another day in Harry's house to recover. Harry had new plans:

"I'll go to Las Casas myself. Perhaps Timber can come with me. I was going back to the States in a fortnight anyway. It doesn't matter if I start a fortnight earlier. First I'll come to the lake with you. Then I'll go to Las Casas with Timber. I must see about your getting out of here myself—

from Las Casas. You can't rely on Mexicans. Don Pepe may come at Easter, or he may not. If he comes then it's all right and you'll hear from him. If he doesn't come it'll still be all right. In that case I'll get you an aeroplane in Las Casas."

It all sounded somewhat unreal, but Harry was determined to save us. He was energy personified and we were grateful. For we were, in fact, far from being "out of the wood".

After two days we went off with Harry and lots of his stores—some of which we left on the savannah between the two rivers—crossed the two rivers with the dinghy and marched along the trail to the lake. This time it was easy because we were not a caravan and had hardly any loads to carry. We voyaged all over the lake with Harry and it was almost as wonderful as we had imagined it. A few days later Kliesing and Paulchen came back from the dump with the provisions. Our missing six iron rations had not been found there, as we had hoped, for the sake of general harmony and peace. But never mind.

*   *   *

The lake.

Through the clear blue water you could see the bottom covered with the characteristic formation of sulphur deposits. The lake water itself contained less sulphur than the Arroyo Mariana. We searched in vain for warm sulphur springs.

We had been told there was a mighty whirlpool at the southern end of the lake, a maelstrom which would capsize any boat. This great whirlpool was caused by a *sumidero*, a subterranean outlet, at the bottom. The idea of such an outlet could not be rejected out of hand. For if the great lake had had no outlet at all, it would long ago have become a salt lake.

However, we could not find a single whirlpool in the whole lake. There was an outlet in the funnel-shaped bay on the eastern bank, but when we saw it, at the end of May, it was dry. Anyway, the dried-up bed which we saw from the Azul can only have been an outlet from the lake during the rainy season.

The first island where we went ashore to discover Maya ruins had a landing place with tall trees and rocks. It looked like a place for meetings and festivals. There were no ruins, but we saw some on the second island. No, not ruins: large pyramids, between ninety and a hundred and twenty feet high, buried beneath the jungle's shroud—a northern and a southern pyramid. On the northern one a well-preserved sacrificial stone cleft by strong tree roots.

It was exciting to stand on this island in a large, mysterious lake, surrounded by overwhelmingly beautiful and deserted country, and to follow the traces of an ancient people who had built and abandoned places of worship there and had never returned to them—a people whose last descendants we had met and befriended.

In Guatemala and Mexico pyramids are as common as castles in Europe. "Our" pyramids cannot be compared with the great ruins of Chichen Itza, Palenque or Cobán. Our pyramids were impressive, solid buildings, but the architecture was not great and they were bare of decoration. Stone had been joined to stone with clean, precise workmanship. Where vaults might have been there were none. The vault was not known to them. Primitive ruins . . .

On the other hand, what a huge population must have lived round the lake for it to have been possible to get the stones up without machines, without a wheel or a pulley, but simply by the use of ramps! What a waste of manpower!

Between the two pyramids was the ball-game court. There is one within the precincts of all Maya and Aztec temples. The game was, after the sacrifice, the second most important religious ritual. It was played with a hard rubber ball six inches in diameter and often painted with phosphorus. This ball had to be driven through a stone ring eight inches in diameter at the two narrow ends of the court, which was here about a hundred and twenty feet long. (The measurements of the ball and the stone ring are from Chichen Itza.) It was a difficult and strenuous game, played until the players were exhausted or—which was often—carried off the field injured or dead. It must have been difficult to drive the heavy ball through the narrow rings, since the players were only allowed to touch it with their shoulders, their hips or their buttocks, but never with their hands or feet. The court was divided into a day side (at the southern pyramid) and a night side (northern pyramid), and the game was played between these with the phosphorescent ball. Ball-game and human sacrifice were conditions for the continuation of the world. They were the highlights of the periodical feasts in honour of the various gods, feasts when the lake must have been alive with thousands of canoes . . .

Thousands of canoes filled with people in festive mood, with musicians playing flutes and drums. Drums and flutes everywhere—on the lake, on all the islands, on the hills . . . Priests and feathered, painted and masked dancers on the pyramids of the temple island, where the death-cries of the victims were drowned in blood and ecstasy and in the cries of the festive crowd . . .

At night fires on all the islands, fires on the mountains of the Chamhuitz range, fires in all the bays of the lake and in the great city which may, perhaps, yet be discovered there . . . For there must have been a great population living round this lake. Whether there ever was a city is an open question, but that the islands were "sacred islands" cannot be doubted. The five largest and most important ones are in the south-eastern part of the lake; there are three small ones off the south-western shore and a solitary one in the north. Of the south-eastern islands only one has pyramids and a ball-game court. Another, very small, island has traces of walls, the remains of a pyramid or a temple. The rest of the islands have nothing, as far as we could see—least of all any trace of a secular settlement.

The settlements must have been on the southern shore and in the valleys of the Chamhuitz. The whole wild and empty area now without a single human being must have been densely populated after the end of the New Empire (the Maya Empire in Yucatan). A powerful nation lived here once, and its centre was the lake with the sacred islands.

Spanish Conquistadores' accounts of a fabulous "Empire of the Lacandones" were not an exaggeration. Even Barrios Leal's reports speak mysteriously of a legendary "city". If it did exist, it could only have been beyond the northern shores of the lake, between the Sierra Perlas and the Sierra Caribe.

We looked at the terrain. It was the only terrain which could have accommodated a settlement of any size. We could not stay long enough to make an intensive search; it would have taken months of roaming and hacking through the jungle, and the rainy season was imminent. (I do not envy any race which has to live through the seven months of rain there.) But even if the rainy season had not been imminent we could not have done it. We were far too run down after our adventure on the Azul. With our restricted means we could not even have cleared the pyramids on the island. And if we had, we would probably have found little more than stones, dirt and mould.

Compared with the forest our time on the lake was sheer holiday, yet there was still far too much forest around the lake and we had had a bellyful of forest! We wanted to leave.

Timber was very much better. He had trouble only with the fat worms under his skin because they had begun to stir. Kliesing's had begun to stir, too. The rest of us were better off in that respect. But that was not why we wanted to get away from the lake. And Harry? Harry was blissfully happy.

Harry, the perfect hermit, had been living there for five years, but he had no archaeological ambitions. His main concern was for his last Lacandones, and he said they would not go back to the lake, or if they did it would only be under great difficulties. He said that in his proposal to UNESCO for the creation of a reservation for the last of the Lacandones he would have to suggest the Chamhuitz.

We agreed with him.

I hope that he succeeds in his plans. They are based on an intimate knowledge of the people and the country, they are practicable and sensible.

They are more than sensible.

They are humane—and they would do honour to Mexico and UNESCO.

*　　　*　　　*

Harry. When we first met him, for about ten minutes in the court of the "Dolphin Hotel" in Comitán, Harry had seemed very strange. Now he had become a friend, a selfless friend, a friend such as one rarely meets. I am not speaking lightly or glibly. We had been together for a considerable length of time and in pretty rum circumstances, circumstances where one learns a man's real worth.

One morning Harry and Timber departed.

"You'll have to stay here, won't you, to get the atmosphere?" Timber said.

"Look at him," my wife said. "He comes from Canada to Mexico, practically dies of the atmosphere and thinks *we* aren't absolutely sick of it."

"You know my place," Harry said. "If you run short of anything go and help yourselves."

We thanked Harry. He waved our thanks aside.

"Those days on the lake were a wonderful experience. As soon as I get to New York I'm going to buy myself one of those folding canoes, a Klepper Aerius. It's easy to transport and a much better craft than the Canadian canoe. When I've got it I'll go on the lake again."

It took us, many days to carry our boats, tents and equipment to the Perlas and across to the landing-strip. Harry had described its position to us. I doubt if we should ever have found it but for a small hut which Don Pepe had built there for *monteros*, forest rangers. In the hut we found a note from Harry to Don Pepe:

TRY TO GET TO THE LAKE IMMEDIATELY. FOUR EUROPEANS IN DANGER OF THEIR LIVES. STARVING AND SICK—MUST BE TAKEN BY PLANE TO THE HIGHLANDS AT ONCE.

We were deeply embarrassed and very glad to be able to tear up the melodramatic but kindly meant SOS. We were in fine shape. We had lost weight but, apart from Paulchen, we were in better health and spirits than we had been for years. It had been a strenuous journey but it had left us extremely fit.

The airstrip had once been cleared to a length of five hundred yards and a width of fifty feet. Now it was just bumpy savannah overgrown with grass six feet high. A helicopter, perhaps even a light Cessna or a similar aircraft might land there—but never a heavy twin-engined plane!

We pitched our tents at the edge of this improbable airport and waited for developments.

The very next day Chan Bor and Nabora appeared. Her small, fat puppy had by now developed into a full-grown, yelping cur.

Two days later Bor came. There was great joy in meeting old friends. No, there was nothing new to tell. All went well with the Lacandones.

Our friends paddled home again. Peace and quiet enveloped our unhopeful airport.

It was very hot on the savannah. Not a breath of air stirred the trees. It was close on Easter.

In all Spanish-speaking countries the *semana santa*, Holy Week, is the greatest and longest Church festival. It is becoming increasingly a secular holiday, an occasion for making long journeys. We therefore reckoned on Don Pepe's party arriving in one, even two aircraft from Maundy Thursday onwards.

It was strange to find, after such a long time, traces left by men who had been neither Lacandones nor Mayas, but from our own world: the ghostly jungle airstrip; worn-out and rusty iron parts; the hut full of empty bottles, tins, cobwebs, dirty, mouldy beans and Harry's note—and then not to see a human being after all.

Hard as we searched, there was not a human being to be seen. Even our friends the Lacandones had crept back into their hide-outs.

A shooting party which would come to us out of the blue— what a joke!

My wife and I had gone hunting again during the long days of waiting for the aircraft, but do you think we got a single edible bird in this wonderful, spacious unspoiled country?

We saw our Amazon kingfisher again, and the tracks of jaguars in the thickets. We saw toucans, araras, even the somersault-bird and the maize snake. But we did not see an anaconda nor the lovable tree bears. No "Hush!" bird frightened us, and not a single pavo looked curiously at the gun-barrel, to say nothing of *Dromococcoyx phasianellus rufigularis* . . .

On the Azul we had lived amongst the animals as though we were back in the Golden Age, but here, where the country was just as deserted, in spite of the airstrip, the Lacandones in their hide-outs and the cobwebbed hut, the edible animals had left, only because man had left his indelible mark in his fleeting but deadly footsteps.

I tried to imagine the shooting party . . .

Maundy Thursday.

No aircraft.

On Good Friday there was nothing either.

On the Saturday we waited till the early afternoon. We had calculated that they could not arrive much later than eleven o'clock if the pilots wanted to fly back after depositing the party.

After another fruitless wait we were just off to the Perlas for a swim when Bor, clad in his best robe, arrived with K'in and Kayūm. They had come down the Jataté in their canoe and wanted to hear the news. They knew that Don Pepe had intended coming, and Bor wanted to discuss a number of matters with him. The two men got on well. Our Lacandon friends spent the night in our camp. Now we were quite sure that the aircraft would arrive early on Easter Sunday and we got everything ready for the umpteenth time.

Each day the sun shone hotter out of the cloudless sky.

No aircraft . . .

Bor and his companions paddled home disappointed.

It became evident to us that everything now depended entirely on Harry and Timber. From our point of view Harry's decision to leave a fortnight early and take the matter in hand personally had been the right one. Since Don Pepe had obviously given up the idea of a shooting party, Harry and Timber would send us an aircraft at once, or at least a messenger. We calculated that they must have reached Las Casas some time ago. If they sent us an aircraft and not a messenger it might arrive on Easter Monday . . .

But even Easter Monday, which was slightly dull with high cloud, and "cooler"—an ideal day for flying—did not bring an aircraft of any description.

Actually it was pleasant, doing nothing in the hot, deserted country with its savannah, its forest, two rivers within easy reach and the invisible Lacandones. In the mornings we got hot and sweaty because we could not bathe for fear of missing the aircraft which never came and never would come. But when, of an afternoon, we went bathing in the clear, cool

Perlas, because nothing would come, we felt fresh again and everything was wonderful, if somewhat monotonous.

Food, for instance, became monotonous. Erbswurst, no fruit, nothing fresh, more sugar-starvation. At home we drink tea and coffee without sugar, but there we craved for it again. There was no sugar in the hut, but there were black beans. God bless black beans. We took some of them and from time to time I took some of the dry tobacco leaves hanging beneath the grass roof. We made a note of everything we took because we wanted to pay Don Pepe for it when we met him in Las Casas.

There would be sugar in Harry's hut, if the ants had not already got at it, but it was a day's journey there and back, and we dared not risk going because of the aircraft which did not come. By then we had been waiting by the airstrip for seven days.

Eight days—still no aircraft.

None on the ninth. Nor on the tenth. We were nonplussed.

Again, no aircraft appeared on the morning of the eleventh day . . .

We gave up, because the sun was already nearing the zenith. Then, just as we were crumbling up the last piece of Erbswurst and Paulchen was cooking beans we heard a humming sound in the air.

The heat cast a thick haze over everything.

We jumped up, leaving the tent and the fire, and ran to the airstrip and shouted to one another: "They're coming!" And we heard the sound rising and falling, like the drone of a large bomber, but we saw nothing because of the heat haze which was so thick you could have cut it with a knife.

It was a large aeroplane. I wondered how it was going to land on the bumpy airstrip in the alang-alang grass on the small savannah in the heart of the forest without crashing. We hoped the pilot would not be put off when he saw where he was supposed to come down, but then we heard the humming go farther and farther away until it finally died out altogether.

And that was that.

It must have been a large airliner en route for British Honduras or Tegucigalpa which had got a little off course. Then we heard the throbbing sound again. This time it came nearer and nearer . . . It was obvious that the crew was looking for the savannah!

Suddenly it appeared out of the haze—large, twin-engined, white and glistening. We waved like mad with our white sheets, and they saw us.

The plane flew over us, went away again, returned in a wide sweep and came in to make a perfect landing over the trees. It was breath-taking.

Kliesing was filming. I took photographs.

They touched down on this wild and dangerous terrain more elegantly than our Super-Constellation at Frankfurt later. They did not even need to use the last hundred and fifty feet of the "runway". They then turned in the fifty foot width of the strip and, throbbing and swaying, taxied slowly towards us . . .

It was a wonderful aeroplane. White with red stripes. From it stepped two tall Mexicans, Captain Luna and his co-pilot. They were splendid men and immediately offered us cigarettes. They thought we were out of tobacco and half-dead.

"We couldn't make it before," Luna explained. "There were too many forest fires on the first half of the route and visibility was practically nil."

No Harry! No Timber!

Don Enrique had left, Luna said. The other one, the young señor, was ill at his hotel . . .

Good God!

There was a letter from Harry. He was leaving Las Casas that night for the United States. He told us to look up Don

Pepe and wished us good luck. He expected us to go and visit him at his home in Vermont, only sixty miles from New York. There was a lot more in the letter, but we could not finish reading it just then. We had to leave as soon as possible otherwise the heavy machine would not get off the ground. I told Luna we could pack up within an hour.

He said we could take an hour and a half. The folding canoes had long been packed, of course. There only remained the tents, the kitchen equipment and a number of odds and ends.

Chan Bor and Nabora appeared and benefited to the extent of another lot of things which we no longer needed.

The heat became more and more oppressive. After three-quarters of an hour the pilots grew anxious, wondering whether they would be able to get the heavy machine up through the thick heat haze. They said it would become increasingly difficult.

We were ready within the hour.

Suddenly my wife appeared dressed smartly in a skirt and a clean blouse. Suddenly my wife looked frighteningly normal again. After going about for more than two months only in the craziest of costumes or quite naked it was a strange sight.

Suddenly, out of breath, Bor arrived.

The Lacandones have a sixth sense: they'll hear an aircraft when it's still fifty miles or more away somewhere over their forests. Bor had started out from his hut two hours earlier and had paddled like a racing canoeist to be in time to say good-bye to us.

The engines roared . . . The first trees . . . Below us!

We had asked Luna to fly over the lake, but we could see only the southern shore through the shimmer, and we never caught even a glimpse of the islands.

After that we saw nothing but forest. A sea of forest along every horizon.

We had expected this sight; but when it came it broke over us like a spring flood. This aerial view of this forest-sea —our forest!—which surged in endless waves over hazy mountains and horizons and all the chasms, and where you could not see a house, a settlement, nor any sign of human life—this view of the monstrous forest was more frightening than our day-to-day existence in it had ever been.

*   *   *

The aeroplane looked beautiful externally, with its red stripes and big aerial, but there was no radio connection with anywhere, because the valves were missing in both the transmitter and the receiver. The great instrument panel was impressive, but nothing worked. The altimeter went backwards after ten thousand feet. The amount of fuel left in the tanks was a matter for guesswork, or very nearly. Luna's co-pilot had measured it with his belt before we took off.

The door in the fuselage, which was big enough to stroll about in, was kept shut by means of a simple hook. If you undid it you could step off the plane in mid-air without the slightest trouble. Altogether a really sporting kind of flying, if I may say so. Everything was done by sight, hearing, instinct and possibly even smell.

Afterwards my wife told me she had kept assuring herself that the two Mexicans wanted to get home, too.

They were the two most experienced bush-pilots in the whole of Chiapas. Captain Luna owned the plane and they chartered it out, generally flying bags of coffee from fincas in the upper Chiapas to Las Casas or Tuxtla Gutiérrez. They had never come to the San Quintin savannah before, but found it at once with the help of a very sketchy aerial map and intuition.

As we soared over the forests of the Lacandones I finished reading Harry's letter.

They had made their way back in forced marches . . .

From Las Margaritas, however, they got a bus to Comitán, and from Comitán one to Las Casas. You know what Mexican buses are like—Noah's Arks. So our friends arrived in Las Casa crushed and somewhat creased, but when Harry learnt that the great shooting expedition was cancelled he at once started to look for pilots and a trustworthy plane. In the whole of Las Casas they could not find one large enough to take us and our kit, then, so Harry wrote, Don Pepe tried to rescue the unknown Europeans who needed help. He at once tried to telephone Luna in El Real to ask him to bring his big plane to Las Casas. Unfortunately the telephone did not work, because in burning their maize fields after the harvest, the Chamulas had burnt the telephone poles down, too.

So Don Pepe wrote a letter which was flown to El Real in his own Cessna. He sent a small aircraft to get a large aircraft to get us "out of the wood" . . . But in El Real they had run out of high-octane fuel.

Now even if you *can* measure with your belt the amount of fuel in a tank, you can still only fly if it is the right sort of fuel.

Don Pepe's pilot flew the Cessna back, and Don Pepe sent a tanker with high-octane fuel to meet the plane on an airstrip half-way.

After refuelling, Luna and his co-pilot flew to Las Casas to find out from Don Pepe and Harry where they were to pick us up. They thought it over for a night at the hotel "El Jardin" then, after much persuasion from Harry, agreed and set off, but nearly missed us because of the forest fires and the haze shrouding the jungle. Harry wrote that Timber had to stay in bed, but that it was only the after-effects of the journey and possibly a little dysentery. He would be all right. But it was a good idea for him to stay in bed rather than come and meet us at the airfield. However, Don Pepe would be there. This from Harry, and all in the air, with still no sign of a break in the forest, or any human habitation. Nothing.

Let me say right away that Luna did not charge us more than what would be a very reasonable fare for a taxi from Frankfurt to Berlin. He asked a price lower than any European or American company would ask just to let a plane take off.

A day or two later I asked Don Pepe what we owed *him*. He had incurred heavy expenses on our behalf: the telephone which did not work because the poles had been burnt down; the aircraft he had dispatched with the letter; the tanker with the fuel . . .

Don Pepe looked at me for a moment, then said: "*Nada*, Don Herberto. Nothing . . ."

We reached the highlands. Later we lost our way. We noticed the fact because the two Mexicans began to quarrel and grew more and more agitated, but above a river valley in the upper reaches of the Jataté Luna suddenly gave a shout which filled us all with hope. He had found his bearing again, and banked to speed off in quite a different direction.

A little later Luna put the machine down gently and smoothly on Las Casas airfield.

There were crowds of people and lots of cars. There might have been an ambulance there . . .

We were given an overwhelming reception.

The plane was three hours overdue and the wildest rumours had been circulating.

We climbed out.

A lot of people we did not know rushed up to us, among them Don Pepe.

We shook hands with Don Pepe.

We shook hands with everybody.

We were back to civilization.

INDEX

251

INDEX